Brian Easton is a research economist and social statistician who works as a consultant and holds academic teaching or research appointments at the University of Auckland, the Central Institute of Technology, the Centre for Social Policy Research, the Institute of Executive Development, the Research Project on Economic Planning, and the Wellington Medical School. He has written widely on New Zealand economic, political, and social issues, and is the regular economics columnist at the Listener. This book developed out of a course at the Tamaki Campus of the University of Auckland, where he is a Visiting Senior Lecturer in Politics.

THE COMMERCIALISATION
OF NEW ZEALAND

Brian Easton

AUCKLAND
UNIVERSITY PRESS

First published 1997
Reprinted 1997
AUCKLAND UNIVERSITY PRESS
University of Auckland
Private Bag 92019
Auckland

ISBN 1 86940 173 5

Typeset by Auckland University Press
Printed by GP Print, Wellington

Contents

Preface

IN 1994 BARRY GUSTAFSON, PROFESSOR OF POLITICAL STUDIES AND Dean of Arts of the Tamaki Campus of the University of Auckland, invited me to teach a course in public policy to second year political studies students. This book arises out of that course. It is based on a series of research papers I have had published over the last few years, some of which have been updated and reorganised, plus some additional material prepared for the course.

Because this was a course primarily for Arts students, I have focused on the application of commercialist ideas into areas where it would not be normally thought they belonged. Thus the book passes lightly over their application to industrial policy, which in any case is less controversial, and there is little discussion of macroeconomic policy. These are matters which I have discussed in my other books, *Getting the Supply-side to Work* (1994) and *In Stormy Seas* (1997). An important advantage of doing this is that the economics required to understand the issues is not so complicated. Where necessary, the required economics is explained in the book.

I also decided to limit the material on distributional policy, not least in order to keep the span of the course tractable. (In any case I am writing a separate book on this topic.) For a similar reason I excluded Maori policy. Moreover, what has happened to the Maori is far more complex than just commercialisation. (I would like to write a book on that one day too.) The case studies reflect various topics with which I have been engaged over the years.

The book is not just a collection of previously published papers. There is not a single chapter which keeps its original form; some consist of an amalgamation of and excerpts from a number of papers; all have additional material and are updated; and some are completely new. However, I acknowledge the original sources in the bibliography, and express gratitude here to their publishers for enabling me to try out and disseminate some of the material earlier.

I have included in the bibliography many references which are not mentioned elsewhere in the book, so that it is a source on the New Zealand reforms in its own right. Because inevitably there are a number of my own publications in any one year in it, I have used a slightly more elaborate reference system in citing my own work in the notes.

Inevitably, given that the book is based on a decade of work, I am indebted to numerous people. Those who should be acknowledged include Rob Bowie, Phillida Bunkle, Graham Bush, Ruth Butterworth, Elizabeth Caffin, Ellen Dannin, Hans Delbrück, Nancy Devlin, Chandra Dixon, Rosemary du Plessis, Geoff Fougere, Rolf Gerritsen, Don Gilling, Alan Gray, Barry Gustafson, George Hughes, Anthony Hubbard, Keith Jackson, Sally Jackman, Bruce Jesson, Rex Jones, Geoff Lealand, Elizabeth McLeay, Jim Marshall, John Martin, Andrew O'Brien, Brad Patterson, Roger Proctor, Bryan Philpott, Bill Renwick, Bill Rosenberg, Peter Simpson, Andrew Sharp, Tony Simpson, Mike Smith, Suzanne Snively, Susan St John, Nicholas Tarling, John Tizard, Jack Vowles, Pat Walsh, John Yeabsley. Any oversight does not mean I have not appreciated others' contributions. Theirs will have been mentioned in the original publications. Among the institutions and their staff which have been especially supportive over the years are the Centre for Social Policy Research of Massey University, the Central Institute of Technology, the Department of Political Studies of the University of Auckland, the Department of Public Health of the Wellington School of Medicine of the University of Otago, the Institute of Executive Development of Massey University, the New Zealand Engineering Printing and Manufacturing Union, the *New Zealand Listener*, and The Research Project on Economic Planning.

I am also grateful to the efficient work of the Auckland University Press in producing an attractive book, on time. Special thanks to the Committee, to the Director Elizabeth Caffin, to Simon Cauchi who did the copy-editing and indexing, to Katrina Duncan for the typesetting, and to the publisher's reader who made numerous useful suggestions.

The list of acknowledgements does not include my students. They have been fun to teach. One cannot interact with lively young minds without learning something. Thank you to them, to Chandra Dixon with whom it has been a pleasure to share the teaching burden, and to Barry Gustafson and the University of Auckland who gave me the opportunity to work with them.

Brian Easton
17 December 1996

PROLOGUE

A Coiled Spring

PROLOGUE

A Coiled Spring

FOLLOWING THE INTRODUCTION OF REFRIGERATION IN THE EARLY 1880s, New Zealand developed as a specialist pastoral exporter of meat, wool, and dairy products, mainly to Britain. Before that, distance from markets had confined the economy to exported quarried resources (especially gold) and wool, tallow, and grain. The freezing technology opened up the possibility of exporting over long distances carcasses and butter and cheese, while Britain's open market for foodstuffs provided a large and profitable destination. [1]

Throughout the first half of the twentieth century New Zealand steadily developed high-productivity farming based on sheep and cows, the sheep providing meat and wool and the cows dairy products (with export beef herds developing later). It was a technology which involved the sophisticated growing of grass, which was first processed by an animal and then, in turn, further processed in the shearing sheds or freezing works or dairy factory. In export terms New Zealand was a processed-grass monoculture. Its state of dependence was such that in a typical year between 1920 and 1950 over 90 percent of exports were wool, meat, or dairy, and over 60 percent of those exports went to Britain.

Given a favourable climate, but not especially suitable soils, this high-technology pastoral export strategy lifted New Zealand to one of the highest standards of living in the world through most of the twentieth century. However it was a third-world commodity export strategy. Despite the prosperity it generated, the economy suffered from the two standard defects of commodity exporting: price volatility and vulnerability to competition from others.

These issues were acute in the early 1930s. The response was to evolve mechanisms designed to insulate the economy from price fluctuations. On the export side this mainly involved smoothing farm income by allowing producer boards to borrow from the

3

Reserve Bank. On the import side there could be some overseas borrowing to smooth export revenue deficits, but there also evolved a complex, comprehensive, and erratic system of domestic protection to save foreign funds and generate jobs (for pastoral farming is not labour-intensive). External protection tended to be via import controls (first imposed in 1938) and tariffs, but it was supported by internal interventions including price controls, licensing requirements, and the threat of the use of such measures against firms which did not comply with the intention of policy.

The theory of effective insulation requires the correct forecasting of the average level of the commodity terms of trade (export prices relative to import prices). In fact the post-war world was changing, depressing the average return for pastoral producers. Britain was less willing to permit unlimited imports of foodstuffs, not least because it was beginning to support its own farmers—a carry-over from the increased self-sufficiency of the war days. Ominously, Britain was not alone in this increasing of support for farmers. A key element of the European Union was the Common Agricultural Policy which over-produced dairy and meat products; the surpluses were dumped into third-world markets, depressing New Zealand export prices. The United States and other rich Northern Hemisphere producers behaved little better. Although wool, an industrial input, was not subject to the same border discrimination, its market was being undermined by the rise of synthetic alternatives. Butter was similarly undermined by margarine. The markets and prices for processed grass were under pressure in the post-war era. After a some skirmishes, the great collapse was in late 1966, when the terms of trade fell sharply. Except for a misleading recovery during the world commodity boom of 1972–1973, they have remained depressed relative to the first half of the post-war era.

DIVERSIFICATION: 1966–1979

Faced by a decline in pastoral profitability the economy diversified out of pastoral farming into other export activities, and into markets other than Britain. The diversification was spectacular. Farming moved into a wide range of horticultural products (most notably kiwifruit) and, to a lesser extent, goat meat and venison. Land was diversified into forestry, while plantations established in the 1930s began the exporting of sawn wood, chips, pulp, paper, and other wood products. There was a boom in fishing. Electricity was exported in aluminium refined from imported bauxite. Raw iron sands were shipped to Japan. Inbound tourism developed, becoming New Zealand's largest single foreign-exchange earner.

There was also manufacturing diversification and exporting, especially with further processing of the resources. Carcasses became boned out, wool was scoured, dairy product exports were extended to variety cheeses (and not just cheddar), casein, dairy-based desserts, and even milk-based pharmaceuticals. A nice little line developed in the export of dairy equipment and scouring equipment. Later there were exports of farm advisory services and farming computer software.

Markets were also diversified as Table 0.1 shows. By the 1990s, Australia, Japan, the United States and Greater China were all more important than Britain, as was now the rest of the European Union. In total East Asia took more than a third of exports.

Table 0.1: Export destinations for New Zealand

	Percent of Total		
	1952	1965	1994
Britain	65.5	50.8	6.0
Other 1990 European Community	12.0	17.1	9.5
United States	11.4	12.3	11.3
Australia	1.5	4.7	20.9
Japan	1.5	4.3	14.6
Greater China	*0.0	0.7	7.7
Middle East	*0.0	0.1	3.4
Other Asia	*0.9	1.2	12.8
Oceania	*0.6	1.2	4.0
Latin & Central America	*0.9	1.5	3.8
Canada	2.2	1.4	1.8
Eastern Europe	*1.5	1.0	1.1
Other	*2.0	3.7	3.1
TOTAL	100.0	100.0	100.0

Source:*New Zealand Official Year Book* (various years).
*Some exports to area groups may be in 'other'.

These changes were socially demanding because they involved cultural diversity. Halal killing for Middle East markets had to be instituted into the freezing works; products had to be rewrapped and marketing redesigned for new territories. The home away from home that was Britain no longer dominated export thinking. New Zealand exporting is still commodity-based, but today there is a greater diversity of commodities and destinations.

John Gould shows that New Zealand exports were highly concentrated in product and country terms in 1965 compared to those of other OECD countries; they were near average by 1980.[2] The diversification effort was a major one, and that plus the fall of the terms of trade slowed down the rate of economic growth in New Zealand in the 1970s. But the changes had been almost entirely in the export sector with little modification to the highly protected and insulated domestic sector up to 1979.

RELUCTANT INTERNAL RESTRUCTURING: 1979–1984

By the late 1970s the New Zealand economy faced six major problems.

1. While there had been considerable external diversification, the domestic economy was still insulated, and lacked the responsiveness that the external sector required. For example:

- Foreign exchange dealing involved a government-licensed cartel of the trading banks, who charged high margins. The diversification generated more exporters who needed more complicated services.
- Domestic regulation of transport forced the use of rail services which were costly and often of inferior quality.
- Import licensing meant that the exporter was not always able to obtain the most competitive inputs of raw materials and services.[3]

2. An increasingly sophisticated population, especially the well-travelled rising urban middle class, were not always able to obtain the consumer goods and services they desired. For instance:

- Price controls on bread discouraged the establishment of specialty varieties and specialty bread shops, which appeared when they were removed in 1979.

- Shopping, drinking, and dining facilities were often restricted to hours that were inconvenient for the customer.
- Import controls restricted entry for desired products.

3. New Zealand faced a complicated energy problem. While traditionally self-sufficient in electricity and coal, New Zealand had imported transport fuels. In the late 1960s the Maui gas field was found, then the fourth biggest in the world, in size far out-stripping the standard industrial uses for gas in New Zealand. Adding to this excess energy supply was a growing excess of hydro power in the South Island. Meanwhile world oil prices rose in the 1970s (and fell in the mid 1980s).

4. New Zealand was in a strong inflationary mode (compared to other OECD countries). Typically the annual inflation rate exceeded 10 percent throughout the 1970s.

5. There was a severe fiscal deficit; that is, the New Zealand government was spending much more than its revenue. The deficit was hidden by inflation because while the government debt grew in nominal terms, the value of the old debt was reduced in real terms. At the same time the deficit contributed to inflation by its monetary injection, and increased pressure on resources. In a further complication which is typical of the times, interest rate controls were used to keep down the cost of government debt, but they distorted investment decisions. When the wage freeze was introduced, there were income tax reductions to make the controls more palatable, adding to the deficit.

The economy was riddled with interventions introduced to mitigate unfortunate side-effects of earlier interventions. In turn they required further interventions to deal with their side-effects. No one understood, or could understand, the total impact of all the interventions, because they were so numerous, complicated, and interactive. But there was an increasing view that they were bad, especially for key growth sectors.

6. The system of government suffered from a 'sclerosis': it was increasingly unable to tackle anything but the most urgent problems. Its structures and processes had evolved to the point where there was little rationality in them, and yet they could not be rationalised. Examples appear in later chapters of this study, so only one need be given here. In 1982 the extraordinary variety of legal statuses of the various state-owned enter-

prises could only be explained by historical experience.[4] Yet attempts to create a more coherent system were stalled.

This could be explained by the personality of Prime Minister Robert Muldoon, who had been radical in the late 1960s when first appointed to the finance portfolio but, as so often happens with such politicians, was now reluctant to countenance further change. However there is a more general explanation. Mancur Olson, in his *The Rise and Decline of Nations*, argued that a society which enjoyed political stability would generate powerful special interest groups which would reduce the flexibility of administrative and political response to new circumstances and shocks.[5] Although the study did not become a significant part of the New Zealand debate until some years after the reforms began, it could have been a Bible for the reformers. The extraordinary political stability of the post-war era—dominated in 29 out of the 35 years to 1984 by one party, National, but where in truth there was much policy agreement with the other party, Labour—meant that the pressure groups seemed to have a headlock on political and administrative innovation. The sclerosis was all the more evident given the dramatic changes to the external sector, and their pressure on the domestic sector.

The first two problems were tackled in the 1979 budget, which introduced a program of reducing external protection, and subsequently with a phasing out of some domestic interventions. Although there had been market liberalisation going back to the 1950s, there was a marked quickening up to 1982, and some continuation beyond.

The energy problem was tackled by a program known colloquially as 'Think Big', in which large energy-intensive manufacturing uses were encouraged, and gas was reticulated throughout the North Island. Think Big was controversial, although the major public debate hardly covered what, with hindsight, was the major issue. Although there was some recognition that there was a downside risk to the strategy if oil prices fell, little attention was given to who would bear that risk. Prices fell well below expectations. In every case the arrangements with the private investor were such that any loss was borne by the general public (usually the taxpayer, but sometimes the motorist). It was a good example of a situation where intervention was so complicated that no one knew what the effects would be if something went wrong. So the Think Big strategy heightened the fundamental tension in economic policy. Pressures from consumers and the diversifying export sector were for market liberalisation, while the energy-based program was highly interventionist.

These tensions were further heightened when in June 1982 the Muldoon government imposed a price-and-wage freeze of draconian intensity in terms of scope (almost total) and length (almost two years). A one-seat majority meant that the government had to be seen to be doing something about inflation—and quickly, given the possibility of a by-election. The conflict with market liberalisation, in which prices are meant to be flexible, is obvious enough, and the above story of the unintended consequences of price controls on bread choice illustrates the complex outcomes of the controls. Even more complicated was the way out of the controls: how was a wage and price explosion to be prevented when they ended?

Admittedly the government continued to liberalise slowly, especially when that would put downward pressure on prices: foreign exchange dealing was opened up to all reputable comers, restrictions on inland freight transport favouring rail were dropped, while Closer Economic Relations (CER) promoted free trade with Australia. Nevertheless, those in the external sector found themselves under an increasing tension of all sorts of restrictions in their domestic markets, while they sold in much more open overseas markets. Such export subsidies manufacturers and farmers received were being threatened by countervailing measures in the exporters' markets. The government, led by the increasingly unpopular Robert Muldoon, gave the impression it was at best reluctant to liberalise, and eager to intervene. Consumer choice remained restricted.

Rex Fairburn's 'Conversation in the Bush', from his poem *Dominion*, goes:

'Observe the young and tender frond
'of this punga: shaped and curved
'like the scroll of a fiddle: fit instrument
'to play archaic tunes.'
        'I see
'the shape of a coiled spring.'

9

Many saw the New Zealand which elected a Labour government in July 1984 as a green and pleasant land. Events proved it was more a coiled spring.

PART ONE

The Ideas

1

The Genesis of the Commercialisation Strategy: From 'Think Big' to Privatisation

THE 1984 LABOUR ELECTION MANIFESTO PROMISED TO LIBERALISE the economy; that is, to use the market to regulate resource decisions more and to rely less on government intervention, especially with regard to border protection. But there was also a considerable commitment to a centralised system of directing investment. Incoming Prime Minister David Lange had announced in 1984 'the election of a Labour Government has ended the move towards privatisation of state ventures by the National Government', rejecting the limited privatisation proposals in National's 1984 election manifesto.

Throughout 1986—and much of 1987—most Labour ministers opposed privatisation. Yet by the end of its term, the Fourth Labour government was privatising many state trading operations (arguably more than the previous three Labour governments had nationalised), and applying commercialist principles to many other activities as well. This chapter traces the policy process leading to the corporatisation and privatisation programs which set the precedent for the wider commercialisation.

LIBERALISATION AND COMMERCIALISATION

Liberalisation is the opening of markets to competition, replacing such interventions as barriers to entry, price controls, licences, and restrictions on some activities, compulsion on others. It may also include the removal of advantages, disadvantages, subsidies,

13

and taxes which discriminate between different firms, or different related markets. Liberalisation was not a peculiarity of post-1984 policy. The previous National government had also been liberalising markets, albeit slowly.

Liberalisation involves increasing the use of the competitive market as a means of regulating the economy, perhaps because it is judged the most effective means of dealing with a particular problem.

For instance, a government might repeal various restrictions on pollution-generating actions, replacing them with a tax or a system of transferable licences. That would be a 'more market' solution, and the shift would be one of economic liberalisation. Note that in doing this, the government need not have any less commitment to treating the pollution as an economic bad, nor any less of a commitment to reduce pollution. Rather it judges the use of the market mechanism is a superior means of regulating pollution.

'Commercialisation', defined in detail in the next chapter, involves using as much as possible the model of private business enterprise to organise economic (and even non-economic) activity. This chapter is primarily concerned with the policies of corporatisation and privatisation. 'Corporatisation' is the activity of requiring a publicly owned agency to behave as if it were a private corporation. In this chapter 'privatisation' refers to the selling into private ownership of a publicly owned business operation or asset. Commercialisation need not be associated with liberalisation. Uncompetitive markets, notably monopolies, are a feature of private enterprise. The privatisation program of the Thatcher government often sold the state asset with its market monopoly intact. Conversely market liberalisation can occur without commercialisation. However, Treasury saw commercialisation and liberalisation as intimately linked.

THE PROTECTION DEBATE

This chapter's theme is the crucial role of the 'Think Big' program in the development of the commercialisation policy. In a way the story begins with the protection debate.

The history of external protection in New Zealand goes back to the 1880s, while a high protection regime was introduced in

1938 and maintained thereafter.[1] For one of the world's rich countries the overall level of border protection was high. Particularly contentious was import licensing, which guaranteed a domestic market to New Zealand producers (often sole producers), irrespective of their cost structure. There was a vociferous and energetic minority of economists who supported the continuation of this protection,[2] but the large majority of the economics profession favoured reductions in external protection, particularly the elimination of import licences.[3] By 1981, even those in the Department of Trade and Industry had doubts as to the effectiveness of their department's traditional role of protecting and assisting industry. Note that while the debate focused on external protection there was the recognition that internal protection was also involved.[4]

There were two outcomes of the debate important to this story. The first was a Treasury study of costs of protection in the mid 1970s, which concluded that the static allocative losses from misallocation of resources from the protection regime were not high.[5] So Treasury focused on dynamic losses, and the outcome was concerns about managerial efficiency. It was argued that assistance protected inefficient managers, and discouraged entrepreneurial initiative, and that the resulting lack of dynamism was a major reason for the perceived poor performance of the New Zealand economy. Linked to this was the idea of macroeconomic 'accommodation', the notion that the government managed the macroeconomy and the protection regime to bail out any firm or interest group which got into difficulties. This, it was argued, encouraged irresponsible and economically inefficient commercial behaviour.

The second lesson was a recognition that protection often involves assisting one firm or industry at the expense of others. Officials became increasingly less confident in their ability to choose worthy candidates for assistance, at the expense of others. This doubt led to such slogans as the 'inability of the government to pick winners', and the notion that the private sector was more capable.

THE PROJECT EVALUATION DEBATE

Cost–benefit analysis (CBA), developed overseas from the 1950s, began to be used by individual government departments in the late 1960s. CBA is a means of assisting the government to decide which projects should go ahead, including private sector projects which required government assistance. Since the New Zealand economy involved widespread interventions, even moderately sized private sector projects often had to be considered.

Initially each government department had its own rules for applying CBA, but this negated the technique's purpose of imposing a consistent assessment on all projects where some government assistance was involved. In the early 1970s Treasury set up (almost) consistent rules for all government departments.

CBA involves calculating the costs and benefits of the project and comparing the two sums. If benefits exceed costs the project gets approval. Measurement of costs and benefits are at 'social' prices. A contentious matter was the treatment of costs and benefits over time. The combination technique is called 'discounting', which equates future costs and benefits to current ones, by reducing them by a proportion related to the time into the future. While it was accepted in principle, there was considerable disagreement as to the correct proportion, the 'discount rate' set by Treasury at 10 per cent real (i.e. after adjusting for inflation). The discount rate is not dissimilar to a profit rate. In effect the criteria was setting a requirement of earning on investment of 10 percent above inflation. The rate also affects the pace of exploitation of the environment, a high rate giving a lower valuation to the future. Thus there was opposition from an odd alliance of the private sector, who thought the discount rate was far above a reasonable private sector profit rate, and the environmentalists, who thought it led to environmentally destructive outcomes. It was also criticised by academic economists and by many other officials in government departments. Although Treasury had the final say among economists because of its position in the advice structure, its recommendation could be, and was, overturned at Cabinet level, by the acceptance of projects which failed the 10 percent hurdle.

The heated squabble was so focused upon the discount rate that other issues were ignored. Firms and agencies often found they could make benefits exceed costs despite the given discount rate, by including optimistic assumptions about key parameters. The CBA was calculated before the event, and there were rarely any penalties if the analysis subsequently proved incorrect. All the private sector had to ensure was that its private profit targets were attained. Given that, and given a satisfactory CBA outcome, the firm would become eligible for any government assistance. Public sector enterprises had even more incentive to miscalculate, because although the CBA imputed a required return of 10 percent above inflation the capital was advanced to them at interest rates typically below inflation, giving an enormous cushion to any miscalculation.

The officials were aware of the public sector interest rate anomaly, and regularly recommended increasing the interest rate charged to public enterprises to market levels—not least to ease the fiscal position. But the connection with the CBA criteria does not seem to have been made. More generally the 'enforcement issue', how to ensure the plans in a CBA are carried out, does not seem to have been prominent in their considerations.

Even more crucial was the insufficient assessment of the (downside) risk in the project evaluation. Admittedly there was an (often inadequate) allowance for contingencies, and usually there was a sensitivity analysis of some of the crucial assumptions. However, little official attention appears to have been given as to who would bear any losses. The CBAs evaluated aggregate social welfare, ignoring the distribution of the welfare gains and losses. For instance a project in which the richest gained a net benefit of 100, and the poorest made a loss of 99 would be passed by the CBA criteria, since the aggregate net gain to the country was 1. This concentration on 'efficiency' (i.e. treating a dollar as having the same value to every person) remains a feature of Treasury analysis, right through the Rogernomics period.

Another issue is what happens if the actual outcome is a loss. There is nothing in the sensitivity analysis of the CBA to indicate how the loss would be shared, just as there is nothing in the CBA to indicate who are the beneficiaries.

Thus the project evaluation procedures had a number of grave problems—what was the right discount rate, how was the evaluation to be enforced, who bore the burden if the project failed—which were addressed poorly if at all. While these defects were important when the technique was applied to small projects, the Think Big evaluation exercises involved much higher stakes, and CBA failed.

17

THINK BIG

Originally 'Think Big' was applied to a group of large energy-based investments. Subsequently it was applied to virtually any big investment project mooted in the early 1980s. The original energy-based projects were driven by four factors:

1 the finding of the Maui gas field in 1968, and the take-or-pay agreement signed in 1973, which would deliver vast quantities of natural gas into the New Zealand economy from the late 1970s and for which there were insufficient existing markets;
2 the over-investment in electricity generation in the mid 1970s which would also oversupply energy—this time electricity—from the late 1970s;
3 the oil price hikes of 1973 and 1979 and the widely held belief that oil prices—and so world energy prices—would continue to rise relative to overall prices; and
4 the forestry planting program begun in the 1950s now coming to harvest, creating large investment requirements for processing, much of which was energy-intensive.

For various reasons, including environmental ones, many of the proposed projects were politically contentious. There was also considerable concern that the massive investment demands would crowd out smaller (and perhaps more valuable) businesses. A major public debate took place, and the National government made 'Think Big' a centrepiece of its 1981 election manifesto.

The underlying economic model was the thrust to rapid industrialisation that came out of the economic development literature of the 1950s, and which harked back to Soviet industrialisation in the 1920s and 1930s. The strategy involved unbalanced growth, based upon big, capital-intensive, government-promoted (and often protected) industries which, through a series of linkages with other industries, would drag the rest of the economy with them into a process of sustained self-generating growth. The strategy had not been successful in the third-world countries and had fallen out of favour. But even with hindsight one can argue that if the strategy was going to succeed anywhere in the world, New Zealand was close to the ideal—providing the world energy price followed the predicted rising path.

The New Zealand projects avoided the corruption that dogged the third-world equivalents, hit severe construction cost overruns in some projects but not others, and probably crowded out some alternative developments through a lift in the real exchange rate. Some projects, it appears, would have been disasters under virtually any scenario. Others would have succeeded if world oil prices had not collapsed. For instance, the synthetic petrol plant was expected to break even at $US25 a barrel, around half the predicted figure at the time. By the time it came on stream (near budget), world oil prices were well below $US20 a barrel.

There was considerable resistance to the program from many officials, although without detailed papers it is difficult to give a comprehensive account. The public impression is that the criticisms were based upon the neoclassical models of economic allocation from which CBA is derived, rather than the critique of the more dynamic unbalanced growth model. The debate was wide-ranging, including the extent of the incorporation of environmental factors, disputes over the projected prices (particularly the economic value of electricity and gas), and the inevitable disagreement over the appropriate discount rate. The individual projects rarely attained a return of 10 percent real without some massaging of the numbers. Sometimes the government simply abandoned the hurdle altogether and accepted lower returns.

Official advice was generally against proceeding with most of the projects, but the officials lost. It was not just that much of their advice was rejected. Subsequent events show they were usually correct, although perhaps for the wrong reasons, for few contemplated the low oil prices of the mid 1980s. Nor should we assume the officials were always right. Late 1984 Treasury estimates—after the construction stage—gave a return on the projects of 6 percent p.a. real, which as Graeme Wells suggested was not too bad after the event.[6]

And while the officials were ultimately right, the debate failed to focus on the crucial issues of who bore the risk and how plans might be enforced, because it was centred on Treasury-determined CBA criteria. In consequence, little notice was taken of the fact that the downside risk was borne by the taxpayer. As each project failed, the fiscal burden rose.

AN ALTERNATIVE APPROACH

The outcome of the Think Big proposals was seen as a disaster, although the officials tended to explain the failure as an example of the Muldoon policies rather than an outcome of their policy advice framework. The CBA framework, developed in the early 1970s, was not only under attack by the rest of the economics profession, but it had manifestly failed in restraining the excesses of Think Big.

One alternative was to reconstruct and strengthen the CBA framework. That would have involved a recognition that it was part of a planning framework. But intervention, be it co-ordinated in a plan or ad hoc as with Muldoon, was not attractive to the officials.

As often happens, the solution came from struggling with different problems, which appeared to have little to do with the Think Big projects. Telecommunications, an industry with rapid growth of demand and technology, and highly capital-intensive production, was another area where the government was the major investor. How was the government to decide upon its investing, funding, and pricing? The traditional answer was to use CBA, but the officials working on the problem began to see imitation of the private market as an alternative. The inspiration was not theirs alone. The first publicly available paper shows they were greatly influenced by overseas thinking, including that of the Chicago school.[7]

At first Treasury did not fully adopt the approach. *Economic Management*, the 1984 Treasury post-election briefing, uses it, but not wholeheartedly. The strongest exposition is in an appendix which cautiously advocates some privatisation. Yet the analysis became increasingly convincing to Treasury and its 1987 post-election briefing, *Government Management*, explicitly and strongly advocated privatisation of government trading activities. The commercialisation strategy solved a number of Treasury concerns.

First, it provided a justification for the withdrawal of industrial protection and assistance. No longer would officials have to advise upon, and politicians decide upon, the 'picking of winners'. Moreover by placing explicit responsibility in the hands of private sector managers, the responsibility for accommodating their failures is reduced.

Second, it provided a ready alternative to CBA for invest-ment decisions. Economic liberalisation (including the com-mercialisation of the state-owned enterprises) would mean, Treasury supposed, that market prices would move close to the value society placed on those resources, so there would be no need for that adjustment. The corporation's internal discount rate for financial decisions became the relevant one for the ex-ercise, thus avoiding the dispute over the right one (although it sneaked back in when Treasury had to set a target rate of return on its shareholder equity). Corporations would recognise that they had to live with the decisions they had made, thus solving the enforcement problem. And as long as there was no govern-ment money, no government guarantees, and no government subsidies, none of the risk would be born directly by the state.

Third, the approach gave an account for the poor growth performance of the New Zealand economy. This included the traditional account, which came from the protection debate, that government intervention was leading to misallocation of resources, particularly of investment and especially in the gov-ernment enterprise sector. The new story added that the inter-ventions redirected managerial initiative from productivity seeking to 'rent seeking'; that is, manipulating the political environment to the advantage of the firm without any gains in actual output.

Fourth, the government was no longer to be exposed to underwriting private sector mistakes and, in addition, the gov-ernment fiscal position would be improved because state-owned enterprises would no longer be implicitly subsidised by low interest charges, nor would their investments appear as govern-ment spending.

Fifth, in a Treasury squeezed between revenue shortages and spending pressures, it was easy to believe the (unproven) notion that if only the public sector was run on private sector lines it would attain the essential public objectives at a lower cost (since the theory said that the private sector was always more efficient than the public sector).

Finally, there was no need to admit the failure of the CBA framework. Rather it could be quietly dropped as opportunities to use it were eliminated. Those private sector economists who had specialised in the technique eased over to corporatisation and privatisation analysis.

THE POLITICIANS' RESPONSE

Labour has been the natural party of Think Big. Selecting winners was practised by each of the three previous Labour governments, and Douglas's 1980 *There's Got to Be a Better Way!* shows him as the biggest of the 'Think Biggers'. But between 1980 and 1984 the restructurers moved away from intervention,[8] although the 1984 manifesto had promised a substantial government-directed investment fund.

The new government avoided this promise by establishing a committee to investigate the proposal. The resulting report was broadly opposed to intervention, although there was a dissent from the union minority.[9] Ironically for those who fought for the fund in the manifesto, the outcome was the establishment of the Economic Development Commission, which has maintained a strong anti-interventionist stand.

How Labour was captured by the commercialisation strategy is sketched in Chapter 5. Certainly the critics of 'Think Big' in opposition found it politically advantageous to play up the scheme's failures. The rhetoric moved them to an anti-interventionist stance. But this is not the same thing as commercialisation.

While commercialisation/corporatisation principles were creeping into government policy from the November 1984 budget, probably the watershed was the *Economic Statement* of December 1985, which announced a set of principles for state-owned enterprises (SOEs) that produced goods on a commercial basis. These included the following:

- Responsibility for non-commercial objectives was to be separated from major trading SOEs.
- Managers were to be given the principal objective of running the SOEs as successful business enterprises.
- Managers were to be given responsibility for deciding how they achieved performance objectives agreed with ministers, and were to be held accountable to ministers and Parliament.
- The advantages and disadvantages which SOEs had, including 'unnecessary' barriers to competition, were to be removed so that 'commercial criteria will provide a fair assessment of managerial performance'.
- Each SOE was to be reconstructed according to its commercial

purpose under the guidance of boards comprising, generally, private sector members.

These principles were added to by the statement of *Principles Guiding the 1986 Expenditure Review*[10] (which also put the trading activities of departments which were not SOEs on a more commercial basis), and the *Statement on Government Expenditure Reform*.[11] None of the three statements is explicit about the form of ownership. The eventual outcome, corporatisation, was to simulate as closely as possible private sector ownership, with the shareholding being held by two ministers: a structure ideal for privatisation. Yet Roger Douglas describes these changes in terms of public expenditure control, and even denied they were directed towards eventual privatisation.[12]

It seems likely the majority of Cabinet went down this path without fully understanding its implications. During 1986 at least three senior and involved ministers stated that the intention was to improve the delivery of social spending and there was no intention to privatise the SOEs. Politicians rarely lie blatantly (although they are well known for being economical with the truth). That subsequent events contradicted the three and Douglas, suggests the politicians did not understand the political implications of the course they had embarked upon, just as they did not foresee that corporatisation was a step towards privatisation.

FROM CORPORATISATION TO PRIVATISATION

Treasury did. They had indicated in their 1984 post-election briefing that they supported privatisation, they set up the corporatisation program to facilitate it, and Treasury officials were heard to explain to sympathetic business audiences that corporatisation was a step to eventual privatisation. Their position was probably that even if this government did not go all the way, a subsequent government would.

Perhaps the day came earlier than they expected. In early 1987 government announced it would sell shares in the Bank of New Zealand and Petrocorp. The (June) 1987 Budget announced the selling of all the government shares in NZ Steel and the DFC, the selling of a quarter of its equity in Air New Zealand, and that other SOEs would be authorised to issue up to a quarter of their capital in state enterprise equity bonds, a form of non-voting public share holding. The December 1987 *Economic Statement* committed the government to a much more extensive form of privatisation, fully selling the state-owned enterprises which had been corporatised. So corporatisation and privatisation proceeded, much as Treasury had envisaged, under Labour and under the following National government. The official reason presented was that they were a means of getting down government debt, but in reality they were a part of the commercialisation strategy.

2

The Economic Theory of Commercialisation

IN THE PREVIOUS CHAPTER WE SAW HOW THE FOURTH LABOUR government converted its state-owned enterprises into business corporations, with shareholding ministers, and then sold its equity (shares) in these businesses to the private sector. Other government assets were also sold off—privatised.

The term 'privatisation' is sometimes extended to arrangements whereby a public agency contracts out work to the private sector. Today cleaning (and other services) in many hospitals, which used to be managed by the area health boards using their own employees, is contracted out to private businesses, who employ the workers, carrying out the task for the Crown health enterprise. Other examples include the State Services Commission hiring an agency to search for a departmental chief executive, Treasury hiring a consultant to provide some report which in the past would have been prepared internally, or the National Provident Fund hiring a private sector firm to manage its investment fund.

User pays might also be thought of as 'privatisation' (of the demand side), although this may be extending the meaning of the word too far. Or how are we to describe the notion behind legislation that implies that government agencies should be run as closely as possible like private businesses? Or what about the rules which put the government accounts on the same basis as the private sector? Better to use a more encompassing term, keeping 'privatisation' to where the asset ownership or service supply is in private hands.

This more encompassing term is 'commercialisation', which may be defined as 'the application of business (or commercial)

25

principles to the public sector (or a particular public sector activity)'. Note that the term applies both to circumstances where the application is practical and where it is impracticable. It is a theme of this book that commercialisation ceased to be a practical solution to various pressing problems, but became an all-encompassing application to all public sector activity, whether or not there was a problem. The 'if it ain't broke don't fix it' approach was replaced by an 'if it ain't commercialised it's broke' mentality. Just as the mythological innkeeper Procrustes insisted all travellers should exactly fit his beds—stretching them or truncating them to achieve this—the policy became that all government activity had to be made as commercial as possible. The underlying philosophy was 'business is always best'. The policy problem became why an activity was not being run on business lines.

How did this approach arise? That is one of the themes of this book, but briefly the commercialisation model proved successful in some key areas, such as the management of state-owned enterprises, and was extended to other areas, irrespective of its appropriateness, replacing the old paradigm of public sector management. Since commercialisation is advantageous to the private sector, there evolved a synergistic political liaison between the parts of the public sector enthused with the theory of commercialisation and the parts of the private sector which were its beneficiaries.

Yet the theory of commercialisation is not entirely a matter of ideology. There are some economic principles which indicate both when commercialisation may succeed and when it is likely to fail.

THE EFFICACY OF THE MARKET

This is not an economics textbook, so we simply report a substantial body of economic theory as follows. The market may be thought of as a signalling system which co-ordinates the decisions of the various actors in an economy. It has two key features. First, under certain circumstances (details to be outlined shortly), the price signals reflect the social value of the resources being used or traded. Second, the signalling system is self-enforcing, in that the actors obey the signals out of self-interest.

The central notion here is that the price system sends signals which reflect social values that people act on. If you go into a shop and purchase a loaf of bread for a dollar, the price signal of the dollar says that the social cost of producing that bread was one dollar. Presumably your purchase reflects your belief that the bread is worth to you at least one dollar, so you are better off, and society (or, in this case, the shopkeeper) is no worse off, because it has exchanged something which was worth a dollar, for a coin which can be exchanged for something worth at least another dollar.

If every economic transaction—including trade but also the transformation (production) and use of goods and services— takes place under conditions in which individuals participate only if the transaction makes them better off, then it may be there is an ongoing increase in the general welfare of the individuals as each transaction occurs. Even before the modern computer was invented, economists saw the market economy as a computing device which enabled the economy to attain some maximum welfare. This simple idea hides a minefield of complexities, which economists have been struggling with since at least the time of Adam Smith, and which no short account can summarise. But there are some critical issues for our purposes.

First, observe that whether the loaf is worth a dollar to a person not only reflects her or his personal circumstances and preferences, but also the quantum of money (or income) possessed. A person down to their last dollar is much less likely to part with it for the bread than a millionaire. Thus any social value embodied in the prices reflects the distribution of income and wealth in the nation. If the distribution was different the price signals might be different.

Second, we have to suppose that the individual has a clear idea as to what they are purchasing. This is not simply a matter that sometimes one sells an old couch without knowing there are some fifty-dollar banknotes stuffed down the back. In many cases the product being transacted is extremely complex, with multi-faceted aspects—a car, a medical service—so there is a problem about how well informed the purchaser is.

Third, sometimes the transaction may have side-effects which may be detrimental or beneficial to those not involved in the transactions and whose interests are not taken into consideration. The traditional example was a production process involving chimney smoke which pollutes the air, with soot descending on the neighbours' washing. (Ironically while such polluting does not happen so much today, there is now the problem of the greenhouse effect, where carbon emissions into the atmosphere contribute to global warming. Today's 'neighbourhood' may be the whole world.) The soot involves the neighbours in additional costs which are not usually taken into consideration during the market transaction. Thus the price signals of the value of the good to the purchaser may not reflect the full social cost. Such phenomena are called 'externalities', and may be briefly defined as those costs and benefits of a transaction which are not taken into consideration during the (internal) decisions concerned with the transaction. Externalities need not be detrimental.

Fourth, a standard market framework may be practically impossible. For instance, it has not been practical to charge for a broadcasting transmission. Eventually cheap effective charging systems may be developed, but there are always other things in a society for which the market is totally inapplicable. How does it incorporate the values of honesty and kindness, for example?

Fifth, in order to have some social optimum we require that the transformations and trade use the minimum possible resources. This is the 'efficiency' criterion. (See Chapter 3.) To use more would be to waste resources which could be used elsewhere to produce other goods and services, and an even better social outcome. A means of attaining this efficiency—one which is assumed in the market models we are considering here—is that the transactions take place in competitive markets, where 'competition' means that there are numerous agents (firms) buying and selling (consuming and producing) in the market, none of which has significant market power (or influence). If there is not the competition, then the agents have less incentive to seek the most efficient (least wasteful) means of operations. A more complicated case is where there is a monopolist, because even though its internal operations are efficient, it will use its market power to set prices above the level which reflects social costs, so distorting the market signalling system.

This brief review of the strengths and weaknesses of the market casts some doubts upon the efficacy of the market for achieving best economic outcomes. The next question is harder. What is the alternative?

Before answering the question specifically, the general point must be made that there is no perfect solution to organising something as complex as human society. Every method of organisation resolves some of the difficulties, but other difficulties remain, are compounded, or are created. In practice there have to be compromises, in which the worst outcomes are blunted, but some inevitable issues remain unresolved.

All the easy solutions to social problems have almost always been adopted, for the obvious reason that they are easy. The difficult problems, for which there are no easy solutions, are left. This is not to argue that improvements are impossible. First, society may want to change its trade-offs between what is acceptable and what is not. For instance, past solutions treated women in ways which are likely to be unacceptable today. Second, new circumstances may offer new possibilities for solution. If free-to-air broadcasting evolved because charging was expensive, the feasibility of pay-TV opens new possibilities which may (or may not) lead to a better broadcasting system.

DESIGNING AN ECONOMIC SYSTEM

There is not the room here to discuss all the possible designs of an economic system, even were we to confine ourselves to possibilities for late-twentieth-century New Zealand. Instead we begin with the vision of a social democrat, Australian social theorist Michael Pusey, author of the influential *Economic Rationalism in Canberra*, who wrote:

> A first assumption of social democrats everywhere is that nation societies (and federations such as the emerging Europe) have not one coordinating structure but two. On the one side they have states, bureaucracies and the law, and on the other, economies, markets and money. It is with these structures we collectively coordinate our relations with the rest of the world, our work, our social interactions, and most other aspects of life we understand as 'civil society' and normatively define with notions of citizenship, democracy, and human rights.[1]

While we may wish to refine the details of Pusey's account, the notion of there being at least two co-ordinating systems of social activities is central to a modern democracy. Sometimes it uses bureaucratic co-ordination, sometimes market co-ordination, and often a mixture of the two.

29

However this vision does not tell us which co-ordinating system is to be used in any particular situation. For a social democrat, that is a pragmatic decision in which the various advantages and disadvantages of outcomes are weighed. Very often some mix of the two modes of co-ordination are synthesised. Chapters later in the book examine particular cases.

As it happens the production and distribution of most goods and services is left to the market mechanism, with a minimum of bureaucratic intervention. Even under the most interfering period during the Muldoon regime the production and purchase of bread was largely determined by market behaviour, as was that of other goods and services. Indeed it is very difficult for the bureaucratic mechanism to override the market mechanism, where the conditions described above—of the market acting as a enforceable signalling system for social value—apply.

Where the conditions do not quite apply, so that the signalling is not quite perfect, it may nevertheless be better to rely on the market mechanism, since the alternative is likely to be much less satisfactory. Sometimes the bureaucratic mechanism will operate so as to enhance the market mechanism. The appendix describes how complicated bureaucratic interventions in the environment were replaced in the 1980s with ones based more on the market mechanism. Another example is the conscious strategy of 'internalising externalities' by levying excise duty on alcohol and tobacco, so that their market price better signals the social costs of their consumption, which are otherwise ignored by drinkers and smokers.

The advantage of the market mechanism is not only that it can often (albeit roughly) signal the social value of resources. It is also self-enforcing. On the other hand the cost–benefit analysis approach, discussed in the previous chapter, is also a signalling system, but it is not self-enforcing. If proponents of a Think Big project changed key project parameters in order to get their desired outcome, they could do so with impunity, because there was no penalty for getting a CBA wrong—not to them, only to the economy.

THE SELF-ENFORCING MARKET

To explain the strengths and weaknesses of the self-enforcing market mechanism we use 'principal–agent' analysis, and contrast a standard economic transaction where the self-enforcement works well, with a medical one, where it is markedly less effective. An agency relationship arises when one party (the agent) acts in the interests of another party (the principal). There are two crucial differences between the agent and principal: a divergence in interests between the two parties, and an asymmetry—an imbalance—of information between them. How are the interests of the principal and agent to be reconciled?

Consider a standard market transaction of purchasing bread. Suppose a person, who in this case is the principal, goes to a shop to purchase the bread, where the shop assistant is the agent. As well as the transfer of product and money,

- someone decides on the transaction;
- someone funds the transaction;
- someone/thing regulates the transaction.

In the case of the purchase of bread the situation is this:

- the decider is the principal (the shopper);
- the funder is the principal;
- the regulator is competition backed by the law.

Note that the agent's interest is to sell the bread for the highest possible price, while the principal has an interest in the quality of the bread and in buying it at the lowest possible price. The agent probably knows much more about the quality of the bread, its cost, and the going price in other shops. Yet the principal purchases from the shop, usually without looking at every other possibility and usually with only the most cursory assessment of the bread.

What makes a transaction possible despite the divergence in interests and the asymmetry of information? The answer is complex, and related to the regulatory environment:

- It is a repeated transaction. If shoppers get a bad deal they do not have to go back to the shop again. This is an incentive for the agent to perform well on the principal's behalf to get the best long-run return.
- Competition is crucial. If the shopper had to go back to the same shop every week perhaps the service would not be as good.
- The transaction is underpinned by law. Few shoppers know their exact rights, but if anything dreadful happens—say a

mouse inside the bread—there are channels for redress. The mere threat of litigation and public exposure keeps most shop owners very mindful of their customers' interest: a court case is not only expensive, it could also be ruinous to the shop-keeper's reputation.

- Although there is asymmetry of information between the purchaser and provider, it is not great, and in this case the 'suck it and see' test is relatively inexpensive.

There is a sort of 'miracle' of the supply of bread, for there is no dictator or bureaucracy who decrees that it should happen. Despite involving numerous people—cereal farmers, truckers, millers, bakers, and shopkeepers—most of whom are anonymous as far as the consumer is concerned, the market co-ordinates all their activities to provide the bread required. Principal–agent theory points out that in each transaction through to the consumer the incentives are aligned so that the myriad of complex transactions are effectively co-ordinated to supply us with our daily bread.

However, in most medical transactions the principal (the patient) is unlikely to be the decider. One of the reasons patients go to a medical professional (the agent) is because they do not have the technical information to diagnose and treat their conditions. In principle an unscrupulous doctor could commit the patient to all manner of treatment, without the patient being able to judge the appropriateness of the therapies.

Not only are patients typically not the deciders, at least not practically, but they are rarely the full funders. The incidence of disease is erratic. The patient may have medical insurance, while the community also moderates a full user-pays approach to health care for reasons of equity, and because private medical insurance is not an especially efficient way of covering for the erratic incidence.

If the decider is not the funder, the principal and the agent—that is, the patient and the doctor—have an interest in pursuing a transaction (a treatment) without reference to the cost, since it will be borne by someone else. This is obviously true for the public health system, but it also applies to private medical insurance. Practically the patient and doctor can conspire against the medical insurer to generate treatments which are not in the insurer's interests, nor in those of the economy as a whole. The resulting outcome can be very inefficient.

Because the principal—the patient—is not the decider, competition does not work as a regulator; and, as the American experience shows, law—at least malpractice law—is not especially effective either. That is why most countries use additional regulators such as professional ethics, supervision, peer reviews, requirements for informed consent, controls over clinicians' use of hospital resources, and the direct involvement of government ministries in the minutiae of medical practice.

To summarise, in comparison to the standard market transaction, the typical medical transaction is as follows. While the provider (the health professional) is again the agent, and the receiver (the patient) is again the principal (but may not be the purchaser),

- the decider is usually the agent (not the principal);
- the funder is usually someone else (not the principal);
- the regulator is competition backed by the law (as occurs in the standard market transaction) plus a range of other regulatory mechanisms.

As the self-enforcement mechanism of the market fails, bureaucratic mechanisms come into play.

The reader will observe here a very pragmatic account of the choice, in any particular instance, between the degree a society uses the bureaucratic mechanism and the degree to which it uses the market mechanism for co-ordination. Both the market mechanism and the bureaucratic mechanism are practical means to a higher end. However, the commercialisation strategy was not simply a practical application. It was enthusiastically applied to situations which economic analysis by itself could not justify. Indeed commercialisation seemed to become an end in itself. Its justification was ideological.

IS PRIVATE OWNERSHIP SO MUCH BETTER THAN PUBLIC OWNERSHIP?

Although Richard Prebble, the Minister of State-Owned Enterprises in the Labour government, justified privatisation as a means of retiring debt, the main justification for the sale of state-owned assets was the claim it would generate gains in efficiency. Debt retirement is not a favoured argument by most economists, because it gives the impression that the fiscal stance may be relaxed, with the proceeds from sales going to additional spending and/or tax reductions.[2] But are there efficiency gains to be made? That rests on the question as to whether a privately owned enterprise is more efficient than a publicly owned one. Some would answer ideologically, but positive economic theory gives far more cautious answers.

For the economy to be efficient, it is necessary that firms seek efficiency. It can be shown that under certain (competitive) conditions this is equivalent to firms seeking to maximise their profits. But do they? A number of economists have argued that corporations in monopolistic or quasi-monopolistic markets do not. Rather the managers use the firms' market advantage to make sufficient profits to satisfy shareholders and then seek other goals such as higher managerial remuneration, status, technological excellence, and maximum turnover.[3] The managers are agents who would not align their interests with those of their shareholders. Yet these principals, it is argued, have few means of controlling their agents. Such behaviour is likely to frustrate the efficacy of the market as an enforceable signalling mechanism.

An ingenious resolution was to accept the possibility that corporate managers would avoid maximising profits if they could, but to argue that the sharemarket was a market for corporate ownership. Firms which were not maximising profits would be taken over by hungry corporate raiders, who would pay the shareholders a premium for their shares above that justified by the market earnings and replace the management with one which would pursue efficiency. By doing so the raiders would make a sufficient increase in the firm's profit to recoup their takeover costs, and still leave themselves a profit. This possibility of takeover and managerial redundancy, it was argued, was sufficient to keep managers seeking maximum profits rather that some other objective.

Perhaps the theory sounded more plausible in the heady days before the 1987 sharemarket crash when mergers were popular. The theory is perhaps less intuitively convincing in the more subdued 1990s, as firms which survived the crash regret their ill-considered mergers, and when demergers and selling off disparate business activities are common.

One prediction from the theory is that firms which are not subject to the threat of takeover are likely to be less efficient than firms that are subject to market disciplines. The former includes firms which are government-owned. The ideologist would think the theory proves that publicly owned businesses are less efficient; the scientist would test the proposition. (Some evidence suggests that firms with one or a few significant shareholders perform better, because of the closer shareholder supervision of management. If this is true, it might suggest that wholly government-owned firms will perform better than the market average.)

In the New Zealand privatisation debate, there was considerable romanticism about the efficacy of the private sector, perhaps understandably, when officials and politicians have had so little business experience. The claim by Jennings and Cameron that 'the empirical studies are almost unanimous in finding evidence of superior efficiency for private sector firms',[4] a sentiment repeated in Treasury's 1987 post-election briefing,[5] may be put down to enthusiasm rather than a hard-headed reading of the research. Any systematic survey of the research evidence has to be cautious in its conclusions. A not untypical summary is 'privatisation through asset sale can in some circumstances be worthwhile, yielding a reduction in resource waste in the overall economy'.[6] Among the exceptions the writers identify are cases where there is monopoly or there is government regulation. In conditions of full competition the publicly owned firm is likely to be about as efficient as a privately owned one.

There is one other obvious exception. Suppose the government instructs its businesses not to pursue profit but to seek some other objective (or objectives). Then the firm will not be efficient based on a measure of its profits. If the firm is later given a profit objective, as occurred under the State-Owned Enterprises Act, there will be substantial gains in efficiency on this measure (and perhaps on others, depending on the previous objectives), even though the firm remains in public ownership.[7] The empirical evidence suggests that once a government-owned enterprise is required to pursue profits it becomes about as efficient (on a profit maximisation criterion) as the same firm in private ownership.

Not that this convinces ideologists.

Appendix: Applying More-Market to the Environment

While environmentalism is becoming a potent political force, most environmentalists have not abandoned material values. Undoubtedly some have, living in circumstances others would consider primitive and uncomfortable, or forgoing high-income-earning opportunities to campaign for the goals they believe in. But the majority of environmental supporters are willing to make only limited sacrifices: donations, a little time to sign a petition or attend a rally. Basically they desire material welfare and the environment.

There is an apparent exception when people appear to be willing to trade off material gains for environmental objectives. However, that often involves trading off someone else's material gains. The classic case was the dispute over the West Coast native forests, when the locals claimed the environmentalists were willing to destroy West Coasters' jobs (in the forestry, allied, and servicing industries) in order to preserve the indigenous forests.

The implications of this need to be teased out. Characteristically, environmental policy involves public bads, that is outputs which are not wanted (such as pollution). Typically private market decisions result in an over-supply of public bads, so there is ongoing political pressure for measures to decrease the total production of environmental bads. (There is also the converse, which is equally unsatisfactory, of the market under-supplying public goods—outputs that are desired but not profitable to produce.) Measures intended to decrease the production of environmental bads will reduce the production of some associated private goods and services and will leave their producers and the consumers worse off. Thus there are almost always distributional consequences from environmental policies.

Consider the issue of global warming, which is the result of the emission of carbon dioxide and methane into the air, typically as by-products of some process which is producing desired goods and services. Because increases in the gases result in increases in air temperatures (global warming) which is judged detrimental, they are economic bads. But the emitters of the bads do not pay for their discharges, and so do not take into consideration in their business decisions or profit calculations any impact

of the emissions on the environment. In so far as there is a reduction of emission of the carbon-based gases, and a net gain in
overall social welfare, there is also likely to be a reduction in the
profitability and welfare of the producers and the consumers of
the products which caused the emissions. If a coal-fired power
station is closed, the miners who supplied the coal, the owners
of and workers in the power station, and the consumers of its
electricity (among others) are likely to be worse off.

In the past environmental decision making was based on
heavy administrative interventions overruling the market. In
some places the interventions were even directly to the detriment
of the environment. Price controls on indigenous timber resulted
in rimu being used for packing cases and similar low-quality
uses. Underpricing of electricity resulted in its increased intensity
of use, and additional pressures on rivers and lakes in order to
supply the additional demand. Here would be a coming together
of the 'more-market' advocates and the environmentalists.

THE MARKET AND THE ENVIRONMENT

Although there was a commonality of interests between the economic advisers and the environmentalists against those interventions which encouraged environmental depletions, there are
other situations where the market might be detrimental to the
environment. However, a burgeoning development in the area
of economics and law enabled further commonality. If by the
1970s some New Zealand economists were using the literature,
the majority of the environmental movement were unaware of
the intellectual underpinnings—even in the early 1990s. Yet the
approach became central to the reforms. The foundation of the
approach is the Coase Theorem, one of those amazing insights,
rich with subtle implications. It can be expressed in a number
of ways, but may be stated as:

> Providing the property rights of a resource are fully and un-
> ambiguously allocated, and transaction costs are zero, the use of
> the resource will be independent of the property rights.[1]

We illustrate the theorem with a classic example. Suppose
there is a proposal for an airport which will generate noise, dis-
turbing residents in an adjacent suburb. The property rights of

making a noise might be allocated to the airport land owners, or to the residents. In the first case the airport can go ahead, ignoring the residents' interests. In the second the residents can prohibit the aircraft noise. However in the first case the residents might purchase the airport land thus preventing the building and the noise. In the second case the airport might purchase from the residents the right to make the noise. The theorem states that if both options are possible (and the costs of transacting the deals are zero) then the ultimate use of the land for the airport will be independent of who was given the initial rights to make, or prohibit, the noise. What this means is the use of the land resource, and the level of noise pollution from the airport, can be settled by market processes with less recourse to legal processes, providing the property rights are well specified (and the transactions cost small).

Ergo, by being more precise about property rights associated with resources various environmental dilemmas can be resolved at least to some extent, with an improvement in efficiency. Thus there was considerable activity in the 1980s with the aim of clarifying the property rights associated with resource ownership:

- In 1983 the right to catch deep sea fish was transferred to a system of 'individual transferable quotas' (ITQs). The almost permanent quotas could be used or sold by the private owners, typically fishing companies. The theory was that giving fishers unambiguous, but limited, rights to catch specified fish would enable the maximum harvesting of the fishery without depletion. The quota does not give the company ownership of the fish, only of the right to catch it. But what about by-catches when other fish is caught by accident? What if research shows the existing ITQs exceed the optimal level?
- In 1989 the right to use a section of the radio frequency spectrum was leased out, with property rights not unlike the ITQs. The original proposal by Treasury to the Royal Commission on Broadcasting involved a system where disputes (e.g. from interference) would be settled in court. However since most of such infringements would be minor, and expensive to settle through the usual legal process, a simpler administrative system was set up as a first stage. Transaction costs can be important.
- In 1986 ITQs were extended to inshore fishing. The allocation rule tended to exclude Maori inshore fishers. The resulting

protest ultimately led to the Sealords deal in which the Crown gave the Maori a greater involvement in all (including deep-sea) fishing in exchange for the abolition of Maori fishing claims under common and statute law.[2] The application of the principles implied in Coase's Theorem gives no guidance to who initially should be allocated the property rights. (In other cases the government avoided the problem by taking the rights itself, and then selling them to the highest bidder.)

As well as the problems of defining the property rights precisely, limiting the transaction costs (which may involve a non-market involvement), and making the initial allocation of the rights, there is another complicated effect, which at first looks unimportant, but which ultimately limited the use of market solutions to environmental issues.

Suppose a piece of land is ideal for a piggery. Applying Coase's Theorem, the use of the land should not be affected by its ownership. But consider a situation where the owners might be pork eaters or not. Possibly the ownership of the property rights might affect the income distribution between pork eaters and pork abstainers, and so affect market demand for pork. In this case the use of the land depends upon who owns it. Implicit in the Coase Theorem is the notion that the distribution of the property rights (and so the income it generates) does not affect demand and prices in the economy.

The example just given is so tenuous that one might well treat this caveat as of little importance. But the distributional property rights cannot be so easily dismissed. A key issue is the rights that unborn generations have in current resources. If we could ask them, a future generation might well have a different view of the rate we should deplete an oil field, in contrast to the view of this generation. An ingenious (but partial) resolution of this conflict was introduced in the Resource Management Act. But first, the developments between 1984 and 1989 should be examined.

REORGANISING THE ENVIRONMENT

The 1984 Labour caucus contained a number of committed environmentalists, few of whom were Rogernomes committed to commercialisation solutions. At an early stage, however, they found a common interest with the economic reformers, with-drawing subsidies, price controls, and other interventions which encouraged environment depletion.

This was reinforced by the state sector reorganisation conse-quential on the corporatisation of the state-owned enterprises. A process of accretion had resulted in a number of agencies having both commercial functions and conservation ones. Frequently these were thought to be in conflict. How could the New Zealand Forest Service both manage indigenous forest for conservation, and at the same time manage other forests for commercial tim-ber production, especially when there were disputes over some forests as to which end they should be used for? How could the Department of Lands and Survey both develop some lands and conserve others?

We do not here detail the reorganisation, but a number of gov-ernment agencies were created—the Ministry for the Environ-ment to advise the government of environmental matters, the Department of Conservation responsible for the heritage holdings of the state—while the Commissioner for the Environment be-came a Parliamentary Commissioner to advise Parliament rather than government. (Note the characteristic separation of roles: a *policy* advising ministry, an *operations* department, and a parlia-mentary commission to *audit* performance. The regulatory role was located in local government and the health system.)

Together with its record on nuclear-free ships, the Labour government was able to fight the 1987 election on a platform of having a viable and progressive environmental policy.

THE RESOURCE MANAGEMENT ACT

The next major phase was a sweeping reform of all the legislation which regulated the environment, culminating in the Resource Management Act passed in 1991. In particular, cost–benefit analysis, with all its defects described earlier, was being used to regulate the use of resources. If the regulation could be put on a market basis there would be no need to use CBA.

Corporatisation had abolished the need for a public sector dis-count rate for investment decisions in state trading activities—the mechanism by which the market allocates resource use over time, and hence allocates rights between generations. Left to themselves businesses would use their required rate of return for commercial investment as an implicit discount rate. Typically this would give a high real discount rate which would encourage resource depletion. Such a resolution was not acceptable to environmentalists.

More-marketers also raised the question of the necessity at all for town planning with its various direct controls and related interventions. The Coase Theorem suggests that a full market system left to itself, with property rights fully allocated, would make administrative interventions unnecessary, or at least less necessary. But as the earlier examples illustrate, there are real difficulties with a simple market strategy: how can one unambiguously identify all the property rights? what about the transaction costs? who receives the property rights?

The resolution to these two issues, embedded in the Resource Management Act (RMA), was ingenious, although experience has yet to determine whether it is practical, as the transaction costs involved may well be onerous. First, a system of planning via tribunals was maintained, but more decisions were left to the market, rather than tribunal direction. Meanwhile transaction costs were put up front, and (hopefully) minimised.

Crucially, Section 5 of the RMA states 'the purpose of this Act is to promote sustainable management of natural and physical resources'. But within that framework of sustainability the RMA tends to permit the best commercial option. In simple terms the RMA tells any project promoter to select, from all the options that are sustainable with respect to natural and physical resources, the one which the promoter prefers (which is likely to be the most profitable).[3] In this way, the RMA sets up a system which allocates the property rights between current and future generations by giving the latter in principle a veto over the unsustainable use of resources. In effect the discount rate over natural resource use (mining excepted) is zero. For all other decisions the much higher commercial discount rate can be used.

CONCLUSION: THE POLITICS OF THE REFORMS

The introduction of market mechanisms into the regulation of resources and the environment was one of the most successful economic reforms. There was no single reason for this, but the following constellation contributed.

Unlike the other microeconomic reforms, the environmental changes were not dependent upon macroeconomic success, or at least were not so judged by the general population. As a rule the introduction of the market was not seen as central to the environmental reforms, although it was.

Second, the more-market environmental reforms seem to have involved big gains in efficiency, probably more than in many of the other cases. To put it the other way around, the previous system of environmental regulation was so clumsy and inefficient that it was possible to make some simple changes which gave substantial gains, at least as seen by those who care about environmental issues.

Third, the reforms involved a comfortable relationship between the environmentalists and the government. In many cases—such as the identification of those resources transferred to the Department of Conservation, and the development of the RMA—there was close liaison between the lobby groups and the officials. The establishment of the 'pro-green' Ministry for the Environment and Department of Conservation gave environmentalists government agencies aligned with their interests.

This is not to say that the environmentalists agreed at the beginning with the reforms. If there had been a referendum in 1984 proposing the widespread introduction of more-market into environmental regulation it would have certainly lost by a wide margin among the greenies. Yet today most would accept that most of the more-market changes which occurred were beneficial to environmental management.

Perhaps key to this was that the reforms were pragmatic and practical, not driven by the extremism which was so dominant in other economic reforms. As a rule, there were not commercial possibilities for big profits. In the few cases where there were— the fishing ITQs, for example—there have been acute political difficulties which have not yet been resolved. Possibly the removal of ambiguity of the property rights of the resources gave sufficient increase in the value of the assets so that the most active players could be compensated.

This pragmatism means that many issues are left unresolved, while the new regime has yet to be tested as rigorously as the old one. That challenge does not seem far out. The overbuilding of energy supply in the 1970s and the economic stagnation of the 1980s meant there was not the same need for additional energy

production in the 1990s. As the task of adding to power generation capacity reappears, the new regime will be challenged. Perhaps the economic stagnation of the 1980s eased the growing
pressures on the environment, giving the chance for the reforms
to bed in without transitional mishap. We may be seeing a return
to the more direct conflict between the environmentalists and the
developers and business.

Yet it is not at all evident that there is a widespread acceptance
of the more-market framework of the environmental reforms by
the majority of the environmentalists. By lobbying for energy conservation measures using non-market solutions (such as subsidies
and prohibition) many environmentalists are again arguing that
the market signals are not giving a socially optimum outcome.
The significant lobby which wants to return to the use of subsidies and more direct interventions on this and other issues shows
that the reforms have yet to win the hearts and minds of all
greenies. It may well prove impossible: while more-market can
improve some aspects of environmental and resource management, there are significant areas which remain intractable to market solutions.

3

The Abandoning of Equity

BETWEEN 1984 AND 1991 THE PUBLIC POLICY OBJECTIVE OF EQUITY, IN any of its meanings of the 1970s, was increasingly abandoned. There was no single moment when this occurred, as happened with employment policy when the Labour government revoked the priority of full employment in its 1987 election manifesto. Rather, a series of incremental decisions were made, each of which reduced the priority of the equity objective, until eventually the government could introduce policies almost obliviously of their impact on the deprived.

There was no coherent and cogent account of the nation's concept of equity in the 1970s. Here we look at three themes—the platitudes of such agencies as the New Zealand Planning Council (NZPC), the 1972 Royal Commission on Social Security (RCSS) and the theme of poverty, and the Muldoon practice of 'Pareto incrementalism'. These three Ps—platitudes, poverty, and Pareto—all played a role in the events after 1984.

Platitudes

There were various attempts in the decade prior to 1984 to construct some sort of consensus in social policy. It amounted to little more than waffle. For example the NZPC document *Issues in Social Equity* says:

> For the purposes of this study, equity has been defined as social justice, or 'getting a fair go'. Attitudes towards fairness depend on the individual point of view, but the sum of individual feelings influences the degree of confidence which society has in itself and its institutions. Thus, in the interests of enhancing the cohesion and well-being of society, govern-

ments should be aware of and monitor feelings about equity.

It is necessary to make a distinction between equity and equality; they are associated but different. An over-emphasis on equality would ignore essential differences between people. Equity is therefore a more justifiable, and more feasible, goal for society.[1]

This is quoted at length, partly because there is an interesting echo later, but also to emphasise the primitive level of the analysis. The introduction by the NZPC chairman shrewdly describes the report as a 'grievance list', and remarks that there was a 'widespread lack of consensus among New Zealanders on what represents fairness in our relations with one another.' Indeed the report gives the impression that New Zealanders—or more precisely those involved in the project—had no coherent notion of equity, or its principles and issues, but had numerous complaints about the state of society, which could be summarised in the childish 'it isn't fair'.

Poverty

There was a second strand in the 1970s, which the Planning Council and government agencies in general tended to ignore, or at best to make passing reference to. It arose out of the deliberations of the 1972 Royal Commission on Social Security, which codified the existing social security system, offering a set of underlying principles, and provided a platform for future development. A notion the Royal Commission proposed was that:

The aims of the system should be
(i) First, to enable everyone to sustain life and health;
(ii) Second, to ensure, within limitations which may be imposed by physical or other disabilities, that everyone is able to enjoy a standard of living much like that of the rest of the community, and thus is able to feel a sense of participation in and belonging to the community.
(iii) Third, where income maintenance alone is insufficient (for example, for a physically disabled person), to improve by other means, as far as possible, the quality of life available.[2]

The original set of principles referred to the social security system, but they became adopted in the wider context of the community as a whole. It is then not a big step to say that where the objectives of the system were not met, the society was failing, and could be said to be inequitable.

The subsequent analysis evolved mainly around poverty, where it was argued that a household was 'poor' which had insufficient income and resources, so that they were unable to participate in and belong to their community. But there is a wider interpretation. Someone may have sufficient income, but still not be able to adequately participate in their community—someone of homosexual inclination before the law reform, say, or a person with mobility limitations who may not have adequate access to buildings important in community life. Moreover the RCSS does not offer a complete account of equity, because it wrote little about the distribution of income above the poverty line, or the distributional principles behind the funding of support for the poor. Nevertheless while it is difficult to operationalise the notion of participation and belonging, this notion is not as platitudinous (or vague) as that which the NZPC was pursuing.

Pareto

We do not know to what extent the platitudes of the NZPC report, or some other equally vague concept of fairness, were important in Robert Muldoon's thinking as Minister of Finance and Prime Minister. We do know that he was influenced by the poverty research in the family policy element of his income tax changes.[3] Equity considerations affected his policy making in other ways.

When officials proposed a policy, Muldoon would often ask who would be made worse off by it. The officials would then be told to see whether anything could be done to prevent or ameliorate these deleterious effects. Implicit in this approach is a vision which sees the current system as fair (or equitable), and a change which makes anyone worse off is unfair or inequitable. This might be called 'Pareto incrementalism'. Vilfredo Pareto was the Italian social scientist who is associated with the criterion that a change improves welfare if someone is better off, and nobody is worse off. Pareto incrementalism is the strategy that a policy initiative should not make anyone worse off.

It is nigh on impossible to run an economic policy on such a principle. It was one of the sources of sclerosis. However Muldoon's high inflating economy had fiscal creep, where incomes move into higher tax brackets, and so average taxes tended to rise. The additional revenue this generated (relative to the rise in inflation) gave the means by which the Pareto incrementalism could be pursued. Sometimes, in desperation, Muldoon would actively damage the interests of a group, preferably one which was politically weak, not a supporter of his government, or which the majority of the public might think were justifiably made worse off. But generally he avoided such measures.

Was Muldoon inherently a Pareto incrementalist? He certainly liked to give the impression that he was more decisive, and willing to make enemies. But for two of his three terms, he headed a National government elected with fewer votes than the Labour opposition, and with a narrow majority in Parliament. Alienating potential supporters was something he could ill afford. Moreover for much of his term in office, the real economy was growing slowly and was difficult to manage. The Muldoon we see was a child of his times.

FROM 1984 TO 1990

The July 1984 election introduced a new style of government, which approached the equity issues in quite different ways, which may still be summarised under the previous three headings.

Platitudes
In 1986 the Labour government established the Royal Commission on Social Policy (RCSP), which reported in April 1988 (Chapter 8). The RCSP offered no codification of existing practice, no grand vision of what that code meant, and no foundation on which to build. It carried out widespread consultation. The 6000 plus submissions were summarised as 'Voice, Choice, and Safe Prospect'.

> *Voice* People want to name the world, to be heard and understood, to have someone who would listen, to have their say in matters which affected them directly, to have their say in policy . . .
> *Choice* People wanted to be in a position to choose freely from amongst alternatives, to have alternatives available, to value diversity, not to have majority views imposed willy-nilly . . .
> *Safe Prospect* . . . guardianship of the people resource; guardianship of the physical resource; guardianship of the nation.[4]

Note how the voice and choice objectives in particular are written about what individuals want from society, not what sort of society they want. There is some distance between these submissions and the RCSS objective of 'participation in and belonging to the community'. Had the objective been abandoned in the sixteen years between the two commissions?

The authors say their method was to 'let the people speak', but did their report accurately reflect people's concerns? By its actions and choices, such as the contents of the series of booklets it put out to stimulate discussion, the RCSP would tend to focus the public responses in particular ways. For instance, the coded responses to submissions do not include 'equity', nor do they include 'poverty' or 'social deprivation', nor any other expression which might include these notions (e.g. 'fairness').[5] The lowest single reported term is 'entitlements' mentioned in 17 of the submissions. It seems most unlikely that less than 17 submissions mentioned poverty.

The contents of the RCSP's own report also suggest a deliberate avoidance. In the 4004 pages just 2 address poverty. In over 1.5 million words, the term 'poverty' was used 157 times and 'poor' 342 times (including occasions when the use was not related to social deprivation). By contrast 'Maori' was used 6278 times, and 'woman' or 'women' were used 2313 times. What is especially extraordinary is that concerns about poverty and social deprivation had been central in the history of the development of social policy, the subject of enquiry. By turning its back on poverty, the RCSP cut itself off from any intellectual roots. Instead it continued the tradition of NZPC platitudes. Not surprisingly the RCSP had little influence on the subsequent debate (as over the 1990/1991 spending cuts). In contrast the RCSS is still quoted to this day.

Poverty

The study of poverty was quieter in the 1980s than in the 1970s. In the earlier period there was a great flowering of research, but there were few new innovations after 1984. The technical reason for the failure of the new research developments was that they were more expensive and the public resources were not available for original and innovative research. Such work that was done was repeating the work of the 1970s and updating it.

There was a second important reason for the lack of focus on poverty. Despite the tendency to assume that deprivation and inequality are always increasing, the evidence is that for much of the 1980s it was not. Apparently the Labour government, perhaps through some primal instinct, was still looking after some of its own supporters. For instance the real benefit level was maintained through to March 1989—perhaps even rising a little.[6] It was cut in 1989 and 1990 (in a period when real market incomes were falling), but even then not markedly below the level it had been set at in 1975. Again, although the 1987 Labour Relations Act was meant to reform unions and industrial relations, it was not meant to undermine the protections the workers had in the past. Meanwhile the more comprehensive family support benefit (introduced as the family care benefit in 1984) lifted the incomes of some poor families.

It is true that average real incomes were falling through much of Labour's administration, and unemployment rising, which made distributional policy difficult (since government revenue was not as great as if production and employment had been rising). Overall there was a mild increase in poverty proportions over the 1980s. In 1981/2 11.6 percent of the population were below the RCSS-based Benefit Datum Line (BDL), and by 1989/90 it was only 12.9 percent.[7] This was not anywhere near the numbers that pessimists expected, and while there was anecdote to demonstrate there were poor people, the numbers were not rising rapidly.

Pareto

Pareto incrementalism, the rule that there should be no change other than one in which everybody was better off, made the Muldoon regime sclerotic. But consider removing all the interventions at once. Then everyone will be worse off from the loss of the few interventions that benefited them, and better off from the removal of all the remainder. Suppose everybody (or almost everybody) is better off as a result, or that there is sufficient improvement in welfare so that those (or most of those) who are worse off can be compensated. The analysis can be further refined by arguing that the main beneficiaries of many of the interventions were not entitled to the gain, and so theirs could be abolished without an injustice. The example most frequently cited was holders of import licences who took a toll on every import for which a licence was used, although they did nothing other than possess the licence. The Labour government talked about sweeping away such 'privilege'.

Practically, it is not possible to do everything at once, but there evolved the 'blitzkrieg' approach, described in Chapter 5, where the new policies were imposed quickly—a far cry from Muldoon's incrementalism. But how can we be sure that the conditions for the underlying overall improvement in public welfare apply?

Recall the economic theory which says that under certain assumptions an economy which has no interventions in the market will have a higher GDP than one in which there are interventions. More strictly, it demonstrates that under these assumptions, a market economy where there is no intervention is Pareto-efficient (the situation where it is only possible to make one person better off by making another person worse off), while one where there are interventions is not. By removing all the interventions the resulting economy will be better off, in that those who are better off can compensate those who are worse off.

What was assumed, then, was that removal of the interventions would generate economic growth, which would generate jobs (so the unemployed and redeployed would be better off), and additional fiscal revenue which could be used to give tax cuts to low income people and raise benefits. Unfortunately economic growth did not happen. While the rest of the world grew in the late 1980s, the New Zealand economy stagnated. Thus there was nothing to compensate those who unjustly suffered from the change. So the reforms pressed on with a slightly different, and easier to understand, analysis. They were, it was said, to seek 'efficiency'.

Now the term 'efficiency' is not a simple one in economics. It involves a variety of notions, not all of which are mutually compatible. The easiest to understand is *production efficiency* (sometimes called 'technical efficiency'), which means that no resources are being wasted in the production process. A factory which had unutilised buildings or plant would be inefficient in that it can make the same output without having to use those resources. For an economy to be *Pareto-efficient* it has to be production efficient. Otherwise the under-utilised (and misutilised) resources could be deployed elsewhere, with the extra production making some people better off. On the other hand production efficiency may not mean necessarily Pareto-efficiency. Suppose a factory made only left-footed shoes, albeit efficiently. Switch it to half its time making right-footed shoes, and everyone with right feet would be better off.

However, there is a third form of 'efficiency', which reduces to an increase in real GDP, or potential real GDP, irrespective of the distributional consequences. This notion of *uncompensated efficiency* comes from the economist Nicholas Kaldor, and relies on there being a potential Pareto-efficiency, that is, those who are worse off from the greater GDP could be compensated out of the gain. But it does not require the compensation to happen, as the following example illustrates. Suppose a tax reduction gave the richest man in the country an extra $1,000,001, which was funded by taking $1 off each of a million poor, the remaining dollar coming from the savings in the tax department from having to collect less revenue. That would be an increase in real GDP by $1, and hence an increase in uncompensated efficiency, even though there was a deterioration in equity. Thus this focus on uncompensated efficiency suppresses equity considerations altogether. This focus increasingly underpinned policy, although the notion was rarely expounded, so that the public was confused in its mind with the two previous notions.

The trick is that once the mind is locked on to uncompensated efficiency, underpinned by a theory that a commercialist strategy generates the highest level of uncompensated efficiency, then any justification for intervention for reasons of equity may be ignored, since it was argued they would reduce uncompensated efficiency. The obscuration was furthered by shifting from judging policies by their 'outcome' (in distributional terms who were better off and worse off) and instead arguing the case for 'process'—especially commercial processes after 1984. Thus more-market economic mechanisms were deemed right per se, irrespective of their outcomes—an advantageous position for the reformers since they did not have to look at the—often disastrous—consequences of their policies. As a result the Rogernomics debate became a curious non-dialogue with one side saying 'we put the right policies in place', and the other saying 'look at the consequences'.

THE 1988 TAX REFORM

This is illustrated by the flat-tax proposal in the December 1987 package, and the subsequent tax reform. The advocates said low tax rates on rich people were good, irrespective of the distributional consequences. In fact the flat-tax proposal—that there would be a uniform rate of income tax on all incomes—was abandoned in part because there were going to be large numbers of low-income people who would be worse off. The subsequent tax reform, after the flat-tax proposal got dumped by Prime Minister Lange, reduced income tax levels substantially for those on high incomes—from 48 percent at the top to 33 percent. The result was a substantial increase in the incomes of those on high incomes. Typically those in the top tenth of income recipients were about 25 percent better off.[8] Their good fortune was offset by the reductions in the share of the bottom four-fifths, as various tax concessions (proportionally more valuable to the poor), were withdrawn.

However, the withdrawn tax concessions were insufficient to fund all the reductions. The fiscal trick had been that the concessions had been withdrawn over the whole of the 1988/9 year, but the income tax cuts applied for only half of it. This left a long-term fiscal deficit, only partly covered by the GST hike from 10 to 12.5 percent in the subsequent year, and the small real benefit cuts achieved by changing from twice yearly to once yearly indexation. Other short-term measures such as the sale of public assets hid the deficit temporarily. Labour left office in 1990 with an underlying structural budget deficit.

THE 1990 AND 1991 PACKAGE

After the election the new National government was confronted by a budget deficit (which they exaggerated by adding in any new policies promised by Labour). Given that it wanted to address this deficit the government had two options: to revoke some of the tax cuts or to cut government spending. National chose the second.

Almost all social security benefits for adults were cut, usually to well below the RCSS poverty line. Entitlement conditions were also cut. Not unexpectedly, the benefit cuts caused widespread distress among those who depended upon them, a distress which was compounded by the sharp rise in unemployment that occurred at the time. The proportion below the poverty line rose from 12.9 percent in 1989/90 to 16.3 percent in 1992/93, an increase of over a quarter.[9] The distress was so great that there was a concerted outcry from the general public, led by the churches and community welfare organisations, and backed by survey and anecdotal evidence.

Such was the public outcry, and the visible evidence of hardship, that there was a perceptible change in government policies. In line with public opinion, the government announced it would pay more attention to increased funding (especially of education and health) rather than cutting taxes. Surreptitiously it eased the stringent tests on entitlements, adding special needs grants. The National government was not able to resurrect the central role of 'belonging to' and 'participation in' the community, and instead introduced the objective of 'social cohesion'. Recall the *Issues in Social Equity*'s 'in the interests of enhancing the cohesion and well-being of society, governments should be aware of and monitor feelings about equity'. However, whatever its goal, the government appeared to have little idea as to how to implement it.

Thus there has been a substantial downgrading, if not abandoning, of equity considerations in public policy, nicely illustrated in the appendix to Chapter 5, where Treasury advises on the labour market, and does not discuss its distributional and social welfare roles, nor any adverse effects on the poor caused by the measures it was advocating. The consequences of its policies were deemed irrelevant.

4

Commercialism versus Culture

IN THE NORMAL COURSE OF THE PUBLIC POLICY PROCESS TREASURY would be asked for advice on the economic implications of broadcasting issues, while the resource demands of public broadcasting—both the licence fee and their funding and investment requirements—would also closely involve Treasury. In September and December 1985 it submitted evidence to the Royal Commission on Broadcasting, defining Treasury's goals as maximising 'net social benefit' and focusing on 'audience benefit'.

> Total audience benefits can be derived from the preferences of individual consumers. . . . a consumer's choice between watching a particular TV programme and, say, gardening reflects a personal valuation. . . . A convenient way of comparing these trade-offs is to express them in dollar terms by asking the question: 'what would you be willing to pay rather than go without this programme?' The aggregation of individual consumers' 'willingness to pay' for a particular . . . service can be regarded as a collective valuation of it, and this collective valuation can then be used as an estimation of the product's social benefit.[1]

The Treasury statement is not very different from the standard textbook, and for many purposes the definition proves a workable objective for policy issues. For instance, suppose we were concerned about supplying apples and oranges. It would take a little time, but most people could be convinced that the best allocation of the fruit would be that which maximised the net social benefit, measured by willingness to pay. There would be the minor caveat that the consumers were informed about the characteristics of the fruit, and the major one that their ability to pay—their income—was fairly allocated.

The approach may be traced back to the utilitarianism of Jeremy Bentham and James Mill, in which a person's welfare may be judged by a measure of utility. The approach has been modified and elaborated by economists over the subsequent two centuries, but the most important modification, by John Stuart Mill no less, tends to be overlooked. When he tried to codify his mentor's and his father's system in his essay *Utilitarianism*, Mill found what appears to be a fatal weakness in the notion of a simple utility objective. Different pleasures seem to have a different quality to them. Mill resolved it by providing a hierarchy of utilities/pleasures, which culminated in the following passage:

> It is better to be a human being dissatisfied than a pig satisfied; better to be Socrates dissatisfied than a fool satisfied. And if the fool, or the pig, are of a different opinion, it is because they only know their own side of the question. The other party to the comparison knows both sides.[2]

TREASURY AND CULTURE

This objection underlies the cross-examination by Tony Simpson, representing the Public Service Association (which includes broadcasters among its members), of the Assistant Secretary who presented Treasury evidence. Here are some (edited) excerpts which illustrate some of the critical issues.

After noting that Treasury uses in its evidence the expression 'contribution to cultural heritage', Simpson asked

> *Simpson*: Are you aware that the expression 'cultural heritage' is part of the vocabulary used in an international cultural debate to refer to a conservative cultural position in political terms?
> *Treasury*: No.
> *Simpson*: The sense is that heritage refers to a primary value on past cultural experience rather than present cultural experience. Is that what was meant by Treasury in using the phrase in its submission?
> *Treasury*: No, I don't think so. I would prefer a more general definition of it, I guess.
> *Simpson*: What does the Treasury understand to be the expression 'contribution to cultural heritage'?
> *Treasury*: You would be labouring for a more precise definition, I'm afraid, Mr Simpson.

Simpson: It's quite an important matter you know.

Treasury: Yes. I'm not sure if I'm game enough to try but I guess it's important to a lot of people to see and experience things which help them establish their identity in a society in which they live. Whether as a member of that society in general or as a member of some group with which they feel cultural affinity within it. And that programming, television and radio can help with that.

Simpson: Would you agree with the general definition of culture as being an expression of the patterns of meaning within a society?

Treasury: Yes. You put what I tried to say much more succinctly.[3]

The spontaneous attempt by the Treasury official to define culture was commendable, but one is left with the impression that such issues had not been discussed in any detail within Treasury in the course of the preparation of their evidence. Perhaps Treasury did not see this as a part of their remit but the following interchange from a long sequence on the role of local content requirements shows cultural issues impinging upon economic ones.

Simpson: The Australian experience suggests that local content requirements in the form of a quota does in fact foster national culture. What is your view of that?

Treasury: Yes, I would accept that on the particular definition of the national culture being used. But I would question whether that definition in fact means an increase in local programming equates with an increase in fostering a national culture equates with an increase in social benefit.

Simpson: Why do you say the expression of national culture is not of itself a social benefit necessarily?

Treasury: The definition of national culture has become so heterodox that it seems to me that it encompasses a range of programmes to which a large number of people might strongly disagree that there was a benefit.[4]

The discussion drifts away at this point, which may be fortunate for Treasury, for an economist is in very deep water. The notion of social benefit contains the assumption of a set of stable personal preferences embodied in some context, which might be described as the individual's culture. Simpson has a notion of culture evolving, in which case the preferences may not be stable. If this sounds a bit theoretical, consider the 'Goodnight Kiwi' which became a cultural icon to the point where it was sometimes shown early to enable young children to see it before going to bed, and Goodnight Kiwi brand products were sold.[5] How does an economist incorporate that into the analysis? Before the icon existed it was easy enough. After it was established it is easy enough, but how do we get a path between these two times? Can we compare the economists' social benefit before and after these two events?

What has happened is that the economic analysis here is treating culture like, say, marbles. If there was a quota which required a minimum amount of time each week devoted to marbles most would agree that would be against the social benefit. The somewhat narrower treatment by Treasury led to the following exchange.

Simpson: Are you saying that the higher the quality the higher the audience?

Treasury: I'm saying that that's a measure of the quality of the programme.

Simpson: Are you saying that if more people watch it, it is a good quality programme?

Treasury: In the commercial system, yes.

Simpson: That is an eccentric definition of quality if I may say so.

Treasury: It's not your definition of quality.

Simpson: It certainly isn't. I wouldn't wish to author it in any form.

Treasury: Quality is in the eye of the beholder.

Simpson: The eye of a large number of beholders increase the quality is what I took you to be saying.

Treasury: To some extent yes.

Simpson: Would it surprise you if I told you the Miss New Zealand Show is the most popular, the most watched New Zealand programme on television?

Treasury: No. It wouldn't.

Simpson: One presumes that by your definition of quality broadcasting you would like to see the Broadcasting Corporation or broadcasters in general doing more of that sort of thing, and that is the Treasury view.

Treasury: The Treasury's view is that in respect of its commercial role that the Broadcasting Corporation should make those decisions on the basis of audience size.

Simpson: We're not really talking about what the Broadcasting Corporation might do, are we? We are talking about what might

happen if under the Treasury's proposals there were more Miss New Zealand Shows. Treasury would not be nonplussed but more liable to be delighted would it not?
Treasury: You could probably conclude that. Absolutely delighted.[6]

Before we judge Treasury's delight, it is worth noting one of their concerns is to avoid making judgements about 'quality' in Simpson's sense of the word. (But he is not defending 'high culture' at this point.) Economists find difficulty with the Reithian view that there exists somebody who should impose his, or her, values on other people's choices. This can be seen most clearly by imagining a Lord Reith who decided how many apples and/or oranges each should eat. But does this apply to cultural services, especially in the light of Mill's hierarchy of pigs and philosophers?

TREASURY AND COMMERCIALISATION

The reason Treasury came to be delighted is clarified by this interchange:

> *Simpson*: Don't you say in your submission the purpose of a state owned enterprise is to be measured purely in financial and economic terms? That is to produce certain market directed rates on its investment and so forth?
> *Treasury*: Yes. It is quite in order for cultural products to be produced by an organisation which is commercial in its objectives. The way one ensures that the product will meet whatever specifications are required in cultural terms is to contract with an organisation to produce them.[7]

This Treasury notion of broadcasting being primarily a commercial organisation is repeated in other places:

> *Treasury*: The BCNZ is primarily a commercial broadcasting business funded by revenues.[8]

and

> *Simpson*: So you are asking the Broadcasting Corporation to conform to your general theory of State Owned Enterprises?
> *Treasury*: Yes.

Simpson: Rather than assess itself in the terms of its own objectives and dynamic?[9]
Treasury: Yes. Because it has external accountability in terms of its financial performance.[10]

The reason that Treasury would be delighted to have more Miss New Zealand shows on television is nothing to do with its judgement of the content. Rather, a commercially oriented broadcaster would put on more shows, because of the audience response. The implicit assumption is that this would increase net social benefit.

But would it? Suppose most of the audience did not care very much about the show, but tended to watch it because there was a tiny margin of benefits over the costs of watching the alternative program. Suppose too, there was a group of non-watchers who intensely disliked the show. Under such circumstances it is quite possible that the show would be a net social cost, rather than a benefit.

But non-watchers generally do not have any means of directly expressing their dislike. Treasury definition of net social benefit requires there to be the possibility of the dislikers paying ('bribing') the broadcasters not to put on the show. If their payments exceed those payments of the audience for watching the show, then it would not go ahead. Instead, the commercial mechanism driving the broadcasting is advertising, who are purchasing audience time by size and mix.

It is a very circuitous route to get from advertising-driven commercial broadcasting to net social benefit. Given the need for an assumption of stable consumer preferences, there is probably an unbridgeable chasm somewhere along the track. Moreover the track passes through a swamp when it considers the audience who find advertising detracts from their pleasure (benefit). This may be directly or indirectly, when the advertising results in cuts in the program. Treasury appears to have assumed the route is direct, simple and short, but they provide no case that it is.

Commercialisation is presented as a value-free objective despite being loaded with values. These values are unavoidable; not including a valuation of culture in one's objective is a valuation of culture as zero.

A related issue of some concern is captured nicely by Simpson recalling the dictum of American journalist A. J. Liebling, 'the publisher bites the editor's lip'.[11] If the primary purpose of the publishing or broadcasting is the pursuit of commercial objectives, it seems likely that the bitten editor is going to be inhibited from being critical of commercial aspirations and mechanisms.

The same problem arises in the cultural sphere. Cultural identity involves a degree of cultural autonomy. The Pakeha cannot run a proper Maori media system. Treasury took the view that abandoning government-imposed barriers to entry (such as requiring a licence awarded by a tribunal) would lead to a more competitive and diversified broadcasting system. However, as its evidence under cross-examination admitted, entrance into the industry would be confined to those with 'a large sum of capital' who were prepared to risk it. A lot of cultural activities do not have the ready access to this capital, and may be worse off as a result of the changed rules of entry.

Although not discussed in any depth in front of the Royal Commission, some American theorists have gone a step further and argued that there is a civil right of having access to use of the media.[12] Commercialism would be a very hit-and-miss means of having that right expressed.

Commercial broadcasting has thus far been couched in terms of advertising-driven commercialism. The possibility of user-pay broadcasting, which, not needing any advertising, has fascinated economists, became actuality with Sky Television. However because set-up costs are high, the technology involves strong economies of scale—average costs fall dramatically as use increases—so again these new ventures depend upon a large audience.

Another advocated solution—this time only quasi-commercial—is audience funded/donated broadcasting. While practically it has a role, the excesses of religious television in the United States suggest the role is limited, and in any case still confined to large audiences.

In summary it is difficult to see in an entirely commercially driven broadcasting system how either the cultural objectives that Tony Simpson aspired to, or the net social benefit objectives that Treasury said it aspired to, will be reasonably effectively attained. It is tempting to leave the last words with Simpson and the Treasury Assistant Secretary.

Simpson: I am suggesting two things. The first is that although continually pressed, the Treasury has been unable to provide me with concrete examples of how the system you propose would improve the programmes received by viewers and listeners. That is so is it not?

Treasury: By and large that is true. Yes. But that is because you misunderstand the nature of our submission, Mr Simpson.

Simpson: I think I understand it only too well Mr —

Treasury: There is little evidence that you do.

Simpson: The second point I would like to put to you is that the broadcasting system which Treasury is proposing is a singularly arid piece of cultural expression. What have you to say to that?

Treasury: Well, I disagree with that assertion.[13]

(There is a more sinister story, if only hearsay. Simpson was the sort of counsel every expert witness fears; someone more familiar with some of the areas of expertise than the witness. But the barristers who cross-examined the Treasury officials, while not experts, did grievous damage to Treasury's credibility and case. The technical and economic issues belong to another venue, but one Treasury official (not the Assistant Secretary), badly bruised from the cross-examination, is said to have muttered as he left the room, 'You bastards think you have been very clever. It took us ten years to get Forestry, and we'll get you too.' These may not have been the exact words, but the story became one of the urban myths of broadcasting.)

COMMERCIALISM AND CULTURE

The late Warren Mayne remarked that Treasury 'in its most inventive "mad dog" maverick mood pushed the more-market deregulatory scenario to its outer limits', with potentially 'bizarre consequences'. What actually happened to broadcasting is described in the appendix. The issue applies not only to broadcasting, however, as we shall see.

Appendix: The Broadcasting Reforms

It is very easy to argue that there is something special about some economic commodity such as broadcasting, but to overlook that there are other activities which are just as special, such as hard-copy periodicals. A good magazine shop sells over 5000 titles. They range from daily newspapers to monthly science journals, from gardening to financial investment. In a big city there will be dozens of competitors also selling titles, as well as specialist shops for ethnic language literature, rock music, obscure political views, and so on. Alternatively there is subscription by post. This extraordinarily rich supply in response to a myriad of public demands is provided without significant government involvement other than the framework for normal commerce.

What special characteristics, if any, does broadcasting have which mean that the government has to treat it specially, including providing non-commercial funding? Why cannot funding be left to the market? It is not hard to see radio and television as providers of magazine type services, albeit using a different method of delivery. How are they fundamentally different?

ROYAL COMMISSION ON BROADCASTING

In the early 1980s broadcasting faced a number of issues including:

- new technologies—video, cable and satellite television, and FM radio;
- the ongoing issue of the management of the public broadcasting system;
- private radio, and a third private channel (introduced in 1989);
- Maori, in particular, and minority ethnic broadcasting;
- the independence and the accountability of the broadcasting system.

The Royal Commission on Broadcasting and Related Telecommunications in New Zealand was commissioned to consider such questions in February 1985. But its recommendations in its report of September 1986 were hardly implemented. Instead, we have had Treasury's alternative vision of commercialisation of the public system, and the opening up of broadcasting to competition. The general thrust was for the full commercialisation of broadcasting, in practice an advertising-driven system.

Treasury put its evidence to the Royal Commission in three broad sections which illustrate this general conclusion.[1] The first on the management of the radio frequency spectrum (RFS) argued for its privatisation, and regulation via commercial relations, relying on the Coase approach. The proposal was, however, very impractical and the outcome could have been extremely inefficient because of the transaction costs. Court cases would have been necessary to deal with minor frequency interference, better organised spectrum owners would have chosen configurations which would have been detrimental to the users, and the competitive solution would only have practically worked for radio, but not for TV where there were few players and entry costs are very high.

Treasury's proposals for the government-owned Broadcasting Corporation (BCNZ) can also be dealt with quickly. It thought it should be corporatised. One supposes the ultimate destination was privatisation, although that Treasury agenda was not public at that time.

The one Treasury proposal from this section which has been wholeheartedly rejected was the recommendation of the abolition of the TV Licence (now called Broadcasting) Fee. Treasury recommended that instead the government make grants from departmental votes to provide non-commercial broadcasting services, with the ironic consequence that Treasury would have obtained more political control over the media, in that it would have been recommending on each departmental grant for broadcasting.

The discussion on advertising-driven broadcasting was muddled, ignoring the economies of scale which are crucial in terms of production and distribution, the inability of broadcasters to charge consumers for their product (although this is less true now with pay and cable TV), and any conflict in interest between advertisers and audience. The best way of understanding the Treasury proposal is to assume that there is a highly competitive, multiple-supplier, advertising-driven broadcasting system. If it exists (and there are not people who object to advertising) then the outcome may well be efficient and in the consumer interest. But this ignores the fundamental problem:

the idealised system does not, and probably cannot ever, exist. Not surprisingly Treasury then concluded that there is no great justification for government intervention. It opposed content regulation, and considered whether there are equity grounds for intervention.

Treasury concluded that non-commercial broadcasting favours the well-off and in that sense is anti-poor. Even so, the rich have as much right as the poor to have collective means used to meet their demands, if the market cannot do so. Thus the state might provide cultural facilities such as museums, recreation facilities, orchestras, without charge or subsidy from general funds—even though the rich may use them more—providing the overall government revenue and expenditure system is progressive—if that is a social objective. The report also reflected briefly on merit goods arguments, which it dismisses, although the argument is put naively, ignoring such issues as political independence, national integrity, and cultural attainment.

Most of the Treasury case was rejected by the Royal Commission, although they comment there was not enough evidence presented for the Commission to come to an overall conclusion on the economic issues. The Royal Commission reflected a view of economic, social, and cultural management from the 1970s, while Treasury's was of the commercialised economic regime of the 1980s.

SPECIAL ECONOMIC CHARACTERISTICS OF BROADCASTING

There are two special justifications for a high degree of state intervention which should be quickly rejected. In the past some special measures might have been justified on the grounds that broadcasting was a monopoly. But today there is typically a substantial choice of radio stations, three commercial television channels, often pay-channels, and a supply of commercial videos (plus films). Many households are likely to have cable television within a generation.

Also dismissed is the Reithian argument that the government is duty-bound to manage the broadcasting system so that it is 'uplifting'. There would be little agreement in New Zealand as to who should be our next Reith—or James Shelley, his local equivalent.[2] Any attempt to 'lift up' broadcasting services is likely to be manipulated for baser ends. That does not mean there should be no government subsidised classical music program or whatever. All that is being argued is that more subtlety than a simple Reithian justification is needed.

There appear to be two important economic features of the broadcasting media which distinguish them from magazines. The first is that most programs, especially television ones, have high fixed costs relative to total costs of supply. That means they experience substantial economies of scale—with average costs falling significantly as numbers viewing increase.

Once there are economies of scale the market ceases to be fully efficient. Economies of scale are common, but providing they are small—the average cost of supply is not too far from the marginal cost—the inefficiency of market delivery is small. Thus while economies of scale exist for periodicals—it being cheaper to produce the last one than to produce the first—they are not so great as to seriously damage the efficiency of market supply. In the case of broadcasting the divergence is much greater.

The analysis is further complicated by international dumping, for that is the effect of foreign producers selling their programs at prices far below their costs of production—at marginal costs rather than average costs. This does not happen to the same extent in the magazine market, for although there may be price variations by countries, the differences are not as great as in television where a multimillion dollar program may be sold to a New Zealand station at a price of only thousands of dollars.

In so far as there are non-economic objectives in broadcasting, a matter which belongs to the second group of issues, a pure market delivery system would suppress New Zealand supply. But the payment system for broadcasting compounds the dumping story. New Zealanders might prefer New Zealand content programs, and be willing to pay for them over the foreign imports in an ideal world. When you read a magazine, someone—perhaps you, perhaps the dentist—has paid for it. That is not true, as a rule, in the broadcasting market, dominated by free-to-air transmission. Exceptions include pay-television, competing video and film activities, and, in the future, cable television Even here, though, one does not pay per service.

Instead, most commercial television is advertising-driven; that is, the production and transmission are funded by the sale of advertising time. This is not to criticise advertising per se. But it is easy to show that an advertising-driven broadcasting system does not readily maximise social welfare. As a simple example, consider a station choosing between two programs, one of which will attract a small audience who will value their program greatly, and a second which attracts a much larger audience but who are not fussed by the particular program. In the user-pays system of the conventional market, the smaller audience might be able to outbid the large audience, thus maximising the efficiency (as conventionally defined) with which the broadcasting slot was being used. However, without user pays, how would a broadcaster know there were differences in intensity of preferences between the two audiences, for there is no signalling mechanism? That audience surveys do not bother to ask is indicative that this is not the manner in which the broadcasters think. Advertising-funded broadcasting seeks audience size. The medium becomes a vehicle for business purposes, so the audience's needs are only tangential. An advertising-driven service is a commercialised service. The station is likely to take into consideration only audience size in choosing its programs.

It is important to distinguish between a broadcasting system whose purpose is cultural but is subject to market disciplines and a broadcasting system which is to meet market objectives and thereby contribute to culture. Under the current profit-driven requirement TVNZ might think it could make a better dollar providing health services, say. Most people would think that odd, because they see its purpose as providing television. Thus there is a higher objective for the agency than the profit objective it has been set.

THE CULTURAL ROLE OF BROADCASTING

All commodities have non-economic features which are distinctive to themselves. Are there any features of broadcasting services which are so unusually distinctive that we need to take them into consideration when designing any public intervention?

Broadcasting uses resources and hence interacts with the commercial system. Indeed commerce needs broadcasting, not least for advertising, and there are those who would argue it also needs a favourable image in the media. Yet broadcasting may have a purpose beyond merely satisfying consumer wants as defined in the conventional market analysis. Society has various collective objectives, which can neither be reduced to some maximisation of the sum of individual welfare (as defined by conventional economic analysis), nor attained merely by pursuing that maximum economic welfare.

Culture needs to be used in its widest sense of 'the human creation of symbols and artifacts'[3] or, as Nick Perry entitled his book, a 'dominion of signs'.[4] This is much more encompassing than the 'high' culture of the concert program, which for our purposes here has the same fundamental status as popular culture, even though they may be delivered through the broadcasting system by different funding arrangements. Patrick Day's recent study of the radio years up to the early 1960s illustrates well how the new media moulded the New Zealand community.[5]

To what extent does a totally commercial broadcasting system meet the broader cultural needs of a society? There has been a rather interesting legal debate about this issue. The essence of the Maori broadcasting claim, eventually settled in the Privy Council, was that a commercially driven broadcasting system could not meet Maori needs, especially with respect to their concerns for te reo (language) and tikanga (culture). Fortunately the Maori had a principle (set down in the Treaty of Waitangi), and a statutory process by which they could successfully pursue that principle. As a result they have obtained their own publicly funded Maori network. Others in the community are not so fortunate, and yet they may have parallel needs. If, as the courts decided, a commercially based broadcasting system fails one minority, the Maori, then surely it is likely to fail most.

DEMOCRACY AND THE MEDIA

There is no automatic connection between market outcomes (and the maximisation of material welfare) and democracy (or liberty), once we eschew the New Right tautological linkage of the notions. Editorial independence is especially important, as is well illustrated by a New Zealand radio station which broadcast both the BBC World Service and New Zealand-content breakouts, with an extraordinary contrast between the editorial lines of each. BBC independence is an international standard, although clearly there is some contention as to the meaning of 'independence'. The New Zealand breakouts did not even pretend to be independent, but actively espoused a New Right editorial line which also happened to reflect the views of the station's owner.

This is not to object to a magazine or station having an editorial line, and certainly not to columnists and talk-back hosts taking one. What is important in a democracy is that there should be a variety of opinions. But what mechanism is there to prevent media driven by commercial goals from promoting only pro-commercial views or the views of their owners? Suppose the material prosperity that commerce promises to deliver (a promise it may or may not be able to keep) is not the ultimate goal of society. What is there to stop the entire media combining all their forces in order to promote a commercialist doctrine?

There can be no simple solution, but an important mechanism is the way in which the publicly owned broadcasting stations are protected from outside editorial interference. The classic example is, of course, the BBC, which satisfies the ultimate test that when there is an international crisis people turn to it because they can rely on the quality and independence of its reporting. That places a constraint on the rest of the world broadcasting systems, be they government or privately run. In a similar way RNZ and TVNZ set a standard for reporting not only for broadcasting, but also in the printed media as well. That does not mean there is no editorialising in the printed media, but it does constrain them and encourages them to separate opinion from fact. Otherwise the public turns to RNZ and TVNZ.

Because a democracy has higher objectives than materialism, there seems to be a need for some non-commercial mechanism to ensure the elements of editorial balance and independence in at least one part of the total media system, so as to influence the entire system.

THE OUTCOME

People grumble about the magazine industry in terms of the choice available to them, but there is no significant demand for its reform. However, there is a widespread perception that the broadcasting system is failing markedly. The reforms of the 1980s are seen as too pro-market, and the system is failing to deliver on choice (advertising-free programs) and community and culture.

Nevertheless the current broadcasting regime has some advantages compared to the past one. The supply side is regulated almost entirely by market considerations, with the cumbersome licensing system repealed. It seems much more responsive to the introduction of new technologies—although the size of the New Zealand market remains a major restraint. The funding of the international service and the symphony orchestra has been shifted off the broadcasting fee to Parliament, where it more properly belongs.

There is also anecdote, but little hard evidence, that the public broadcasting system is more 'efficient' and less resource-using,[6] although many would argue that such alleged efficiency gains ignore a deterioration in quality of programming and, especially, the increased advertising. There is certainly more broadcasting choice than there was a decade ago, especially in the main centres, although much of the variety would have happened under other regimes also.

An unexpected, and unplanned, taonga from the changes has been Maori broadcasting, with a national network of iwi radio stations, separately funded from the broadcasting fee by the Maori equivalent of the Broadcasting Commission (Te Mangai Paho). Funding is now being provided for Maori television. While the primary purpose of this development is to support Maori cultural and language development, there have been benefits to the non-Maori from the distinctive local Maori television programs, the encouragement of Maori artists valued by the entire community, and news bulletins from Maori perspectives.

Probably the main bugbear to the public is the loss of advertising-free television, and the very high proportion of time commercials take up on the screen. An advertising free channel would be very popular, but the cost is such that it could not be funded from the current broadcasting fee. As a result there has been a policy stand-off. Its resolution is likely to depend upon alternative sources of funding.

Meanwhile, the state-owned Radio New Zealand's commercial network has been privatised in exchange for giving the non-commercial networks of RNZ an independent entity under a parliamentary charter. It would appear that the combined RNZ was not a total success because its commercial and non-commercial activities involve different corporate cultures.

Clearly the nature of the public funding matters. The non-Maori funding agency, the Broadcasting Commission (now known as 'New Zealand on Air') has, excluding some miscellaneous spending, almost two distinct policies towards radio and television. Funding RNZ is a resolution to the issue of providing a non-advertising-driven free-to-air network. Meanwhile the television funding is for New Zealand-made programs, contributing to their costs of production to make such programs competitive with overseas alternatives. The programs themselves are broadcast in association with advertisers, so advertising-free programs are hardly addressed in television. With the exception of the non-commercial and Maori radio, there is little funding for radio production by the Commission.

Not all the changes in the last decade have been bad. There is more choice, the system is more flexible to technological change, developments in Maori broadcasting are heartening, and there have been efficiency gains. Yet the present system is not ideal. Its weakness is that it is too dependent on commercial decisions, so that there are insufficient mechanisms to ensure true public demand and needs are properly incorporated into the system. Commerce does not always produce the best outcomes. Yet very often it is an effective provider of goods and services. When it manifestly fails in a major way, especially where the failure is in as important an activity as broadcasting, we should be willing to contemplate non-commercial mechanisms. Magazines can be left as they are.

PART TWO

The Politics

5

The Troika and the Blitzkreig

IN PRINCIPLE THE MINISTER OF FINANCE IS JUST ANOTHER CABINET minister, but in practice he or she can be as powerful as the prime minister. That power comes from the importance of economic and financial issues in the politics of the country, where no other portfolio is comparable, together with the size and the scope (and the competence) of Treasury, which services the minister. While the prime minister has the constitutional power, including that of appointing and dismissing a minister of finance, in most policy matters the latter has more effect. A rough measure can be seen from the size of the respective offices which service the two positions. In 1995/96, the central activities of the Office of the Prime Minister and Cabinet were voted $4m, while Treasury was voted $59m for its advice role. The imbalance was even greater in earlier years, before the advisory arm of the prime minister's office was built up.

This feature of New Zealand politics was obscured in the 1975 to 1984 period when the Prime Minister, Robert Muldoon, also held the finance portfolio. Even so, it was said that he was too powerful as a result and that the premier should never be minister of finance. The practical equality of the premiership and finance portfolios is moderated by the personalities of the ministers involved. The period of 1984 to 1988 was characterised by a weak Prime Minister relative to an exceptionally strong finance team.

LANGE AND THE MINISTERS OF FINANCE

David Lange's greatest strength was his handling of the government's relations with the New Zealand public, where he had no peer. He was also an able crisis manager, perhaps with the flaw of precipitating unnecessary crises. However his internal management of the government was much less successful, most evidently when he was in conflict with the ministers of finance.

On the other hand over most of the period of Lange's premiership there were three ministers of finance, each an effective politician. The finance team of 1984—sometimes called the 'Troika'—was a unique innovation. In the past there had been a junior minister assisting the minister of finance. This was partly to share an increasingly onerous workload, and it suited the practicalities of the office. The appointment of a second minister became standard with Robert Muldoon. On occasions he even had two associate ministers, but they were junior in ranking, and very much under his direction.

Instead Lange appointed three extremely able politicians, Roger Douglas, Richard Prebble, and David Caygill, ranked fourth, fifth, and seventh in Cabinet, and who in addition held major portfolios of transport and trade and industry. The three ministers (with the parliamentary under-secretary for finance, Trevor de Cleene) had offices on the same floor of the Beehive, which increased their degree of integration.

In contrast the Prime Minister was isolated at the top of the Beehive without any really close associate. Neither Lange nor Deputy Prime Minister Geoffrey Palmer had any competence in economics. (Indeed, they and two of the Troika—Caygill and Prebble—were lawyers, and this suggested a stance of representing their client's views—in this case Treasury's—rather than having independent views of their own.)

The economic direction had started out badly, with little agreement about economic policy in opposition. The 1984 manifesto papered over the differences, relying on what became a characteristic feature of the Labour government, language that was so vague it often had two meanings. Once it was agreed to, the commercialisers, who in government had the power of implementation, interpreted the text in their way, or if necessary ignored it.

Initially Lange also was part of their team, supporting the Troika's policies. The policy process went like this. The Troika, having come to some policy conclusion based on Treasury advice, would persuade Lange and Palmer of its correctness. The tight five would then take a proposal to a Cabinet committee.[1] The recommendations would then go to Cabinet, and then on to caucus. At each step in this decision tier, there was already a majority in agreement. This most obviously applied at the caucus level. The 1984 Cabinet plus the six under-secretaries amounted to 26 (of the caucus total of 55) who usually supported the Cabinet decision under the principle of collective responsibility. Allowing for a few other functionaries (whips, chairpersons of committees, the caucus secretary), and a few reliable loyalists, the Cabinet (which might have been split when it made its decision) had a natural majority in the caucus. (Often the caucus would not even be consulted, because the Cabinet knew it could rely on retrospective acquiescence.) The same process of majoritarian loyalism gave the government its majority in Parliament. Thus the Troika, obtaining the support of Lange and Palmer and a few loyalists in Cabinet, could impose their policies on a House of 90 plus MPs, and so on the country. This was a formidable degree of leverage by a few politicians over the entire country.

Adding to the effectiveness of the Troika was the fact that there was usually no coherent alternative economic policy. While Treasury marked (in the sporting sense, and sometimes in the academic sense too) virtually every other department to some extent (formally because they had to approve its expenditure), there were major areas of economic policy where the only expertise within the government was that of Treasury. Yet when Treasury clashed with another government department on the latter's patch it could rarely win, because there was now within Cabinet a minister who was as well briefed as the Troika.

THE TROIKA

Thus the ministerial structure that Lange chose gave considerable power to the Troika. Given the compliance of the Prime Minister and the inability of the large parliamentary majority to resist policies that they doubted, given the unity of purpose of the three, given the congruence of their purpose with that of the most powerful economic department in the land (whereas Muldoon had been in conflict with his advisers), one could argue the Troika was more powerful even than Muldoon had been.

The broad direction of the Troika's policies was that there

should be greater use of the market in the regulation of the economy, and that the economy should be more open to the outside world. To what extent they were initially committed to full commercialisation of the economy is less clear. It seems likely that the ministers started down the more-market road, and found it leading to the advisers' commercialisation strategy in a way they had not foreseen.

Roger Douglas had been highly interventionist as a minister in the Third Labour government from 1972 to 1975. His 1981 *There's Got to Be a Better Way!* is a confused document. For every sentence that can be read as a precursor of Rogernomics, there is another which shows him still a keen interventionist. His scheme for carpet factories across the country made him one of the greatest 'Think Biggers', although mercifully it was launched while he was in opposition. It is not until 1983 that he seems to be more directly moving towards the economic policies which today we call Rogernomics, under the tutelage of a Treasury official attached to the Labour opposition.[2] When he came to office in 1984 he supported an uncontrolled float of the dollar, but he favoured a retail sales tax and had to be persuaded by Treasury into a GST.

His 1987 autobiography, *Toward Prosperity*, suggests that Douglas's main characteristic is that he was an activist, liking to do things, but rather casual about what exactly they were. In a different economic regime, as occurred in 1972 to 1975, he was happy to be an active interventionist. Douglas was trained as an accountant with little background in economics. His writing has consistently shown a lack of interest in the welfare state. Instead there is a belief that giving people cash income will resolve such issues as the distribution of health and education. Hence his support for a minimum guaranteed income. The policies in his *Unfinished Business* are a continuation of what appears to be a long-held belief.

Richard Prebble was the most ideologically right-wing of the three on economic policy. Treasury officials quickly identified him as the economic dry and 'monetarist' in macroeconomic policy: today he is leader of ACT, the most right-wing of the parliamentary parties.[3] Yet in opposition he had campaigned for a public transport sector subject to government intervention. One guesses that Prebble, trained as a lawyer, had little knowledge of the economist's market theory and its underlying notion of the role of efficiency that drove the reforms. Rather, he was inclined to grab simple economic ideas—bumper slogans he called them—often based on anecdotes, which he waved about with a ferocious intensity. Prebble was the most political animal of the three, a determined negotiator, a good political tactician, with a superb grasp of parliamentary procedure, and a first-class bovver boy. Muldoon loathed Prebble—facing him was like looking in his mirror.

David Caygill was the most unassuming of the three, but was just as crucial to the Troika's success, not least because of his reasonableness. When he became Minister of Finance, after Douglas in 1989, the tone of Treasury changed. Caygill was willing to look for compromises. When funding for the cervical smear campaign was sought, he asked Treasury officials to look around for a source within the budget. When the green element in the caucus wanted something done about lead-free petrol, he put a differential in the petrol tax. Unlike the other two, Caygill majored in economics (and political science), although he then went on to a law degree. The economics course imbued him with a neoclassical market-oriented micro-economics, and was more monetarist than Keynesian. (He was the minister responsible for the Reserve Bank Act.) He had a distaste for political lobbying of the self-seeking kind. Whereas his predecessors in the trade and industry portfolio had their ministerial anteroom filled with those who wanted some handout, Caygill's soon became empty because he refused to offer lobbyists any special concessions, other than to ease the transition to the government's ultimate goal. Caygill was a superb negotiator. Douglas couldn't, and Prebble wouldn't, but Caygill would compromise on detail, providing the fundamental principles of the policy were not endangered.

This is well illustrated in his border policy, which is unique because it is the one substantial part of what we call Rogernomics which was signalled—in detail—in the 1984 Labour Party manifesto. It was a remarkable feat that a party which had been protectionist for over half a century should have promised in its 1984 manifesto substantial reductions in protection. Not that all the caucus agreed with the policy (and it was in part to be offset by the promise of a major investment fund). But in a cobbled-together policy which was designed to hide the deep differences within the opposition caucus between the Douglasites and the interventionists, the border protection policy was a rare exception, indicating that Caygill had persuaded enough of his colleagues to make it acceptable.

When Labour took office, the key economics portfolios were given to Douglasites, and out of that grew Rogernomics. However, it is noteworthy that there was a general acceptance of less government intervention in the economy among a much wider spectrum than the Troika and their acolytes. The Minister of Labour, Stan Rodger, who was only a Rogernome in the most extravagant rhetoric, became 'Sideline Stan' as he resolutely refused to get involved in industrial disputes. He argued that good industrial relations had been compromised by Muldoon's willingness to intervene early and to intervene often, so that the disputants never had reason to settle between themselves, knowing that ministerial intervention would be the ultimate resolution, perhaps with some government subsidy or concession thrown in as a sweetener.

After the 1987 election Lange tried to break up the Troika. Douglas would not give up the finance portfolio, but he was given Michael Cullen, who at that time was considered an anti-Rogernome, as an associate Minister of Finance. (Cullen was also given the social welfare portfolio.) Prebble was also taken out of the associate finance portfolio, and given a group of portfolios which amounted to his being minister of the just-corporatised state-owned trading enterprises. However, the portfolios were subject to Treasury advice, so in effect Prebble remained a Treasury minister (and the Troika remained on the sixth floor of the Beehive).

Caygill also lost associate finance, retained trade and industry, and was given the ministry of health. It was a portfolio he handled with exceptional acumen by announcing he knew nothing about the area and would take a year to master it, so nothing would be done in the period. While little was done publicly or loudly, much was done in preparation and announced quietly. Caygill's successor, Helen Clark, got the kudos. Caygill seems to have diverged quite markedly from the other two in the Troika, in that he made no attempt to commercialise the health area. It would appear that Caygill (like Lange) believed that it was possible to make the business sector more-market, while maintaining a public social service sector. Douglas and Prebble vehemently disagreed.

At some stage Lange began to have private doubts about the

drift of economic policy. Some of his closest advisers were expressing such doubts by mid 1985. But having decided he did not like the direction the commercialisers were going, Lange failed to evolve a coalition of supporters either within Cabinet or within caucus or in the country. There was a 'kitchen cabinet', but it seems to have had nobody of any technical competence sufficient to challenge the Troika. Lange built up his prime ministerial office, but the advisers dealt mainly with putting out fires, and there does not seem to have been a long-term strategy element in it. The Royal Commission on Social Policy was established but proved ineffective. There was a Cabinet Committee on Social Equity, as an ineffectual attempt to resist the push for efficiency, but this too often papered over the differences, in the tradition of the 1984 manifesto, without resolving them. Various advisory committees on social policy, established in December 1987, not only cut across the Royal Commission, but in some cases were captured by commercialisers.

Lange used his power of patronage poorly. The Labour government had said that unlike the Muldoon government it would not put its supporters into the wide range of positions to which it held the power of appointment, but would put the best man or woman for the job. Of course it did not follow this in practice with any purity, but in the economic area it was rare to appoint anti-commercialisers to positions of influence, no matter how competent they were. Instead the government appointed businessmen with little loyalty to Labour (as they proved in 1990). Economists soon learned that public dissent against the current economic policies was not a pathway to opportunity, whereas uncritical loyalty enhanced one's career. When Lange needed economic support for his resistance to economics there was no one in a position of significance who could (or would) support him.

Thus the Prime Minister, unable to oppose a formidable trio of Cabinet ministers with economic portfolios, led the Labour government down the commercialisation path. Resistance from elsewhere in Cabinet and caucus was difficult because there were few alternative sources of economic advice. Those which might have been were repressed.

THE BLITZKRIEG APPROACH TO POLICY MAKING

The Troika's ability to implement policy came not only from its ability to control parliament through the already described process of institutional leverage, but a policy approach with similarities to the blitzkrieg in warfare. In each case the 'lightning strike' involved a policy goal radically different from the existing configuration, to be attained in a short period, following a surprise announcement and a very rapid implementation. While each blitzkrieg was different in detail, the aim each time was to take some substantial aspect of the economic and social framework and transform it profoundly. Policy blitzkriegs were nothing if not audacious.

They were a response to the perceived policy sclerosis which occurred under the previous Prime Minister. The master of the overnight raid, Robert Muldoon rarely risked venturing into any policy development which involved much time between announcement and implementation. Leaving aside Muldoon's own personal style, a major reason was that the consultative process seemed to give almost every major interest group an effective veto. The Troika's blitzkrieg approach was expressly designed to move things along so rapidly that the interest groups were unable to provide effective resistance, and therefore the public's immediate wishes had to be discounted, for fear they could be manipulated by the pressure groups.

Like other successful generals, Douglas has written down his strategy:

- If a solution makes sense in the medium term, go for it without qualification or hesitation. Nothing else delivers a result which will truly satisfy the public.
- Consensus among interest groups on quality decisions rarely, if ever, arises before they are made and implemented. It develops, after they are taken, as the decisions deliver satisfactory results to the public.
- Do not try to advance a step at a time. Define your objectives clearly and move towards them in quantum leaps.
- Vested interests continuously underestimate their own ability to adjust successfully in an environment where the government is rapidly removing privilege across a wide front.
- It is uncertainty, not speed, that endangers the success of structural reform programmes. Speed is an essential ingredient in keeping uncertainty down to the lowest possible level.
- Once the programme begins to be implemented, don't stop until you have completed it. The fire of opponents is much

less accurate if they have to shoot at a rapidly moving target.
• The abolition of privilege is the essence of structural reform.[4]

Douglas's formulation shows no introspection as to how one might decide that a policy solution is right. Given uncertainty of purpose is the greatest threat, the approach requires that all opposition to the reforms must come from 'privilege', or vested interests. There is no room for reflection or an alternative analysis. Once the commitment is made, speed and quantum leaps are essential: anything less is vulnerable to resistance from the vested interests. Under urgency there cannot be consultation, but Douglas thinks the public will support the reforms as it sees the benefits, including the ending of privilege.

This recipe is all the more ironic for being expounded at a meeting of the Mont Pelerin Society, founded by Friedrich von Hayek and honouring Karl Popper, whose social engineering was essentially incrementalist. In contrast the blitzkrieg is 'Plato's dream like the Leninist actuality . . . of an elite political order guided in the exercise of absolute political power by its supposed insight into essential reality'.[5]

The classic policy blitzkrieg was the introduction of GST, a success in contrast with the later Australian experience. Chapter 1 described the successful blitzkrieg of state trading activities with their corporatisation followed by their privatisation. Chapter 9 analyses the health reforms as a failed blitzkrieg.

AFTER THE TROIKA

The inherent political tensions between the policies of Douglas and Prebble and the Labour movement eventually led to the collapse of the Troika's hegemony, and a little later the termination of the Fourth Labour government.

The incoming National government continued both the extreme commercialisation policies and their implementation by blitzkrieg. In December 1990 there was the *Economic and Social Initiative* which aimed to 'redesign' the welfare state, and announced the measure which became the Employment Contracts Act (which redesigned industrial relations law). In July 1991 the process continued with the budget announcements which included redesigning the accident compensation scheme, the health

Table 5.1: Examples of reforms since 1984

Restoring the Market Mechanism

Liberalisation of entry licensing into industry.

Partial liberalisation of occupational licensing.

Removal of other operating barriers to industry.

Removal of price controls.

Removal of import licensing.

Significant decrease in import tariffs.

Establishment of Closer Economic Relations (CER) with Australia.

Removal of financial controls.

Liberalisation of foreign exchange controls.

Floating the exchange rate.

Revision of corporate, personal, and indirect taxation.

Removal of monopoly rights on state trading.

Corporatisation of state trading activities.

Corporatisation of some local authority trading activities.

Review of competition regulation.

Liberalisation of the transport sector.

Liberalisation of financial services sector.

Liberalisation of ports and waterfront work.

Partial liberalisation of energy sector.

Removal of concessions for favoured investment.

Removal concessions for favoured sectors.

Removal of shop trading hours restrictions.

Revision of town and country planning.

Commercialisation of broadcasting.

Commercialisation of science research.

Reforming Core Government Activities

New relations between minister and ministries.

Introduction of accrual-based and balance sheet accounting
for entire public sector.

Changes in appointment procedures of chief executive officers of
government agencies.

Public sector industrial relations put on a similar base to private
sector industrial relations.

Resource management law reform.

Revision of role of producer boards.

Abolition of many quangos and quasi-government organisations.

Program of asset sales.

Reorganisation of core government departments.

Reform of local government.

Reserve Bank given operational independence.

Redesign of Welfare State

Reform of delivery of social welfare provision.

Reform of provision of accident compensation scheme.

Reform of provision of compulsory education.

Reform of provision of health system.

Reform of provision of public housing provision.

Reform of provision of tertiary education provision.

Labour market reform.

Major reductions in relative benefit levels and entitlements.

system, the provision of public housing, and social security. This was the final great thrust of the reformers. Within weeks the government was backing down, and it found itself in constant administrative and political turmoil on all these fronts, experiencing the same cut in its electoral share in the 1993 election as Labour had done in 1990. Only the peculiarities of the First-Past-the-Post (FPP) electoral system gave it a bare majority in Parliament.

What seems to have happened is that from their election in 1990, once more the 'other prime minister' took charge of policy. The new Minister of Finance, Ruth Richardson, was as enthusiastic for change as Douglas. This time the Prime Minister, Jim Bolger, a far more effective politician than Lange, steadily limited her ability to make unilateral policy, especially as the policies led to one political and/or administrative disaster after another. In this he was helped by having close friend and able administrator, Bill Birch, at number three in Cabinet. (Bolger was older and more experienced than Richardson, whereas Lange was younger and less experienced than Douglas.) Various Cabinet committees were put in place, chaired by Bolger with Birch as a deputy, which weakened Richardson's position. By the end of 1991 her power was crumbling. Following the 1993 election Bolger was able to demote her, offering her the position of Minister of Agriculture. She resigned from Cabinet instead, and shortly after left Parliament.

By then blitzkriegs were extinct. Bolger had neither the mandate in the House nor the personal inclination to continue them. The new parliamentary regime, a consequence of the Mixed-Member-Proportional (MMP) electoral system, implemented by referendum in 1993, will veto future blitzkriegs. Since no party would hold a majority of seats, the likelihood that a few politicians can get leverage over the whole house will be severely limited. Undoubtedly pressures for further commercialisation will remain, but in the future the outcome is likely to be settled by administrative infighting, parliamentary scrutiny, and even public consultation. That is what the voters were instinctively voting for when they chose MMP over FPP.

OUTCOMES

Nevertheless the record of the Troika and later the National government led by Richardson in achieving change is impressive. Table 5.1 provides a summary list of the changes. They are astonishing in their breadth, although their quality is more variable and their success has been mixed. Often the successful more-market reforms have been obscured by a macroeconomic policy involving a high real exchange rate, which inhibited the tradeable sector and so was antagonistic to economic growth. Other reforms are still in the balance, some are abject failures. As this study proceeds we shall see that the application of commercialisation principles to non-commercial activities tends to belong to the latter group. A dictionary definition of 'reform' is 'form again'. That does not necessarily lead to an improvement.

6

The Treasury: Philosopher-Kings for Commercialisation

THE DRIVE FOR COMMERCIALISATION CAME FROM TREASURY, THE CHIEF economic and financial advisers to government. Certainly the ministers they advised, and who led government policy, were— at the very least—compliant, while as the next chapter shows the business sector, when it saw the opportunities, became enthusiastic. The task in this chapter is to trace this development, and to evaluate it. To do this we need to begin with a structural change which occurred in the way Treasury managed itself. This is best understood by briefly describing the traditional means by which official advisers operate—the bureaucratic mode of advice. The Ministry of Foreign Affairs and Trade provides one of the best illustrations.

THE BUREAUCRATIC MODE OF ADVICE

One is struck how New Zealand's foreign policy, in the period from the 1930s to the 1980s, shifted from a dependence with a European (British) focus to a degree of independence with a Pacific focus.[1] If the phenomenon was graphed the shown path would not be without its setbacks, but on the whole the trend is one of a steady change. It is especially odd that the trend occurred despite on occasions an unsympathetic government and sometimes an unsympathetic populace.

The shift can be explained by geopolitical-economic forces. But this does not explain how these great forces influenced the individual actions of the officials and the politicians. No one said:

'These are the realities—respond to them as follows'. A second sort of explanation is the 'great man' (and, one day, woman) phenomenon. Sometimes changes are attributed to a visionary politician such as Peter Fraser or Norman Kirk. On occasions a politician will speed up, or slow down, the trend. Perhaps politicians add some momentum to the change, but they are not long enough there to maintain it. A variation of the great man phenomenon is the great civil servant. The ministry dealing with external relations was dominated by Alister McIntosh between 1943 and 1966. Perhaps an exceptionally able permanent head might over such a long period have a vision which informs and drives the direction of policy.

But do we need an explicit vision within the department? Perhaps not. Perhaps the vision is formed in the context of the geopolitical-economic (or whatever) pressures. Consider the practicalities of foreign policy making at the level of the desk officer concerned with day-to-day decisions. He or she is continually faced with issues which require responses. Typically those responses are based on precedents of previous responses, or responses in related areas. A key element of those responses is consistency. Related issues also require related policy responses. The working environment of the official is designed to provide these co-ordinated responses. There are files, the records of previous responses. The official will report to a more senior one who is supervising policy in a wider domain. There are opportunities for discussion between officials. In effect, the ministry has a collective memory, physically embodied in its files and archives, in the learned studies which it commissions or encourages, and in the individual memories of the officials (which are in turned reinforced by maintaining informal contacts with retired officials, with think-tanks, and with people with expertise outside the ministry).

There is also a sense in which the ministry has a collective brain. Each issue which arises is tackled by officials using the collective memory to resolve the issue. Usually the process is incrementalist, and even where there has to be a rapid policy innovation precedent is important. Usually there has been previous discussion and debate, perhaps going back years. Within the ministry there is a conscious practice of promoting debate in order for there to be a diversity of views, which makes it possible to have a more flexible response to new or evolving situations.

There is also a collective 'intelligence', in the sense of information and news collected on the ground. The ministry has officers in its foreign missions, who are collecting data and feeding it back to the centre, where it is added to the collective memory.

These processes give policy that systematic trend, which in the long run dominates the accelerations, decelerations, and reversals, and which seems to suggest that geopolitical-economic forces determine foreign policy in the long run. The collective brain is continually interacting with the external environment through its intelligence. Some resolutions to policy problems are more successful than others because they are more consistent with the overall context. Successful solutions are recalled and re-used as new, apparently related, problems arise. Thus the general direction of policy development is consistent with the external environment—the geopolitical-economic context. We need neither a theory of an invisible hand which directs the overall policy, nor one of a great man thinking issues through.

What has been described here for the ministry concerned with foreign policy is true for most other government agencies, although they do not always do it so well. Sometimes an agency will create policy in a different way. Treasury in the 1980s was an outstanding example of this exception.

POLICY MAKING IN TREASURY

Treasury operated according to the bureaucratic mode until at least the mid 1970s. The details of the breakdown over the subsequent decade are not known but the broad outlines are. The rapid economic change left a precedent-based advice system struggling to cope.

The collective memory began to break down. Apparently the filing system was not carrying the burden required of it by the mid-1980s. Senior staff kept leaving, and the young staff and senior outsiders did not know what the precedents were. In any case few economists study history or the liberal arts, unlike officials in the external affairs ministry. It is no accident that Treasury has turned down the opportunity to commission a history of itself. Its evolution is not one of the interests of the Treasury of today. The vast majority of economists think of the here and now—and the future—and do not expect to learn from the past.

The response to this breakdown of the collective memory was probably not conscious. But we can see how it might evolve. It became necessary to give very great responsibility to junior, recently employed, Treasury officials. As an alternative to ensuring consistency by checking their decisions against a collective memory, they could check them against an analytic framework. Economics provided such a framework. The solution could be evaluated against the principles of the framework, rather than by asking an official whether it was consistent with previous decisions.

This could only work if the framework was sufficiently narrow. Economics is a very broad church, in which distinctive sects cohabit and argue. The debate best known to the public is that between the monetarists and Keynesians on macroeconomic policy. In the 1970s both schools existed within Treasury, as did both sides of other disputes.

One might expect that a good policy advice agency would operate as a broad church, encourage debate, and seek pragmatic outcomes close to the centre of the discipline. But this requires the collective memory of the bureaucracy. Otherwise the difficulty of consistency arises. Treasury cannot have one official using a Keynesian analysis, while a second operating in a related area uses a monetarist one. Similarly it cannot have one official using a leftish environmental analysis when dealing with the soil and water division of the Ministry of Works and Development, while another uses a rightish one when dealing with the irrigation division.

Initially there was no conscious strategy to require consistency, nor was there an awareness that this requirement would involve an extreme version of economics. But ineluctably Treasury was drawn there. By the late 1980s Treasury said its policy conclusions came from 'first principles' (that is, were not based on precedent). Yet ministers and their close advisers observed that the policies were predictably commercialisation ones. This analytic approach to policy making involved a major difference from the bureaucratic one, in that it squeezed out debate and dissent.

Until the arrival of Roger Douglas as minister, the balance favoured the pragmatists over the extremists, although the Chicago school extremists were growing in strength. Douglas tipped the scales towards extremism. Afterwards there was little toleration of difference—even of pragmatism. Those who uncritically agreed were well rewarded: in the private sector with lucrative contracts. Debate became muted, and centres of dissent—inside and outside—were destroyed. A public display of the venom of Treasury towards competition was the occasion at the February 1985 conference of the New Zealand Economists' Association when a group of academics chose to criticise Treasury's 1984 post-election briefing in the opening of the books debate.[2] Competitive pressure against Treasury was also reduced by the withdrawal of funding from the New Zealand Institute of Economic Research which had given the NZIER discretion over its choice of research activities.

The Chicago school version of economics, although extreme, had a number of attractions. It was very different from Muldoon's interventionism. Its simple organising principles ensured that a commercialist policy would almost always be recommended.

Thus the New Zealand Treasury resolved the problem of the breakdown of a collective memory by an analytic approach to policy making, in which a model or set of principles, rather than evolving precedents, determined each decision. Inevitably any such model would be narrow, and would offer little opportunity for challenge and dissent.

THE PRINCIPLES OF TREASURY POLICY MAKING

Irrespective of the mode of operation, the head of any agency ought to be able to predict reasonably accurately the departmental recommendation made by a junior officer. However, in the bureaucratic mode of policy making, the external observer needs to know the welter of precedents, and to be able to judge their relative importance, in order to predict a policy position in any detail. With the analytic approach it is much easier. Here is the set of decision-making principles from which an outsider can predict each Treasury decision, given some of the detail of the context. The ranking of the principles is crucial. A different ranking can lead to a different policy recommendation.

- Rule 1: Treasury is concerned to maintain and increase its power and influence.
- Rule 2: Subject to Rule 1, Treasury is concerned with the tendency for government expenditure to rise, and the govern-

ment accounts to be in deficit. It is consumed with controlling these two phenomena. It is willing to sacrifice the long term in the interests of short-term deficit reduction.

- Rule 3: Subject to Rules 1 and 2, Treasury is committed to an ideology of 'more market' (in its mildest form) or the New Right (in its most extreme form).
- Rule 4: Subject to Rules 1, 2, and 3, Treasury provides advice which promotes the 'economic efficiency' of the economy—that is, uncompensated efficiency (Chapter 3). Because Rule 3 is superior to Rule 4, Treasury advice can ignore inefficiency which arises from its proposals.
- Rule 5: Subject to Rules 1 to 4, Treasury promotes fairness in the economy.
- Rule 6: Objectives such as civil liberties, democracy, ethnic diversity, national identity, 'higher' cultural ends, are ignored, except in so far as they support Rules 1 to 4, and possibly 5.

Rule 1 applies to any institution. What is crucial is Rule 2 and Rule 3, and their relationship to the strategy of commercialisation. In effect we have to ask why Treasury tended to apply the most extreme version of Rule 3.

Rule 2 is what makes Treasury an unusual institution. Other government agencies spend government monies, whereas Treasury is concerned with the raising of the funds, typically by taxation and borrowing. The spenders have little to do with the funding, so this puts Treasury in a unique, if onerous, position (which includes the power to comment on almost every Cabinet paper). As a result Treasury almost invariably opposes every spending proposal. It is for an economist a very odd situation, so peculiar that even Treasury officials sometimes informally commented on it. There is nothing in general economics theory which says that all public spending is inefficient, yet that is the practical stance which Treasury takes. Its position is understandable. Raising tax revenue is not easy. Borrowing involves debt servicing (another form of spending), and the debt may have to be rolled over. This biases Treasury decision-making against spending. Hence their name 'the abominable no-men'.

While generally economics does not automatically condemn all government spending, there are sects within the broad church—most notably Chicago school economics—which are opposed to (almost) all government interventions. Such theories are attractive to the no-men (and no-women). More generally market solutions to economic problems tend to involve lower government spending. The most extreme version of these market solutions is total commercialisation, which is a logical solution to the problem that Treasury faces of restraining public spending. So (and this explains Rules 4 and 5) justifications for government spending get down-graded, reduced to supporting arguments which can be used to bolster higher Rules if they are favourable.

TREASURY AND THE TIGHT PRIOR[3]

There is one further peculiar feature of Treasury decision-making. Treasury literally lacks intelligence. Instead it depends on the collecting of information of other departments and from other sources such as newspapers and financial market commentators. This not only affects its perception of the world, but it means that individual Treasury officials usually have never been close to the 'coal face'. Often they are giving advice on matters with which they have little practical experience, depending at best on anecdote.

Why did not Treasury recognise this weakness? To some extent it did, but addressing the lacuna was not a high priority. Perhaps the willingness to tolerate it arises from the university training most economists get, which typically involves academics as isolated from the practicalities of the economy as their students. By the time the intelligence problem became evident, Treasury was totally committed to the Chicago school approach which emphasises theoretical rigour, at the cost of less attention to empirical facts because they may conflict with the model.

The expression the 'Chicago school of economics' is often used as a term of abuse. That is not the intention here. Melvin Reder, himself a University of Chicago professor, distinguishes Chicago economics from others by the notion of the 'Tight Prior Equilibrium', which

> is rooted in the hypothesis that decision makers so allocate the resources under their control that there is no alternative allocation such that any one decision maker could have his expected utility increased without a reduction occurring in the expected

utility of at least one other decision maker. . . . For Chicago and non-Chicago economists alike, this is a definition of Pareto optimality. . . .[4]

This, in economists' jargon, is the definition of the Pareto optimum discussed in Chapter 3. However, the Chicago school goes a step further, for it assumes that the world is in a nearly Pareto-optimal state, or would be if only governments were to do the absolute minimum of intervention. As Reder describes it, the normative Chicago view is 'anti-statist'.[5] A fuller but brief definition is 'dogmatic liberalism' where policy advice

> is strongly biased towards preserving or establishing
> (i) a maximum (negative) freedom of choice and action for consumers, producers and entrepreneurs,
> (ii) a minimum tax-, welfare-, and interventionist state, and
> (iii) a stable rule bound institutional framework including the monetary regime.[6]

Sometimes this is called 'New Right', defined by *The Fontana Dictionary of Modern Thought* as follows:

> Components of New Right thought have shaped Reaganism and Thatcherism. Those include economic theories associated particularly with Friedman and von Hayek, often described as 'neo-liberal', which exalt capitalism not only for its productive capacity, but its claim to be uniquely conducive to the maintenance of political and social liberty. The New Right thus opposes a strongly interventionist or ownership role for the State in the economy.[7]

In Reder's view the policy position arises out of the tight prior. Chicago-style economists do not believe the world is in exact equilibrium, but they

> tend strongly to appraise their own research standard and that of others by a standard which requires (*inter alia*) that the findings of empirical research be consistent with the implications of standard price theory. . . . Any apparent inconsistency of empirical findings with the theory, or report of behaviour not implied by the theory, is interpreted as anomalous. . . .[8]

The expression 'tight prior' is used in this book in a wider context than Reder's. It refers not just to the tight prior equilibrium, as described by Reder, but to the underlying methodology of the Chicago school and the New Zealand Treasury. Methodologically, a tight prior is a theory almost invulnerable to challenge by empirical evidence. Under challenge, auxiliary hypotheses are added to the core of the theory to protect it from any anomalies or inconsistencies.

Such a tight prior methodology is not just a peculiarity of Chicago economics, for it appears in many other strands of Western thinking. For instance 'Sartre's wonderfully ingenious brain could always think up some escape clause to save the ideal at the expense of reality. The parallel with acceptance of revealed religion is obvious.'[9] The reference to Jean-Paul Sartre is particularly pertinent given that he was a great influence on Roger Kerr, a key Treasury officer in the early stages of this development, and subsequently chief executive officer of the powerful Business Roundtable.

Because Treasury has primarily been involved with policy, its approach has been an extreme version of Chicago's. The tight prior can make one extraordinarily neglectful of relevant experience. Consider the discussion on state-owned enterprises, in the first publicly available paper cited by Treasury as key to their thinking. Some 23 of the 29 overseas references are American, despite the administration of state-owned enterprises being an area where Americans have little experience, let alone the overwhelming absolute advantage the paper's imbalance implies. The curious selection is, no doubt, one of the main reasons why the government advisers were ineluctably drawn to supporting privatisation, since the American experience hardly provides any other model.[10] Or consider:

> Part of an investigation recently undertaken by Treasury into venture capital included a survey of financial arrangements involving risk or venture capital in the capital market. The survey included a number of interviews and telephone conversations with market participants and elicited numerous written responses to a request for information.[11]

The Treasury paper then provides anecdotes from these unstructured interviews, to an apparently casual sample, for 3½ pages. There is no evidence in the paper of any systematic analysis of the survey, other than one paragraph reporting work on New Zealand sharemarket beta coefficients, which is the only reference to local realities.

In a third example indicative of its narrow vision, Treasury provided the Royal Commission on Broadcasting and Related Telecommunications in New Zealand with an article by Fowler and Brenner. Treasury appeared to have made no attempt to seek out, review, or provide to the Commission the subsequent—and numerous—criticisms of their views.[12]

Treasury's econometric standards can be appalling, showing just how casual they were over empirical investigation. In the appendix of their submission on securities law a study examines a data set of 18 years which it splits into two periods of 3 and 15 years and tests for structural change, reflecting different regulatory regimes. It concludes 'the results indicate clearly that factors not operating in period 1 were operating in period 2.' This so-called clarity is muddied by the data set being constructed from different sources, with the first two observations (of the three) coming from one source, the third from a second and the remainder (all fifteen) from a third. Occam's razor would suggest that any observed structural change reflected the different data sources.[13]

The practical failure of an analytic approach dominated by a tight prior is evident in a row between Richardson, the Minister of Finance between 1990 and 1993, and Wyatt Creech, who was Minister of Revenue at the time. In her biography Richardson complains about the unwillingness towards and resistance to the tax changes to which she got Cabinet to agree.[14] However Creech responded by pointing out that they were unworkable. 'The devil [wa]s in the detail.'[15] At one level this might just appear to be a couple of politicians from opposite wings of the same party disputing in public. But it also reflects the vast gap between the theory of taxation expounded by Treasury and the practicalities of implementation, which reduce the relevance of the theory's application to the real world. (For a further example of the tight prior and Treasury, see Chapter 14 on science policy.)

TREASURY AND GOVERNMENT MANAGEMENT

In some ways the key Treasury document was not the 1984 post-election briefing, *Economic Management*, which had a total commitment to more-market, but was only edging towards the full Chicago school position. The dispute was not resolved internally until the arrival of Roger Douglas as minister tipped the balance. By 1987 the commercialisers were in full control, as is evident in the 1987 post-election briefing, *Government Management*. Its basic framework is summarised as

> Government policy needs to move towards a comparative systems approach. This approach invites assessing alternative institutional structures (both private and governmental) according to the processes and outcomes they involve, utilising generally accepted criteria for making social choices.[16]

At a superficial level this statement appears unexceptional. However it has a number of far from subtle difficulties. First, the approach tends to involve static comparison of existing options; there is little advice on how to design the institutional structures, nor awareness of the evolutionary consequences of different institutions. Second, and not surprisingly given the previous section, the approach is almost bereft of empirical content, perhaps particularly where it might contradict the analytic thrust. Third, Treasury's 'generally accepted criteria for making social choices' is far from generally accepted, for it gives priority to uncompensated efficiency over equity, equivalent to favouring the income of the rich over the poor.

The narrowness of the vision is extraordinary. For instance, the treatise states that 'income is the passport to participation in society'.[17] 'Passport' is a poor metaphor, but even so there is no single 'passport' but a whole range of characteristics which enable participation in society, including rights, respect, opportunities, physical access, and employment. It suits the commercialist ideology to ignore these and concentrate on the single characteristic of income, which they claim their policies best deliver. But even here there is an inconsistency, since Treasury policy has been to cut people's social security income, apparently equivalent in their analysis to withdrawing beneficiaries' passports.

These 'oversights' relentlessly direct Treasury to a set of policy conclusions which can only be described as 'New Right'. Some indications are:

- Various statements which while technically true because of soft caveats are presented in a form which are biased towards an anti-government stance. For instance, it is stated that central government 'policies may distort the incentives of individuals'.[18] Then again they may not, or is the expression 'distort' tautological? Another example is 'where trade-offs are posed they need to be evaluated and the virtues of private arrangements not underestimated'.[19] Presumably Treasury is of the opinion that there is no danger of overestimating the value of private arrangements.

- The infatuation with voluntary arrangements—that is, market exchanges[20]—with no acknowledgement that private arrangements can, and do, occur under duress and/or unequal power. An indication of the narrowness of Treasury vision is its statement that 'the major sources of problems with private contracting are uncertainty, informational problems and opportunism.'[21] Many people would think that distributional inequality also posed a major problem.
- The dominance of 'efficiency' as an objective, getting almost five pages of coverage while 'equity' gets two pages, 'liberty' a paragraph, and 'public morals and human dignity' gets a page.[22]
- The conclusion which unequivocally favours private ownership over public ownership of enterprises, and recommends privatisation.[23]

Perhaps the direction of the treatise is summarised in the following statement from the opening chapter on the 'role and limits of government', which says: 'A major theme of the final section is that the state . . . is subject to largely the same pitfalls that face private solutions to social problems plus other ones.'[24] This assertion goes against both common sense and the thrust of New Zealand political development. We need not deny that state intervention can suffer from many of the pitfalls that private enterprise does, or that there can be other problems peculiar to state intervention. But to argue that state intervention suffers from almost all the private market failures and then some, and that there are few, if any, occasions in which state intervention leads to a superior performance over the private market is pure New Right ideology. (Surprisingly, in the light of its own analysis of public agencies, but entirely consistently with the Rule 1 of the principles of Treasury policy making, the one area where Treasury is confident about the superiority of the public service above the private sector is in the defence of its monopoly in giving ultimate economic and financial advice. It argues there are 'conflicts of interest in the advice given by private sector analysts'—but presumably not public sector ones.)[25]

Perhaps Treasury economists have to be reminded of all the standard market failures: justice and defence, property rights where human capital is involved, fairness of income distribution (including rights of the past and of the future), significant transaction costs, environmental effects, insurance where there is moral hazard, markets where there is uncertainty, and so on. And there is little evidence the writers are aware that the market can be destructive to social relations.[26]

An idealisation of the private sector as a model for all human activity pervades the treatise. Yet few Treasury officials had worked in private enterprise. No evidence is provided that private sector efficiency is a standard worth pursuing. Rather *Government Management* adopted the New Right ideological assumption that private activity is a paragon of virtue. By 1987 Treasury was committed to the notion of the superiority of business over government—and a commercialisation strategy.

TREASURY AND DEMOCRACY

'If the government wishes to have a public sector . . . managing its own affairs on a basis comparable with private sector efficiency, major changes in the nature of administration are essential.'[27] But should the objective of government be to pursue private sector efficiency in the idealised form Treasury presents? Most democratic theorists would argue that the point of democratic government is that it has objectives different from private enterprise, and pursues them in a different manner.

The political and constitutional discussion in *Government Management* is a pot-pourri of ideas, which attempts to apply the theoretical analyses described above to the constitutional issues of public sector management.[28] It lacks rigour, but advocates a change in the role of the public service, and its relationship with ministers. Behind this is an 'Americanisation' of the government of New Zealand, without much recognition of the distinctive features of the American political system, its successes and failures, and the peculiarities of American society and economy.

These fundamental changes, perhaps the most important constitutional ones made by the Fourth Labour government, cannot be entirely attributed to Treasury ministers and their advisers, and in part have been justified by improving 'accountability' of government officials and monies. But they partly reflect the New Right's rejection of conventional notions of democracy. As Reder says, ever so tactfully, 'the normative attitude of economic liberals towards the suffrage has often been wobbly, and Chicago has been no exception'.[29] It is not difficult to see in many of the prescriptions of the New Right the objective of stripping power from the democratic process as we know it, and transferring it to a minimally regulated market, that is, to those with the most financial votes. *Government Management* does not show the commitment to liberal democracy which protects it from the charge that it is 'wobbly'.

Plato described humankind chained inside a cave, seeing only the shadows of the world flickering upon the walls. The fortunate few broke their chains and climbed into the sunlight to see the 'reality' which, it will be recalled in Plato's epistemology, is not some real empirical objective world, but a world of ideals. Then they returned to tell the rest of us about what they had seen, claiming the right of philosopher-kings to rule over the rest in a kindly, but anti-democratic, manner.

Government Management reads like a treatise of philosopher-kings. They have seen the ideal; it is private voluntary contracts in an unfettered market. They have not seen, or noticed, the grubby side of the private sector, which became so evidently exposed following the November 1987 share market crash, but was familiar earlier to those well read in business history and/or experienced in business. For the Treasury philosopher-kings there is a pure, flawless ideal of the market, untainted by the practicalities which they suffer as working public sector bureaucrats. It is a charming image, although its relevance to the cave in which we live is far from clear.[30]

In the 1970s Treasury was constrained by its minister (and prime minister) Muldoon, who was both sensitive to the political consequences of proposed policy changes, and powerful enough to resist them. Yet he allowed, albeit apparently grudgingly, changes in a more-market direction, even during the period of his draconian price freeze.

The replacement of the all-powerful Muldoon by Lange, Palmer, and the Troika changed the balance. Now there was no political leadership to resist the changes, while Treasury ministers uncritically adopted them. Treasury advice slewed towards the New Right extremism of commercialisation. The Labour administration did not go the full distance in social policy, perhaps because of an atavistic commitment to the welfare state. That was left to the succeeding National government. Nevertheless even in social policy areas they moved down the road, with prescription charges in health and student loans (and higher fees) in tertiary education. In broadcasting they commercialised as far as they dared.

The role of Treasury changed. Suddenly the abominable no-men were saying yes. Instead of opposing proposals for change (many of which were loony), they were advocating them. Who now was to scrutinise the proposals? *Quis custodiet ipsos custodes?*

Appendix: The Treasury View of the Labour Market

In its *Briefing to the Incoming Government: 1990* Treasury devotes 17 pages to 'The Labour Market'. This appendix reviews that chapter to illustrate the sort of analysis Treasury often provided.

When I was asked to provide this analysis (to go before a select committee on the Employment Contracts Bill in 1991), I did not go directly to the text but first reread various OECD publications on labour market flexibility. I had expected that Treasury would have used the OECD economic analysis to argue that the existing legislation, the 1987 Labour Relations Act, discouraged necessary flexibility, and I wanted to be able to pick up the resonances with the OECD in the post-election briefing. To my astonishment, not only did the chapter ignore the OECD analysis on labour market flexibility but, as will become evident, its argument is almost totally bereft of economic content. Instead it is an ideological account supported by anecdotes and assertions without any systematic analysis or evidence. Especially illuminating is how the objectives in Treasury recommendations are political ones of rights, rather than economic ones such as increased flexibility.

The following is an edited series of extracts from my original evidence.[1] I quote or summarise the Treasury view, together with my point-by-point commentary. Comments added later, and not part of the original evidence, are given in italic.

POLICY CONTEXT: PP. 145–146

Achieving better results will require action on a number of fronts. Especially important for the labour market are:
- fiscal discipline and low inflation . . .
- . . . competitive pressures . . .
- keeping the cost of domestic regulation and taxation of business activities at the lowest possible levels . . .
- ensuring education and training systems are capable. . . .
  The labour market is not uniform. There are demands for a wide variety of skills and abilities. Skilled labour, particularly the most skilled, is scarce while there is an abundance of unskilled.

While this list is uncontroversial, like the rest of the *Briefing* it excluded the impact of overall macroeconomic policy on labour market performance. Perhaps the failure of labour market performance was a failure of macroeconomic policies, while the labour market policies have been effective and adequate.

As the length of unemployment is often a negative indicator to potential employers, this further decreases the chances of employment. To break this vicious cycle it is important to get them back into a regular job. This may require a balanced approach that makes benefits less attractive than work, reduces laws and regulations that lead to the low skilled being priced out of the market, and adopts approaches to benefit administration that help people back into the work force.

No evidence was provided for the assertions that:
- benefits were more attractive than work;
- there were laws and regulations that price the low-skilled out of the market;
- current benefit administration did not help people back into the workforce.

One could well argue the opposite, but it would be pointless to do so here, because the empirical evidence for the Treasury assertions was lacking.

Note that no mention was made of the consequential poverty impacts when these policies are implemented on those who are still unable to obtain a job (or one with a very low wage).

> Initially there will need to be greater variation in wages with changes above the low-skilled end of the labour market where wages are currently above the level at which employers find it worthwhile to employ additional staff. . . .

The prediction that under the policies proposed by Treasury there will be a fall in the nominal wage of unskilled workers was likely to be true (*unskilled wages in fact fell after the Employment Contracts Act was implemented*). The proposition that this will markedly increase employment among the unskilled may not be true (*there was a rise in employment, but from a macroeconomic expansion, not as a result of the Act itself*).[2]

KEY CHARACTERISTICS OF A WELL-FUNCTIONING LABOUR MARKET: P. 146

> Not all eventualities can be foreseen at the beginning of employment, so both parties look for ways to protect their investment [e.g. for the worker in human capital] by improving the potential for an enduring relationship. This often results in complicated and varied terms and conditions of employment.

In practice many of the terms and conditions in the employment 'contract' are unstated, and may even be unforeseen. Typically the implicit contract includes an agreement by the parties to act in good faith.

One difficulty the proposals generated is that following an upheaval in the past practices and the increasing fragmentation of the industrial relations structure it would be necessary to make explicit increasing parts of the implicit contracts. Moreover they will increasingly be enforced in the civil courts, rather than on the worksite by the partners acting in good faith. The transaction costs of the proposed system are likely to be higher than the old.

> The parties to these [employment] arrangements should be

those with the best information and the greatest interest in the outcome. . . .

In the previous system the union was often the best informed on the employee side. Obtaining the information by a single person is very costly, particularly in occupations where there is high turnover, and where technical information (e.g. safety and health hazards) are complex.

A well-functioning labour market can contribute significantly to job creation, income growth and increased national wealth by:
- allowing employment arrangements to reflect the diversity of opportunities and threats facing firms and workers
- allowing the adaptation of firms to changing markets and technology
- allowing adjustment to shortages and excess availability of workers in different regions and occupations
- allowing arrangements that lead to the development of productive skills and expertise for workers and managers
- ensuring that negotiations of employment arrangements are carried out in the interests of firms and workers
- encouraging the co-operative element of employment relations, while recognising firm's and workers' interests can diverge.

A long critique could be made of what amounts to a definition of a 'well-functioning labour market', but only a couple of points will be made here. First, note the personification of the 'labour market'. Most people think a market is a venue where transactions occur. Second, note that the market 'allows'. Treasury sees this personification as passive. Treasury was confused because it muddled the 'labour market' with the 'industrial relations system', which was a major part of the framework in which the labour market operates.

LABOUR MARKET REGULATIONS: PP. 147–150

This section begins with an overview of the legislation covering the labour market. The main focus is the Labour Relations Act 1987, although some other relevant legislation is mentioned in passing. The paragraph does not even mention training and the apprenticeship system.

The overview, while not contentious, is from a perspective aimed at deriving the policy conclusions that appear. Omissions include:

- There was no mention of the prohibition of second-tier contracting,[3] which would enable greater flexibility/diversity in the wage path.
- While the text mentioned the provision where employers with at least 50 workers on each site can opt out of awards subject to a ballot of workers, it does not say this provision was passed in September 1990, and had no time to be effective. Because over 50 percent of the workforce are in enterprises with 50 plus workers, this would have been a major change in industrial relations, if it had been allowed to operate.

The section then goes on to describe 'the performance to date'. Amounting to one-and-a-half pages, the section contains five anecdotes (one explicitly based on a newspaper item), and one marginal item involving empirical evidence.

> . . . there has generally been little movement away from awards to alternative bargaining arrangements.

This statement was disingenuous. There had been increasing use of agreements and composite agreements and awards (that was between one employer and one union or a composition of unions). The September 1990 legislative change was again ignored.

> . . . the system of occupational awards remains entrenched.

The industrial system was moving from its traditional basis of occupational awards towards industry/enterprise structures, where relevant. (See Appendix to Chapter 7.) However many occupations (e.g. teaching, nursing) are industry-specific, and so the concern was not as much an issue as the phrase 'entrenched' implies. Treasury offered no evidence for their claim.

> Awards registered under the Act continue to contain significant restrictions on work practices. Of the awards settled in the 1988/9 wage round, 10% banned part-timers and 27% disallowed casual work. More than 25% of awards required employers to pay part-time and casual workers between 5% and 20% more than full time rates.

No source is cited for these figures. The passage does not tell us a lot, because there may be good reasons for the reported behaviour. For instance, part-time and casual workers well expect a higher pay rate, because of the inconvenience, proportionally higher travelling time, and lower job security.

> It appears that the extent of prohibitions and restrictions is not generally declining.

No evidence was provided for this statement. Trade unionists, more in touch with the reality of the workplace, were vehemently claiming the opposite.

> Awards often have the effect of reserving certain tasks to members of particular trade unions, such as the distinction between the work of watersiders and harbour workers.

The text anecdote was based on a defunct instance, which arose out of specific legislation. No current example was provided, suggesting that the 'often' was an exaggeration.

> As a result the [Labour Relations] Act constrains workers' ability to develop and use new skills.

Yes, for that will be true in any industrial relations system. And yet no. Developments in the 1990 Metal Trades Award (MTA), which enable multiskilling and a career structure for workers, show how an award can do the very opposite. If there had been only individual and enterprise agreements it would have been impossible to move towards the upskilling program of the MTA award. (*As a result of the new legislation the award's upskilling developments broke down. There has been a long period of stagnation in the development of skills training structures.*)

> Changing work practices within an award is difficult and expensive requiring a co-operative effort by employers.

The abolition of awards did not change the issue. Transaction costs for any bargaining arrangement are high, given the complexity of the issues in the explicit (or implicit) contract.

> Being locked into an award is a major restriction on the op-

portunities open to workers and employers, and their ability to respond to the changing environment.

The statement would be less ideological if the 'is' were to be replaced by 'can be'.

> The system of occupational awards is reinforced by restrictions on union contestability and by agreements that unions will not contest each other's coverage.

Treasury misused the economists' notion of 'contestability'. Contestability is about the hit and run supply of a good or service, where there is cost-free exit and entry. The worker is concerned about an ongoing relationship with her or his bargaining agent (union). Exit and re-entry can be costly. It would be little value to a worker to have a bargaining agent which in a time of industrial difficulty skipped the country.

There was no mention in the text of the legislation which requires compulsory coverage ballots every three years—an omission which strengthened the Treasury argument by detaching it from reality.

The summary reads:

> The emerging picture is one of slow and halting improvement in the flexibility of industrial documents and of labour relations. The present framework for labour relations clearly allocates rights and responsibilities. However, it is less successful in ensuring that the labour market has the other desirable characteristics outlined previously. The Labour Relations Act has three fundamental flaws:
> - The legislative rights and privileges are conferred on trade unions and employer associations rather than individual firms and workers, yet the latter parties have better information and incentives to reach agreement.
> - The bargaining agents are not directly and effectively accountable to individual firms and workers, as their roles are set by legislation rather than by choice of the firms and workers.
> - The costs and risks involved for firms and workers in moving to bargaining arrangements that better meet their needs are high and reinforce the position of existing trade unions and employer associations.

The main concern of Treasury seems to be the political one of the preferential position of unions and employer associations, with the effectiveness of the labour market, or the industrial relations system a very secondary concern. The issue of preference for a particular institutional structure has to be assessed in terms of that effectiveness for its purpose, not in terms of some political objective.

REDUCING CONSTRAINTS IN THE LABOUR RELATIONS ACT: PP. 150–152

> The existing legislation confers bargaining rights on trade unions and employer associations. The key requirement is to ensure that these bargaining agents, when their services are needed fully represent workers' and firms' interests. This means that individual workers should have the right to choose bargaining agents to assist contract negotiation.

Note how the text focuses on rights, and not on the measures to improve the performance of the labour market.

> To achieve that, unions must have no legislatively guaranteed coverage rights, so membership rules should be able to cover workers who could be covered by the rules of other unions, and there should be no restrictions on the establishment of bargaining agents or on the minimum number of members covered by a bargaining agent.

The policy prescription ignores the problems of
• free riding by non-union members;
• economies of scale in union (and more, generally, industrial relations) administration;
• information available to workers.
More generally this was an example of the Treasury predilection for ignoring the information and transaction costs at the heart of a lot of recent economic theory, in order to obtain policy prescriptions which suit their objectives.

> The Labour Relations Act itself is an example of limited reforms achieving limited results.
> The main reason for pessimism [for the success of such

'limited' measures] is that the integrity of the legislation may be difficult to maintain through piecemeal reform.

A number of examples of the way interlocking and interrelatedness are then given. Here we find an explicit commitment to the blitzkrieg. Piecemeal reform is not enough.

There is also a section opposing an industry bargaining structure, because it is 'unlikely to achieve the goal of ensuring that employment arrangements reflect the individual firms and workers'. Treasury appears unaware that under the 1987 Act the structure was moving towards a industry plus enterprise system (a process reinforced by the September 1990 amendment). Not surprisingly in terms of its general policies, there was no recognition of the high costs of an enterprise-based structure to small firms, nor the benefits from industry-based structures in terms of mechanisms to upskill the labour force.

There are intermediate steps for the piecemeal reformer:
- the breakout for 50 worker firms into enterprise bargaining was one such step. A moderate Treasury might have favoured lowering the limit to, say, 25 worker firms;
- the removal of the legislative restriction to second-tier arrangements on top of industry awards.

MORE FUNDAMENTAL REFORM: PP. 152–153

The alternative reform Treasury offers

> allow[s] individual workers the freedom to contract with their employer:
> - either individually or collectively at the enterprise level
> - either with or without a bargaining agent of their choice.

The analysis here makes most sense if the reader accepts this paragraph as stating Treasury's political objective. It does not follow from any economic one.

> The approach would . . . be more likely than current arrangements to ensure that wage deals and the related work practices reflected the value of the contribution of workers to the firm . . . make innovation and investment more likely. . . . Decentralised bargaining arrangements are also more likely to allow employ-

ers and employees to strike deals which facilitate training and improve productivity.

This was piety. Because there was no evidence it is difficult to rebut the claim in any detail. What is one to say to the allegation that the previous bargaining arrangements discourage employers and employees from striking 'deals which facilitate training and improve productivity'?

However, Treasury was under a misapprehension if it thought its policies were more likely to 'facilitate training'. That a trained employee can escape to another employer discourages employee–employer co-operation in skills acquisition. That was why the MTA (before it collapsed) was developing training programs and career paths on an industry-wide basis.

For the purposes of the new legislation, a number of related issues will require consideration by policy-makers.
- The desirability of specific legislation allowing workers to act collectively. . . .
- The case for regulating bargaining arrangements. . . .
- The right to strike. . . .
- Concerns about the abuse of market power in the labour market. . . .

It is a characteristic feature of the utopians that they are very vague on the design of the new country. It is no accident that the section on the 'more fundamental reform' was shorter than other sections on 'amending the existing act'.

CONCLUSION: P. 157

Choosing the regulations to apply to the labour market requires an assessment of appropriate balance of risks.

The risks are neither listed nor assessed. Instead the paragraph rushes on to policy objectives in the second sentence.

The key requirements are to reverse the longstanding slow growth in employment, to maintain productivity improvements, and to reduce unemployment.

As was proved subsequently, the key factor in employment generation is economic growth (i.e. the macroeconomy). Productivity growth re-mained poor.[4]

> This argues strongly that policy balances should be changed to favour getting people back into employment.

The sentence is misleading in that it seems to imply that in the past the policy objectives have not been in favour of getting people back into employment.

> The approach should be to push responsibilities for labour relations down to the level of individual workers and enterprises. . . .

The logical connection between this and the previous sentence is unclear.

> With a policy goal of attaining sustainable higher living standards, there would be gains from giving greater freedom to workers and firms to enter into mutually beneficial employment arrangements with minimal external interference.

The grammar of this sentence is as problematic as its logic.

> Such reforms would facilitate enterprise bargaining, rewards for productivity and training, and would encourage more efficient and responsive trade unions. . . .

No evidence was given for these assertions. There was no discussion in the main text that unions were inefficient (and no indication as to what Treasury meant by the notion).

> Fundamental reform, associated with changes in benefit policies which improve incentives to work, may put downward pressure on real wages for some workers.

Agreed, except that 'may' could be replaced with 'almost certainly will'. A few pages earlier Treasury says, without caveats, 'Those currently overpaid will lose unless there are offsetting productivity increases' (p. 154).

> As improvements in labour market performance will depend on changing attitudes of people who have long experience under a more centralised approach.

We have ways of making you love our policies.

> Such improvements are likely to take years to work through fully.

Was this the same Treasury who objected to the 1987 reforms because 'the emerging picture was one of slow and halting improvement in the flexibility of industrial documents and of labour relations' (p. 150)?

> Providing they are supported by sound macroeconomic policies, increased competition throughout the economy, and other policies related to education, training and social welfare benefits, these labour market reforms will contribute to rising standards and higher participation in the workforce in the medium term.

It is fitting that the last sentence in the chapter should be an unsubstantiated promise, with the let-out that the benefits are only going to appear in the long term, and in any case other policies are necessary (a failure in any of which could mean the promised benefits would not occur).

The picture the visitor from Mars would obtain from the Treasury account of the performance of the industrial relations system at the time was that
- awards were the only thing which mattered;
- the awards were mainly occupational;
- there was little change taking place.

This contrasts markedly with what the visitor would observe:
- only about 55 percent of the employee labour force was unionised;
- while there were still occupational-based awards (although many applied to single industries), there was a growing number of industry and enterprise awards. Moreover legislation just passed applying to over 50 percent of the work force (albeit in less than 2 percent of all enterprises) would speed up this process of vertical reorganisation;
- the industrial relations system was in a major transition;
- the system was much more complex than Treasury portrayed.

While the visitor would observe some of the defects which Treasury itemise, they would also observe other effects which offset them to some extent. Surveys showed many small firms valued industry wide awards as a means of keeping their employer transaction costs low, and of pursuing various skill upgrading and career path strategies.

The unbiased visitor would be puzzled about the balance of the advantages and disadvantages of the system. But they might conclude:

- While it may be possible to conceive of an ideal industrial relations system, the ideal was practically unobtainable because of the conflicting demands. (By focusing on one dimension only—as Treasury does—the problem of conflicting demands may be avoided.) In the end improving the system would involve comparing one imperfect system against another, and neither would dominate the other in every aspect of effectiveness.
- There was a host of intangible but nonetheless real effects between the actors in the industrial relations drama—intangibles such as informal understandings, reputation, trust, and common experiences—which consolidate practical industrial relations, resulting in a system which had evolved steadily, rather than rapidly. Relationships between employers and workers (and their bargaining agents), are more akin to marriage than one night stands. These intangibles are integral and valuable parts of the industrial relations system, even though they do not appear to be recognised by Treasury.

It has not been the purpose of this appendix to evaluate the effect of the Employment Contracts Act. That is to be done elsewhere.[5] What has been shown is the thinness of the analysis of Treasury at the time.

7

The Private Sector

BY THE LATE 1970S, THE PEAK BUSINESS ORGANISATIONS, WITH THE exception of the unions, had become committed to a more-market strategy but not, at that stage, to commercialisation.[1] That came later—after Treasury had led the way. Moreover, it was not simply a matter of the private sector business leadership changing its mind, or evolving its thinking. There was a more fundamental change in the leadership, in the 'Establishment'. In effect, there was a revolution—even a coup.

The expression 'Establishment' is used here to cover the group of men (and latterly some women) who are most closely involved in the governing of New Zealand. It includes key politicians, businessmen, and public servants who are influential in decision making and who have a commonality of vision and a networking of relations. There is an ambiguity in the term, but here we use it to cover the 'ill-defined amalgam of institutions, social classes, and forces which represent authority, legitimacy, tradition and the status quo'.[2] The New Zealand Establishment is typically male, older, white, wealthy, middle-class and of middle-class origin, living in Wellington or visiting Wellington regularly. It is relatively cohesive, because it is small, although there is always ambiguity as to who is on its fringes, who is joining, and who is left out.

THE OLD ESTABLISHMENT

The pre-1984 Establishment belonged to the era of pastoral export specialisation. Many had grown up on a farm, were farmers, or depended upon the farm sector (processing, servicing, supply, or finance). There was a minority who were from manufacturing but it was an inward-looking, highly protected activity, whose prestige came from the jobs it created rather than the foreign exchange it earned. Typically members of the Old Establishment were better educated than average for their generation, and had travelled overseas more than average, although much less so than subsequent generations were to do. Most had been through the 1930s Depression and had served in the Second World War. But the following two decades were ones of progress and stability. Ironically, as the generation came to power, the experience of their formative years—late adolescence and early adulthood—was of conditions exactly the opposite to those in which they would govern. They were unready for the challenge the post-1966 economic structure posed.

There were various reasons for this inability to identify the evolving political economy. Nostalgia for the past pervaded their thinking. The pre-1967 world had been so much easier: grow some grass, minimally process it, ship it to Britain, and live on the proceeds. It was a nostalgia reinforced by the hegemony of the farm lobby, which argued that there was no viable alternative strategy. If New Zealand did not export pastoral products, what would the economy do? Import-substituting industrialisation was a poor alternative—at best, a supplement. Very few in the 1960s had any confidence in export-oriented manufacturing.

But if the Old Establishment was unwilling to countenance a revision from within, there were pressures from outside.

THE RISE OF A NEW ESTABLISHMENT

The new generation—typically born in the 1940s—was more urban than its predecessors, and had not gone through the war experience as the Muldoon generation had. Perhaps they were more urbane, more cosmopolitan, better trained too, but if so it was the result of a changing world environment and affluence, rather than of any superior personal merits. In a society which claimed to be egalitarian, these men typically came from the better schools and their fathers were middle-class or higher—farmers, professionals, successful self-employed.

The business community arising from the structural changes of the 1970s was less dependent on farming, and more based in the financial sector and in the new industries that had come to prominence in the previous decade. The new leaders were very much more-market in attitude, despising government intervention, although not unwilling to use it when it was to their benefit. Even so they depended on the government for their success. Political patronage to a range of sinecures gave prestige, reinforced the new network, and provided additional sources of income. Consultants in the private sector benefited from public sector contracts—especially from Treasury—lavished on them. Opportunities for private profit were opened up by privatisation and commercialisation. And government policy favoured their interests, most notably in halving the top marginal income tax rate from 66 percent to 33 percent.

It is true that the Old Establishment would have favoured most of these things too. But it found itself increasingly cut out of appointments, status, and opportunities. Privately the New Right was scathing about them. Basically there was a coup within the establishment. Roger Kerr, chief executive officer of the Business Roundtable from 1986, captured the intergenerational change: 'The average age of chief executives of major companies has dropped ten years. . . . A generation of human capital has been obliterated.'[3]

Patricide is one of the most heinous of crimes, to be justified only by some greater purpose. In New Zealand the coup could not be justified—as happens in the third world—by an external threat, corruption, or communal tensions. So the new coup leaders used ideology as a justification for their seizure of power. Conveniently, Treasury and the New Right offered such a dogma, which involved—as is usual in coups—the exaggeration of the sins of the predecessors.

The simplistic New Right philosophy, advocating the central role of self-interest and restraining government involvement in the regulation of society, was perfect for this purpose. The rising business community adopted it with alacrity.

THE NEW ZEALAND BUSINESS ROUNDTABLE

The flagship of this business revolution was the Business Roundtable, a self-selected lobby group of about 40 chief executives of some of New Zealand's biggest businesses. It had begun quietly in the late 1970s, apparently in imitation of the Australian

Business Roundtable, indicative of the colonial attitudes it exhibits. It became very active in 1986 following the appointment of Kerr from the Treasury think-tank. Thereafter it was the most prominent private sector advocate of the commercialist approach.

It took an active role in promoting policies in—as it said—the 'public interest'. Yet the Business Roundtable ignored any matter where a purist New Right position would infringe their immediate interests. Thus they did not comment on tariff policy, research and development policy, accountancy reform, commercial law reform, or the issue of the substantial donations to political parties made by business (Roundtable businesses prominent among them). When the government began running a large internal deficit in 1991, the Roundtable was silent on the issue, despite having advocated tight deficits earlier. Instead it urged privatisation, and changes in arrangements concerning education, health, and industrial relations in a direction that would favour private enterprise. Meanwhile it opposed electoral reform, which threatened its dominance. So the claim that the Roundtable advocated policies in the public interest even where it conflicted with its business interests cannot be sustained. Tensions between the business and ideological wings of the New Right were avoided by scrupulously ignoring any contradictions.

Nor did the Roundtable lead the commercialisation revolution. Their public commitment occurred well after the strategy was under way, although without their involvement it probably would not have gone as far. The relationship between Treasury and the Roundtable is complicated. No doubt it was constitutionally proper, but there were informal linkages. Former Treasury officials were sometimes hired by the Roundtable, while both the Roundtable and Treasury might hire the same consultant on the same topic. If Treasury had its public advocacy blocked, the Roundtable would often take the case up. Instances included the competition policy reform, student fees, social welfare, health, and labour market reform.

When many of Treasury's policy initiatives were stalled in the late 1980s, following the resignation of Roger Douglas, it was the Roundtable which took over. This is most evident in its leadership of the policy development which resulted in the Employment Contracts Act. The economic policies implemented in the first year of the National government represented the high point of Roundtable influence, although there had been significant achievements under Labour too, including the privatisation program and the 1988 income tax changes. (Companies whose chief executives were members of the Roundtable bought—sometimes in association with other companies—more than half the government assets by value.) The reductions of government spending by the Labour government, required to fund the tax cuts, were no doubt very acceptable to the Roundtable too.

The relationship between the Roundtable and the politicians is more complex. There were links between Labour and the business community before 1984, reflecting the growing disenchantment with Muldoon. The linkages strengthened when the corporatisation program sought suitable business candidates to sit on the boards of the new state corporations. Many of the appointments were men connected to the Roundtable, and the inevitable interaction between those men and the politicians strengthened the ties between Labour and the business community in general, the Roundtable in particular.

These businessmen gave considerable funds to the Labour Cabinet (not the party) for the 1987 election campaign. The most explicitly reported of these donations is that revealed by Alan Hawkins, chief executive of Equiticorp (Equiticorp later collapsed, and Hawkins was incarcerated for two years for fraud). In his autobiography Hawkins reported that his company '. . . made a donation of $250,000 to the Labour Party, or more specifically to Roger Douglas in recognition of the good work he had done in deregulating the New Zealand economy, something Equiticorp had benefited tremendously from'.[4] The magnitude of the donation should be compared with the standard contribution of $15,000 that the largest company, Fletcher Challenge, made at that time to each major party. In contrast the Cabinet war-chest from these Equiticorp-like donations exceeded $3 million.

The appointments not only helped bed in the New Establishment, but typically the appointees were committed to commercialisation generally, and particularly to privatisation, even of the SOEs to which they were appointed. For instance Ron Trotter (knighted by Labour) was chairman of the Business Roundtable, which was publicly advocating privatisation, and chairman of Fletcher Challenge, which was involved in buying a number of state assets. He also chaired the board of Telecom and the State Owned Enterprise Monitoring Group. (He was a director of the Reserve Bank during the mid 1980s, and later chairman of the

National Interim Board during the health reforms (see Chapter 9). The effect of these various appointments was to strengthen the network of the New Establishment, and to place them well in positions of influence in relation to the Labour government.[5]

Initially they got their way to a large extent, but as the Labour government moderated the Douglas commercialisation thrust in 1988, the businessmen turned to supporting the National opposition, especially Ruth Richardson, the spokesperson on finance. Through this they had considerable influence on the National Party's election manifesto and the National government's initial policies, including the Employment Contracts Act, the benefit cuts and state spending cuts, and the accident compensation scheme and health sector reforms. By now other peak organisations had joined them, especially the New Zealand Employers Federation, the Federated Farmers, and the Manufacturers Association.

POLITICAL POSITIONS AND PLAYERS

Figure 7.1: Elites' ideological positions

	MODERNISERS
Engineering Union	R. Richardson/S. Upton
	Treasury
	Business Roundtable
	Financial institutions
	Centre for Independent Studies*
	R. Douglas/R. Prebble/ACT
LEFT	**RIGHT**
Gamma Foundation*	National caucus
Most unions	New Zealand First (W. Peters)
Most Labour Party	Rob Muldoon
NewLabour (J. Anderton)	Planning Council*
	TRADITIONALISTS

* 'Think-tank'

Figure 7.1 divides the area of political discourse into four separate groupings by the two dimensions left/right, and moderniser/traditionalist. The positions of the political elite are illustrated by various individuals and pressure groups. Instructively, the weight of lobby groups in number and influence is in the upper-right quadrant of right modernisers, while there are hardly any effective lobbyists in the left modernising quadrant. The left was largely confined to the traditionalist dimension. This is partly because it has a tendency to be committed nostalgically to the past on economic policy, but also because one of the first things the Labour government did was to discourage (and destroy) institutions that were left modernisers, while its actions reinforced the right modernisers (such as the Roundtable).

But contrast the lobby groups with the populace. A study of voting behaviour of the 1990 election allows us to distinguish seven different voting groups in the 1990 election, together with their percentage shares of the vote, and to allocate them to one or another of the four quadrants, as is shown in Figure 7.2.[6]

Figure 7.2: Populace's ideological positions

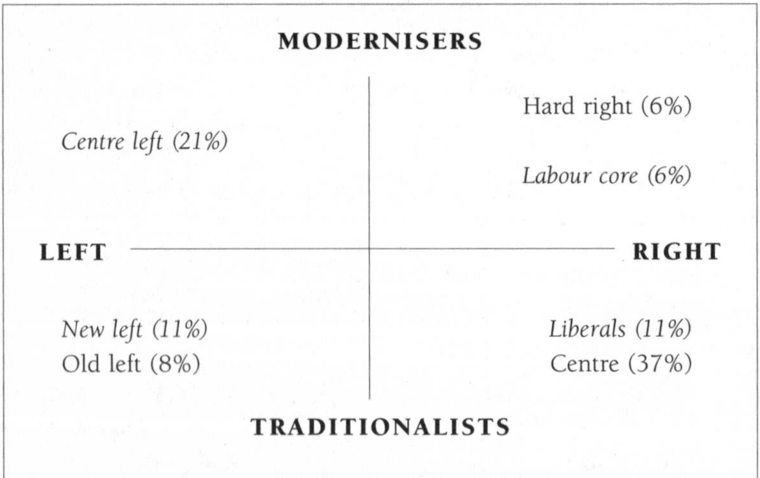

```
                    MODERNISERS

                                    Hard right (6%)
     Centre left (21%)
                                    Labour core (6%)


LEFT ─────────────────────────┼──────────────────── RIGHT


     New left (11%)                Liberals (11%)
     Old left (8%)                 Centre (37%)

                   TRADITIONALISTS
```

Key: social conservatives — roman/Social liberals — italic
Categories and percentages (for the 1990 electorate) from Vowles & Aimer (1993:207)

The most important grouping has been the *right traditionalists* (in the lower-right quadrant), who were almost half of the 1990 electorate, and from them came the base of the Old Establishment. However, they did not have total control and formed a coalition with the *left traditionalists* (in the lower-left quadrant), whose main power-bases were the unions and various left-wing groups, and who provided more of the intellectual input. In any case by the late 1970s the pressures for modernisation tended to force the two groupings together, as the hegemony of the Old Establishment was threatened.

The *left modernisers* (upper-left quadrant) have not been important in political leadership terms, at least on economic policy, although they form the second largest of the seven groups which the study identifies. They have been very influential on environmental, human rights, international relations, race, and women's issues. On economic issues, there has been really only one significant institution, the Engineering Union, reflecting the modernisation pressures that the manufacturing sector has experienced. Instructively, the Engineering Union is one of the few unions that has had to compete against another in its base sector: the smaller Manufacturing and Construction Workers Union, one of the most left-wing traditionalist unions in New Zealand.

The story on the political right is different. An establishment always has a problem of renewal, but the issue is much more acute when the political economy is rapidly changing. The difficulties were perhaps compounded by Prime Minister Muldoon's centralist political and economic style, which ruthlessly eliminated potential successors, and so gave no line of natural succession. Thus the sharp shift in power away from the traditional right to the *modernising right* (upper-right quadrant) has the characteristics of a coup. The businesses which filled the vacuum were not the same as those which had supported Muldoon. At a simple level one generation replaced another. The ideology of the New Right was adopted by the New Establishment.

THE FAUSTIAN DEAL

Douglas promised the Labour Party that, if it abandoned its principles, the resulting policies would generate exceptional levels of economic prosperity. As Chapter 8 reports, the economic outcome has been, in fact, near-stagnation. The promise has still to be fulfilled.

The New Establishment saw the strategy of commercialisation as a means to rid itself of the interference of government in its activities. But independence from the New Zealand government was bought at the price of surrendering the ownership of New Zealand business to overseas concerns, for they covered the gap in the shortage of local savings. Today over half of the members of the Roundtable run firms which are largely overseas-owned. The New Establishment has become a hostage to foreign investors. The deal which gave Faust his power ultimately cost him his soul, or—as we might say in a more secular world—his authority and dignity, his mana. The members of the New Establishment have increasingly become the satraps of foreigners. Ironically those who uncritically adopted a colonial attitude to overseas ideas are now colonials in their finances also.

The resulting combination of a mistrusted Establishment, overseas involvement, and public restlessness makes the politics of the rest of the 1990s as uncertain as at any time in New Zealand's past. Behind this is the complicated issue of the meaning of 'revolution'. Ralf Dahrendorf identifies

> two quite different versions of dramatic change. One is deep change, the transformation of core structures of a society which in the nature of the case takes time; the other is quick change, notably the circulation of those at the top within days or months by highly visible, often violent action. The first might be called social revolution, the second political revolution. The Industrial Revolution was in this sense social, the French Revolution was political.[7]

New Zealand experienced both. The social revolution followed the dramatic change in the economic structure from the mid 1960s, described in the prologue. Dahrendorf is cautioning us to expect further long-term and—from today's vantage point—unpredictable effects which are likely to echo through to the next century. On the back of the social revolution there was a political revolution in the mid 1980s, as a new elite seized power, although not violently.

This political revolution was exactly the sort of extremism that Karl Popper cautions against in his *The Open Society and its Enemies* (written, ironically enough, in New Zealand).[8] For the ideology abandoned incremental pragmatism, which Popper advocated, for the vision of millenarians, which he abhorred. Certainly a Popperian is not surprised that Faust has not benefited as he was promised. With the exception of inflation, economic performance since 1984 has not been impressive. Perhaps if the economy had grown quickly (as it did after 1935, doubling in volume of production in the following decade), the populace would have come in behind the New Right ideals. In fact they have not.[9] The 1993 referendum on the electoral system represents a major revolt by the populace against the New Establishment and its commercialist philosophy.

By late 1991 Prime Minister Bolger understood that inevitable electoral disaster would follow if he continued with the extreme version of the policies, and moderated his government's policies. The weakened commitment to commercialisation could not stop some policies already under way (such as the accident compensation, health, and housing reforms), while a commercialist strategy continued in business areas, with further privatisations. Like the New Establishment the government also found its room to manoeuvre limited by foreign investors. Yet where it could it moderated the extremism. Even so the National government lost almost a quarter of its 1990 votes in the 1993 election, scraping back to government via the oddities of the First-Past-the-Post (FPP) voting system.

But even here the populace revolted, voting for Mixed-Member-Proportional (MMP) representation even though the business sector heavily backed the retention of the FPP system. They did so partly out of anger against an Establishment that had consistently ignored them, but also because MMP seemed to offer the chance of being represented by a government that would take greater cognisance of popular feeling.

The outcome of the 1996 election appears to be a parliament which reflects the pattern of Figure 7.2. The renewed Labour Party plus the Alliance obtained 38 percent of the vote (Figure 7.2 gives the left 40 percent). ACT—the party of Douglas, Richard Prebble, Ruth Richardson, and other vociferous supporters of the commercialisation reforms—obtained 6 percent (comparable to the hard right 6 percent), and almost all the other votes went into traditionalist right parties (although, especially because of its Maori support, the exact location of New Zealand First is problematic).

121

Appendix: The Growing Up of the Unions

The union movement thinks of itself as largely marginalised by and marginally involved in the commercialisation shift. This appendix explores another story, one which advocates of the reforms should be keen to point out. All institutions find it very difficult to reform themselves. Genuine institutional reform involves some external pressure. This case study examines the union experience, but there are numerous others including the corporatisation of state-owned enterprises.

THE ORIGINS OF NEW ZEALAND'S UNION STRUCTURE

The earliest New Zealand unions came from Britain and were organised on a craft (or occupational) basis. Later the Australian union experience was influential, especially for some industry-based unions. The overlapping of occupational (horizontal) and industrial (vertical) union structures has been a persistent feature of New Zealand unionism.

The typical union was very small. As late as 1983 there were 248 unions with 527,545 members, an average of 2127 members per union. However, almost four-fifths of these unions had fewer than 2000 members, covering 16 percent of the unionised workforce. On the other hand, there were 15 unions, each with over 10,000 members, covering more than half of the unionised workforce.[1] Small unions faced considerable difficulties servicing their members.

Yet many small unions persisted. They did so because they were a creation of legislation. Under the law it was feasible for a union never to meet most of its members. All its officers had to do was negotiate the award annually with employers and collect the subscription via an employer levy. Compulsory unionism meant that the worker had no opportunity to opt out, even where he or she was getting no direct services from the union and was being paid above the award rate (which only set minima). Thus it was possible for a single union to organise a handful of members at each of numerous work-sites.

So, together with an historical inertia, unions existed in both horizontal and vertical forms. Often there was more than one union per work-site—the most notorious being at the Tasman mill in Kawerau, where there were 12 unions and frequent and bitter inter-union disputes.

THE NEW ECONOMY AND THE NEED FOR UNION REFORM

One of the major consequences of the external diversification described in the prologue was that increasingly sectors which had been in the protected domestic market found themselves in the exposed external sector. Now the whole of the primary sector was involved in exporting, and not just pastoral farming. Manufacturing increasingly switched from almost solely domestic supply to export supply, either directly or indirectly supplying other exporters. This indirect supply meant that many service activities were also involved in the export effort. (Today the tourism sector is the single biggest foreign-exchange earner.)

The changes made much of the traditional union structure increasingly inappropriate. If the union structure were to be designed from scratch in the new economy, work-site or enterprise arrangements would be likely to prevail. Consider three factories in the same town: one produces timber, one packages dairy food, and the third produces a household durable. Suppose they are all supplying a local market, protected from overseas competition. The industrial relations and pay rates for the three firms could be much the same and, indeed, much the same as those for similar factories in other parts of the country. Now suppose, following the diversification, that the timber is going to Japan, the dairy food to Thailand, and the durables to Australia. Each firm will have a whole range of problems specific to it, arising out of its different markets and marketing conditions. Inevitably industrial relations within the firm will be affected. There will remain some commonalities, but faced by the diverse requirements of exporting each firm will want to adapt its working conditions for its specific markets.

This pressure for work-site specific flexibility was reinforced by two other major changes—increasing technological complexity and changing social demands by workers. The union movement was not insensitive to such pressures. For instance in 1987 the Federation of Labour was replaced by the New Zealand Council of Trade Unions (CTU), which incorporated public sector unions into the peak organisation for the first time. There were constant—not always successful—attempts to give women's concerns a more prominent role in union activities.

Undoubtedly the most important direct source of change in the 1980s was the 1987 Labour Relations Act (LRA) and the provisions in the 1988 State Sector Act which required public sector industrial relations to follow private sector arrangements more closely. The original provisions in the Labour Relations Bill were markedly changed following consultation with (or pressure from) the unions, although the public sector unions were much less successful in changing their legislation.

The requirement that unions registered under the new act had to have at least 1000 workers led to some rather odd and artificial amalgamations of small unions collecting under an umbrella organisation. Nevertheless, by 15 May 1991, when the LRA was repealed, there were 80 unions, of which only 4 had fewer than 1000 members. However, the growth had been in the medium-sized unions, with still only a score of unions with 10,000 members or more, covering 72 percent of workers (compared to 53 percent in 1983). And if there were fewer, larger, and even potentially stronger unions, the structure was still not aligned with the new economy, as the artificial amalgamations illustrated.

In May 1989, the CTU responded to the changing economic circumstances (and the LRA) with *Strategies for Change*,[2] which aimed to encourage voluntary amalgamation and exchange of union members so that the unions might be more closely aligned to an industrial and sectoral structure. Identifying 14 sectors (containing over 100 industries between them), the strategy was that within five years any union would have a presence in only those over which it had total coverage, and in not more than two others. It was hoped that in a particular industry (but not sector) there would be only one or two unions because 'three unions is becoming impracticable; four or more unions is unmanageable'. There is a tone of urgency in the report arguing that 'change is overdue', but there was little progress before the 1991 Employment Contracts Act (ECA) overwhelmed the assumptions upon which it was based.

Another evolving change was the beginning of a move to single enterprise awards for large firms, breaking them out of the national award system, and composite industry awards in which a number of unions combined their awards to a single one, as in the case of the plastics and packaging industry composite award.

One can see these changes as a response to the new economic environment and a movement towards realigning the union structure to one based on industries. However, the changes were ponderously slow. As they were voluntary, an individual union could veto a change. In particular, changes were anathema to the craft-based unions organised across a number of industries and sectors. This is well illustrated by the experience of the clerical workers' unions.

THE CLERICAL WORKERS' UNIONS[3]

The clerical workers' unions were a classic example of horizontally based unions, which organised a few workers on each of numerous work-sites. In 1983 the New Zealand Clerical Workers' Association (NZCWA) had 50,000 members on 20,000 work-sites, or 2½ workers a work-site. Over half the New Zealand Clerical Workers' Union's (NZCWU's) work-sites in 1990 had just one member, and only 3 percent employed more than 20 workers. They were quintessentially a creation of statute. Unionised clerical workers were marginal until the 1936 amendment to the Industrial Conciliation and Arbitration Act. When the statute dramatically changed in 1991 to the Employment Contracts Act (ECA), the union as dramatically collapsed.

There had not been a lot of membership involvement in the unions' activities. Between 1981 and 1990 voter turnout at annual general meetings of the Northern Clerical Union (NCU) fluctuated between 2½ and 5 percent, while only 20 percent took part in the 1989 postal ballot to elect the executive. A similar proportion voted in the 1991 postal ballot to wind up the NZCWU. A 1976 survey of members of the NZCWA found that 68 percent would vote for a voluntary union, and 41 percent would not join it.

The unions' members were predominantly isolated workers on most work-sites, mainly women, often working part-time, and the membership experienced a high turnover. But there were other factors. The Chief Judge of the Labour Court found in 1990 that the NCU's 'rules do not foster democratic principles or nourish the exercise of democratic rights'. Indeed, on occasions the management of some of the unions was thoroughly undemocratic. When the clerical unions were a part of Fintan Patrick Walsh's base in the trade union movement, giving him significant voting power in the Federation of Labour over which he presided, members of the unions were rarely, if ever, consulted on how that power should be exercised. Throughout the academic reports on the union in the 1980s are accounts of power struggles.

The situation was possible because, once an unqualified preference clause was included in the award (that is, during almost all of the unions' post-1936 history), clerical workers had to belong to the relevant union, irrespective of the quality of service they were receiving from it. As the unions themselves on occasions acknowledged, it was virtually impossible to provide any quality of service to members dispersed across so many work-sites. For many members, the dues were just another impost, a tax on their income, for which they received only the vaguest return—if any.

On the other hand, there were dedicated officials of the clerical unions who were conscientious and active about their responsibilities to members, and who were labouring under great difficulties to serve a dispersed membership. Moreover, the unions could make some proud claims for gains for its members, including an active campaign against sexual harassment in the 1980s and their representing women's point of view in the peak union councils.

But when the ECA was introduced in 1991, the clerical workers' unions had little future. By the end of the year the NZCWU had transferred its remaining members to other unions who were better organised on the work-sites, while the two remaining regional unions amalgamated with other unions. Today a clerical worker in the private sector, if unionised, is likely to belong to a multi-occupational union on the work-site and she may see her organiser more frequently than in the past. (But she is less likely to be unionised.)

Peter Franks concludes that 'the union's demise was the result of its dependence on protective legislation, its structural problems, and the failure of its attempts to solve these problems'.[4] The situation was even more complex. An occupational union, organised across a multitude of work-sites, with few workers in most sites, is inherently vulnerable. Only the most supportive legislation enables it to exist. Any significant reduction of that support results in a collapse of the union.

Ironically, one feature of the CTU's *Strategies for Change* had thus been implemented, albeit by the ECA which was otherwise anathema to the union movement. Implicit in the proposal was that many clerical workers would be organised by an industry rather than occupational union, as has occurred under the ECA.

There is a nostalgia about the clerical workers' unions, especially because in later years they were strongly feminist and addressed some crucial labour market issues which affected women. Nevertheless, we might ask whether, in an environment in which clerical workers are organised under enterprise and industry-based unions, the workers are getting a better deal, and whether in the long run the union movement, and workers, will benefit from less gender segregation. Even if the answers to those questions are yes, today many clerical workers get no union support and may well be worse off.

RESPONSES TO THE EMPLOYMENT CONTRACTS BILL (ECB)

We can partly trace union responses to the ECB on the spectrum from independency to dependency on statute. There is some dispute as to what happened. What is not in dispute is that in April 1991, the CTU had a proposal for a 24-hour general stoppage on 30 April. This was defeated on a card vote of 250,122 against and 190,910 in favour. The exact voting lines are not published, but Sarah Heal suggests that the opposition to the national strike included the Educational Institute, Engineering Union, Financial Sector Union, Nurses Union, Post Office Union, Post-Primary Teachers Association, Public Service Association, and in fact 'most of the major unions'.[5] Supporters of the action included the Service Workers' Federation and clerical workers' unions.

Heal attributes the failure to call the national strike to the conservatism of the CTU leadership. Ellen Dannin, in a more reflective study which is nevertheless sympathetic to the notion of national actions, describes the CTU engaging in a complex response which included going around the bill, and talking directly to employers. Many unions despaired of the prospects of significantly modifying, let alone defeating, the bill. She reports how the Engineering Union was giving priority to the transition to the post-LRA environment.[6]

It would seem that those unions opposing the one-day stoppage were more successful in that transition, generally having suffered smaller proportional losses than those who supported the strategy. Those that thought they could survive under the ECA, albeit at a reduced scale, opposed the national stoppage, while those who thought they could not, or that they would suffer most greatly, supported it. Given the greater membership losses among unions which supported or advocated it, if the CTU were to reconsider the 1991 motion, the vote would be even more overwhelmingly opposed to a national stoppage.

What responses had a clerical workers' union to the Employment Contracts Bill when, as subsequent events proved, it was faced with certain demise if it were passed? There were not many, other than to use every means possible to prevent the bill's passage, no matter how low the probability of success. A national strike was a viable strategy for those faced with obliteration under the ECA, even if the proponents knew that a relatively low proportion of their own members would participate. Even a very small probability of success made it worthwhile for the clerical workers' unions, because they had hardly any other strategy.

However, there were more options for those who might survive under the new regime, albeit at a more limited scale. The public sector unions, with a long history of voluntary unionism, knew they had a core of workers they could rely on, although there would be attempts to split off workers into house unions and to non-membership through individual contracts. Private sector unions who had a core of readily unionisable workers knew they would lose some from the abandonment of compulsory unionism, so they needed to maintain as much wavering support as possible around their core. A national strike was only one option, and not a particularly attractive one in comparison to preparing for the new industrial relations environment. Indeed the strike could have reduced that preparation if it diverted energy away from it, and at the same time antagonised both the workers the unions hoped to retain in the new environment and also the more sympathetic employers with whom they hope to work in the future.

Behind the advocacy of the national strike appears to be the belief that it would have been effective. Brian Roper writes about the failure of the CTU 'to organise and lead the kind of generalised strike action that would, at the very least, have forced the National Government to substantially amend (if not withdraw) the legislation'.[7] Was that possible? Would not such an action have strengthened the resolve of the government to proceed with the legislation and to break the union movement, while alienating goodwill among the sympathetic population which was not unionised? In any case, would there have been sufficient worker commitment to such a course? What if the CTU had thrown a party and hardly anyone came? Heal's assessment of the size and effectiveness of the various sporadic actions that happened in lieu of the national strike seems optimistic. She reports a number of such activities, but one gets little sense of their overall size—to what extent they involved a few zealots or were mass actions. The claim that 60,000 people marched against the bill (including those who did so in their lunch time) is either not sourced or attributed to *The People's Voice*. Perhaps as good a test of the counterfactual of what would have happened if there had been a national strike is the experience in the Australian state of Victoria. When the Kennet government introduced a bill based on the New Zealand ECA, mass workers' actions occurred, but they had no effect on the legislation.

THE EFFECT OF IMPLEMENTING THE ECA[8]

In May 1991, when the ECA was implemented, there were 80 unions with 603,118 members. Three and a half years later, in December 1994, there were 82 unions with only 375,906 members. The increase in unions reflected the collapse of the umbrella unions created by the LRA back to their old constituents and the formation, in the public sector and in some private enterprises, of house-unions split off from their traditional unions.

These additional unions disguised the demise of a number of traditional unions which either had collapsed or been absorbed into other unions. The reduction in union coverage was 27 percent. However industrial coverage patterns differed. One group (agriculture, fishing and hunting; mining and related services; construction and building services; and retail, wholesale, cafes, and accommodation) experienced reductions in excess of 60 percent over three years; a second (manufacturing, transport and communication, and finance and business services) lost between 22 and 24 percent; public and community service lost 13 percent; and energy and utility services reported a gain of 15 percent. Excepting the miners, the greatest losses occurred in industries whose organising situation resembled clerical workers —numerous work-sites, few workers per site, women or detached workers, who were often low-skilled. (In 1995, the Engineering Union began a successful recruiting drive in the mining industry.)

There appear to be some stabilities. The CTU covered 86.5 percent of total union membership in 1991 and 79.0 percent in 1994, with TUF covering another 6.2 percent, so that the total of the two peak organisations was 85.2 percent, or almost the same as three years earlier. While there were 20 unions with over 10,000 members in May 1991, covering 72 percent of all unionists, there were only 10 such unions in December 1994 but they now covered 69 percent of unionists. Thus the union movement was becoming more concentrated into relatively fewer unions, but covering a smaller proportion of the workforce.

CONCLUSION

The industrial relations legislation from 1894 to 1991 created unions which were essentially wards of the state, unable to function outside the umbrella of the statute. Unfortunately the resulting union structure reflected an economy which began disappearing in the late 1960s. The union movement was not able to change sufficiently, especially because of the existence of occupational unions organising a few workers in each of numerous work-sites.

Ironically the Employment Contracts Act, whatever its other defects—and the union movement would say there are many— created a union structure much closer to that which the CTU argued for in the late 1980s, although with many fewer members and lower coverage. It was also a structure closer to what might be prescribed for an economy whose external sector is much more diversified and whose domestic economy is much more open to the world. Increasingly there is one, or a co-operating handful, of unions in each industry and more often there is one union per enterprise. Horizontal unions organising a particular occupation in many industries have all but disappeared. The outcome is not perfect, for there are inherent tensions in a union which covers skilled and unskilled workers, while not all unions have faced up to the challenge implied by increasing numbers of women workers.

The economic diversification which began in the 1960s exposed more sectors of the economy to international competition, thereby posing a challenge to the union movement with which it had great difficulty grappling. The difficulty is well illustrated by the fact that few accounts of the events described here include any economic dimension.

This does not mean that industrial relations are totally determined by economic circumstances. But because now each industry (and enterprise) is increasingly exposed to international competition specific to its circumstances, its industrial relations has to be designed to be a part of the response. This suggests that a far greater flexibility in the IR structure is necessary than was the case a couple of decades ago. In particular, the horizontal linkages between firms have to be less rigid. Each enterprise now needs a greater degree of autonomy in setting its pay and conditions.

By shaking off unions over-dependent on state legislation the union movement has freed itself to a greater extent from state control. One suspects that, given the experiences of the decade after 1984, the labour movement will not be keen to return to state dependence again. It might even argue that part of the ineffectiveness of unions—and other agencies of a leftish bent in the 1980s—was that they were too dependent on the state, so that when the state turned on them, their ability to resist was extremely limited. A union movement more outside the apparatus of the state, and less tied to statute, may be able to play a more independent and constructive role in the development of the nation.

8

Was There an Alternative?

THE CLAIM THAT THERE IS NO ALTERNATIVE TO THE COMMERCIALISATION strategy is obviously nonsense, even if it is put in the more deceptive form that the only alternative was the pre-1984 policies of Robert Muldoon. Given the changes to the structure of the New Zealand economy and society, there were going to be changes in the organisation of the economy, most likely in a more-market direction, which would result in less control by the government of the minutiae of New Zealand life. But even so that did not mean that the only alternative was Muldoonism—more-market is a broad church. Instead of looking at what might be an alternative policy process (the subject-matter of the Epilogue), this chapter looks at the potential sources of alternatives.

THE OLD ESTABLISHMENT

Rather than explore every example of the Old Establishment trying to influence policy, this section looks at an example of it in relation to broadcasting policy. In order to get the flavour of those involved it may be best to think of them as the 'Club'. Readers may think of it as the Wellington Club, and perhaps even the institution which bears that name, with the connections and influence of the membership that go with it. We have in mind a somewhat looser group, more identified by its clubbishness. That such a group exists is revealed by the following conclusion to an Institute of Policy Studies publication:

> When the Institute was arranging the seminar from which this book derives, I was concerned that we might not have the expertise required to do justice to its topic. My fears were unfounded.

132

The Institute's network of friends and associates included some relevant expertise.[1]

A 'network of friends and associates' is redolent of a club. How a seminar on broadcasting could leave out Tony Simpson after his brilliant demolition of Treasury proposals for broadcasting reform can only be explained by Simpson not being a member of its network.

The club joined the broadcasting debate late, after much of the Treasury agenda for broadcasting reform had been adopted. The club did not have a very clear vision on broadcasting. Rather it mulled things over, like clubmen sitting in leather-bound chairs with the port and cigars. From conception of the seminar to completion of the publication this casualness abounds. The phrase 'public sector broadcasting', an unusual term in the broadcasting debate, is nowhere defined, despite being the nominal centre of discussion. There are hardly any references in the publication, despite its being a university one, as if the contributors are winging it. Some of the contributions appear to be unedited transcripts of unscripted talk.

Behind this amateurism is a deeper problem. There is no framework for analysis. It is almost as if a group of people were called to discuss the format for a seminar or publication, and found themselves providing the final product. Symposia are difficult to bring together, and publications of the proceedings require quality editing.

The club's problem is nowhere better illustrated than in the brief 1300-word rambling conclusion written after the symposium. Sometimes following an unfocused conference the editor writes a long synthesis, pulling together the underlying themes. But not here. No economist contributed to the symposium, yet the conclusion pontificates: 'An economist is likely to believe . . . that radio and TV are reasonably close substitutes for many consumers. But the paper[s] . . . and the discussion at the seminar generally persuaded me that the two media are much more distinct than I realised.' It is heartening to know that the editor reversed a prejudice, but insulting to economists to suggest they had such a crude view (and doing so demonstrates ignorance of the economic debate). The conclusion then goes to a wonderfully platitudinous paragraph too long to report here. This combination of confusion over the economic issues and platitudinousness continues through the remainder of the conclusion.

What the book's participants seemed to be addressing was the extent to which the current broadcasting system is meeting the needs of the community. Put this way the problem is not of 'public sector broadcasting' (whatever that means) but balance between various means of providing broadcasting services—in simple terms, the balance between commercial and non-commercial broadcasting. By focusing on the public sector only, the account was unbalanced and confused.

The lack of a framework left participants mumbling in their leather chairs at the club rooms. While some of their mumbles are valuable, the overall effect is not. Indeed the impression of someone from a commercialisation perspective would have been to conclude that their worries about government involvement in the broadcasting system were well founded. The advocates for such involvement did not know what they wanted and were hopelessly muddled or, even worse, pursuing their own personal and commercial interests in the name of the public interest. The club—the Old Establishment—offered no alternative.

THE ROYAL COMMISSION ON SOCIAL POLICY

The origins of the 1988 Royal Commission on Social Policy (RCSP) were in a promise in the 1984 Labour Party manifesto to establish one on social security. The intention probably was to repeat the 1972 Royal Commission on Social Security (RCSS), perhaps with a slightly wider scope and more public consultation. Once in government, Labour abandoned most of its manifesto, but the sweeping, radical, and extreme economic liberalisation raised the question of the role of the welfare system in the new economy. There was a strong lobby within government (especially Treasury) and within Cabinet (especially Roger Douglas) for a drastic reform which would have converted the system into a minimalist American one. There was also considerable resistance, notably from Prime Minister David Lange.

In order to resist and delay the pressures, and identify an alternative, Lange extended the manifesto proposal to that of establishing a royal commission on social policy. There followed intense political and bureaucratic infighting.[2] The warrant looks as if it was drawn up by a committee, even to the extent that the same word was spelt in two different ways.[3] The terms of reference were in two parts. The first half set out what was to be investigated, the second set out the standards of a fair society and the principles of the social and economic foundations of New Zealand. Even the membership was fought over in public.[4] The resulting commission of five was sufficiently imbalanced to require a sixth commissioner to be added eleven months later. Once established in October 1986, the commission was further undermined by the establishment of investigating committees which overlapped with its concerns (on hospitals, education, and social security administration) in July 1987, and 17 further taskforces on social policy issues in December 1987 (in addition to the flat tax proposal of the same time). Exhausted by the infighting and the immensity of the task, the RCSP reported early in April 1988.

The commission's report—four volumes and 4004 pages—is perhaps even more extraordinary than the commission's history. One is reminded of Pascal's remark, in one of his *Lettres provinciales*, that he had written a long letter only because he had not had the time to make it shorter. The contents are essays of varying quality—many mediocre, some downright embarrassing, and a few of merit. The essays in the second volume, 'Future Directions', are closest to the commission's own voice. But even the section on 'standards and foundations' hardly meets the commission's own goal of 'a coherent approach to the identification of the goals and values and principles of New Zealand society'.

The RCSP turned its back on the intellectual area of social policy. Tom Marshall's classic definition of social policy is 'the elimination of poverty; the maximisation of welfare; and the pursuit of equality'.[5] The approach is no surprise to New Zealanders. Bill Sutch, a central figure in the development of the modern welfare state, wrote three books on the theme.[6] The 1972 RCSS devoted two chapters to the definition and measurement of poverty. More recently a statement of the leaders of ten churches stated five principles which would grace the report of a royal commission, one of which was 'to give priority to the needs of the poor'.[7] Yet the RCSP almost entirely ignored poverty, covering the topic in a brief two (out of the four thousand) pages.

While some of the Old Establishment worked for the RCSP, the activists and those who made submissions were dominated by dissidents against the reforms, who were not typically members of the establishment. They had little difficulty expressing their distress as to what had happened, but formulating an analysis was beyond them. At best there was an atavistic return to policies of the past, with little observation of the underlying changes that had happened and were happening. The pro-reformers could, and did, dismiss the commission's report and the submissions it received as the work of well-intentioned concerned citizens, who had little understanding of the issues facing New Zealand and could offer no serious alternative.

In this way the Commission's report exacerbated the subsequent attack on the welfare state, by suggesting that those opposed to the commercialists' strategy had no coherent alternative. Ironically, those associated with the RCSP, either as commissioners or writers, did not play a prominent role in the subsequent debate, when the system they supported came under further attack in 1991. Neither did the report itself. The exercise was a double failure, offering neither an alternative direction nor a foundation for defending the status quo.

THE GOVERNMENT SECTOR

Because the commercialisation policy evolved in a single government agency, Treasury, it did not at first dominate the thinking in other government departments. Sometimes those departments stoutly resisted the Treasury proposals, because they disagreed with the theory, and their intelligence told them it was, in any case, not practical.

The best documented example of successful resistance is the development of the Labour Relations Act (LRA).[8] Although Treasury's 1984 post-election briefing advocated a policy similar to that which was eventually enacted, the briefing was written before the balance of power in the Labour government was known. When that was settled, they moved from a more-market to a New Right stance. However their extreme proposals were rejected by the Labour Department, the unions, and ultimately the government.

It could be argued that it was the union connection to the Labour government that made the difference. Undoubtedly they were important, although they were not enthusiastic about the final legislation either. Moreover, the unions were less effective in opposing the State Sector Act (SSA), which aligned public sector industrial relations with those of the private sector set down in the LRA.[9] Admittedly the SSA was a classic blitzkrieg, but the basic difference was that the State Services Commission, which handles public sector industrial relations, favoured the new act, whereas the Labour Department did not favour the Treasury proposals for the private sector. Working closely with its minister, and balanced between Treasury extremism on the one hand and unionist conservatism on the other, the Department had its policy advice largely accepted.

There were other policy areas where Treasury did not get its own way. On securities legislation it was opposed by the Securities Commission, on competition legislation by the Department of Trade and Industry.[10] Later the Ministry for the Environment moderated the more extreme proposals for the Resource Management Act. Where there was no alternative source of government advice, such as over privatisation, the preferred policies were more readily implemented. In the case of broadcasting, the minister had no advice ministry, while the recommendations of the Broadcasting Corporation of New Zealand could be misrepresented or dismissed as self-interest.

Over time the Treasury policy vision spread to other departments: Treasury officials moved to senior positions in them, and those inside tired of dissent or found their career paths blocked. Agencies which were centres of opposition tended to be abolished or gutted: DSIR, Education, Energy, Maori Affairs, Tourism and Publicity, Trade and Industry, Transport, Works and Development. Even a major reorganisation could cripple an advice system, and the new staffing would have an increased proportion of people sympathetic to the Treasury line. The State Sector Act reinforced these trends with its mindset.

There were exceptions. The Department of Labour had to be retained because of the politically popular employment service it ran. The Ministry of the Environment was created as a part of the price for the reorganisation of resources. Its success was more due to the tenacity of commitment of the environmentalists who staffed it than to any alternative economic vision. When the Ministry of Health was confronted by the proposed health reforms in 1991, it chose to focus on its administrative responsibilities, so the reformers, bereft of competence in health administration, were out in a special unit in the Prime Minister's Department.

Only Treasury was unaffected directly by these changes, as it used its monopoly base to eliminate dissent and to protect itself.

There was no alternative agency to press for division into a Treasury and a Ministry of Finance, parallel to the set-up in Australia, and consistent with the Treasury principle of separating policy advice from operations. Its notion of 'contestability of advice' applied only to those areas which Treasury wanted to invade—not to where it was dominant. The new configuration of governance also reduced Treasury to exposure in economic tribunals and other forms of cross-examination (as in the case of the Royal Commission on Broadcasting). The record has been that Treasury officials confronted by a properly briefed counsel have not performed well. Their privileged position in government no longer protects them, nor were their interrogators as easily persuaded as their political masters.

The political success of the commercialisers was not, then, due to some intellectual excellence, some ability to succeed under the rigorous critical and sceptical review traditional to the intellectual process. The reality was that a small group were in the right institutions, and received the right political support, and were able to use their preferential position, to block and destroy alternatives.

THE ECONOMISTS

The reformers sometimes claimed they belonged to the 'mainstream'. But economics is more like the braided Waimakariri than the channelled Waikato. A survey of economists' opinions in 1990 indicates just how diverse the profession was.[11] Here are some of their responses:

- Some 51 percent of all respondents disagreed with the proposition that 'economists agree on the fundamentals'.
- Asked who was 'the modern economist who had made the greatest contribution', 10.6 percent of the respondents said John Maynard Keynes, 9.2 percent said Paul Samuelson (who is generally credited with the neoclassical synthesis, combining Keynesian macroeconomics with neoclassical microeconomics), and 7.4 percent said Milton Friedman, with just about everyone else nowhere. (Some respondents may not have classified Keynes as 'modern' because he died in 1946. All others mentioned were alive.) This response cer-

tainly does not suggest that the Chicago school-dominated reforms were based on the dominant paradigm here (or, from a parallel survey, in the US either).[12]

- When the 1990 group were asked whether 'the basic ideas behind "Rogernomics" were sound', 47 percent agreed and 35 percent agreed with reservations. I remember puzzling over this one when I filled in my questionnaire. What was meant by 'Rogernomics'? If it meant the microeconomic ideas—essentially 'more-market' ones—I agreed with reservations. If it meant the macroeconomic ideas, I disagreed. Or perhaps 'the basic ideas behind Rogernomics' were that we needed a change in economic policy from what had gone before. I could agree to that. Since no definition was offered, it seems likely that different respondents interpreted the question differently. In any case, a not insignificant proportion of the profession disagreed without reservation.

- Some 50 percent of male economists but only 19 percent of female economists disagreed with the proposition 'the free market underpays woman workers', indicating that the gender balance of the profession affects its overall views on some key questions. (There are about six times as many male as female economists in New Zealand.)[13]

- In another indication of position affecting conclusion, and so undermining the notion of a 'value-free' economics, the proportion of university economists who supported Rogernomics was smaller than those in government or business. (But a majority still did.) Business economists were less likely to support government intervention than the academics, with the government economists in between.

- More respondents disagreed than agreed (whether with reservations or not) with the proposition that 'the economic power of trade unions should be curtailed'. This was before the Employment Contracts Act.

The surveys did not indicate an extreme commitment to a commercialist strategy (nor to the monetarist economics which accompanied it). Certainly most economists were 'more-market' in 1980,[14] and more so in 1990, but they were not generally market extremists. There is little evidence that the majority of economists were supporting the full gamut of the future reforms in 1980. Although there was a shift in the following decade, there was still no unanimity, and many had serious reservations. On some issues the majority view appeared to be the opposite. At best it could be claimed that surveys of the economic profession showed that even if commercialisers were not in the centre of any 'mainstream', and although there were few advocates in 1980, the support did increase over the decade.

Yet those economists who disagreed did not, by and large, publicly promote an alternative. They found themselves ignored, their funding cut, access to contracts cut, appointment opportunities denied, and subject to petty harassment.[15] The majority of university economists got on with their teaching, dabbled with research, and grumbled in the tearoom about the theories underpinning the reforms. Challenged, they pointed to their rising teaching loads and perhaps mentioned that the university administrations disliked controversy. This prudence, ironically, meant that economists were in no position to assist their universities when the commercialist policies turned to them.

PUBLIC INTELLECTUALS

John Maynard Keynes once remarked that 'there are, in the present times, two opinions; not, as in former ages, the true and the false, but the outside and the inside'.[16] Edward Said described the role of public intellectual as 'to represent a message or view not only to but for a public and to do so as an outsider, someone who cannot be coopted by a government or corporation.'[17] These critics and consciences of society are outsiders. The public intellectual in Plato's writing is Socrates, a humble seeker of truth and one of society's critics and consciences.

Neither Socrates, nor public intellectuals generally, would have lasted long in Plato's republic governed by philosopher-kings. Nor would have—and Plato is explicit about this—poets and associated artists. In Plato's view poets tell lies. In the same sense, so do public intellectuals because they are continually challenging the 'truth' that philosopher-kings tell. Intellectual control becomes all-important in Plato's republic, for there is only one truth, that held by the philosopher-kings. Any challenge to that truth is treachery.

Fortunately Plato's republic has never dominated human society. There has been at least always one poet, one artist, one intellectual, who has challenged the philosopher-kings' monopoly on the truth, and succeeded—though usually in the long run and often at great personal cost. When the current regime of philosopher-kings came to power in the mid 1980s they were unable to follow Lenin's advice and shoot the intellectuals. Instead there has been a steady squeezing of the centres of intellectual dissent, usually justified by improving the accountability of those involved to the government, as the case studies will illustrate.

Because today's philosopher-kings have an extremely simplistic account of the ideal society, only two forms of public organisation are allowed in their ideal state. One is the business-organised private corporation, the other is the government agency under direct ministerial control. All other organisations are to be converted into one or the other. Ideally they should be converted into business corporations. That is the underlying justification for corporatisation and privatisation. If a business form is not possible, the institution is placed under the direct political control of the minister.

In the old regime it was possible for a public intellectual to exist in the niches created by a miscellany of organisations which were neither purely private corporations nor purely government departments. The philosopher-kings' vision of society led them to destroy all possible resistance centres to their utopian vision.

This applied even in the universities, which are charged by statute to be 'critics and consciences' of society. Roger Kerr, chief executive of the Business Roundtable and recently appointed by the government to a university council, stated: 'You cannot attribute any of [the extraordinary changes in New Zealand] to the intellectual community as represented by the university communities. The faculties have provided critics, but not opinion leaders. In Asia, it [is] people in universities that have pushed governments in free-market directions. Here they have been resisting.'[18] Like many of Kerr's statement this one is not wholly accurate, for there were university personnel who publicly supported the changes (and no doubt are deeply disappointed that the Roundtable has not noticed them). Others have done so selectively, supporting a more-market direction of economic regulation, but not the extremism Kerr expounds. Nevertheless there is something menacing about Kerr's statement.

The record of university economists is discussed in the previous section. Academics from other disciplines played a livelier role on all sides of the public debate, as did some public intellectuals off campus. Yet in contrast to the vigorous role public intellectuals played in the preceding prime ministership of Robert Muldoon,[19] their record after 1984 is disappointing. For instance, among prominent novels there are only Maurice Gee's *Crime Story* and Fiona Kidman's *True Stars*. In part this reflects the sheer difficulty of portraying economic and political events in a fictional form; in part that writers have been concerned with other issues. But with the groundcover destroyed, with the only safe havens managed by the government and business, the remaining options are compliance by avoidance and outright defiance.

Public intellectuals have always had a marginal existence in New Zealand, certainly in comparison with those societies which New Zealanders look to for political and social models. In a seminal essay, first published in 1952, Bill Pearson argued that it was the role of New Zealand intellectuals to wake the public up from its 'fretful sleep'.[20] On some issues they may claim success: foreign affairs, human rights, moral issues, the environment, and the arts and culture. The community of public intellectuals has been much less successful in economic issues.

Yet we may be expecting too much from those public intellectuals in the economic area, especially those outside universities, given the difficulty of the destruction of the niches in which they existed before 1984. First, success typically involves a long gestation period. Second, it is arguable that there have been significant successes in moderating the more extreme instances of commercialisation. The resistance to the commercialisation of health is an instance where public intellectuals played a key role in providing leadership to public dissent. No doubt Said would have approved.

COMMERCIALIST VERSUS CORPORATIST POLICIES[21]

The Australian Labor Government (ALG) chose a 'consensual/corporatist' strategy,[22] whereas the New Zealand Labour Government (NZLG) chose a 'commercialist/monetarist' one. They were similar in that they both chose market liberalisation as a general rule. They were different in that the ALG tended to chose a process of consultation with interested parties in which key interest groups (especially unions) had some influence, while the NZLG was more unilateral, using commercial analogies as a model, even for government decisions. While casual observation might suggest the two policies were similar because both involved liberalisation for the purpose of internationalisation, close analysis shows that they were effectively different, and differently effective.

There is no single simple more-market direction of reform, and at this point the two governments diverged. This was evident in their mode of economic decision making. The ALG consulted key interest groups (most notably the unions), and its economic policy was adapted accordingly. The NZLG began along this path, in imitation of the ALG success, but very soon it began to operate more unilaterally. Why the different paths?

- The Australian institutional system—with its formal constitution, its federal structure, its upper house in which the government is usually in a minority, and its STV electoral system—entrenches checks and balances to unilateral decision making. Policy making in Australia requires the continuous formation of winning coalitions, either parliamentary or extra-parliamentary. New Zealand, on the other side, has a much less formal constitution with fewer checks and balances to implementation of government priorities. Differing constitutional arrangements have affected the structure of the two Labour parties. Despite both being out of national office since 1975, the ALP had formed several state governments. (The NSW Wran Labor government was an exemplar for subsequent ALP pragmatism.) The NZLP had no comparable alternate experience over the period. The ALP had institutionalised factions built into its caucus and decision making. They arose largely from state party bases, but also reflected ideological and policy proclivities. Their existence again encouraged the policy process toward negotiated outcomes. The NZLP caucus is smaller, and did not contain formal factions, but instead was based on shifting networks of loyalties.
- The ALP has ongoing intimate links with its affiliated industrial wing, as symbolised by Bob Hawke's effortless rise from President of the Australian Council of Trade Unions (ACTU) to party leader in under three years. The NZLP had no such record of close links at the personal or career level. The only minister in the 1984 NZLG with a long union background was Stan Rodger, a past president of the Public Service Association

(PSA), ranked number 14 in a Cabinet of 20. The weakness was reinforced by the state of the peak trade union organisation in the early 1980s. The Federation of Labour (FOL) excluded powerful public sector unions such as the PSA. In contrast to the Australian experience, relations between the union movement and the NZLP tended to be distant at the personal level, indicative of the organisational situation.

- Personalities have some role in political destiny. Both Australian Treasurer Paul Keating and Roger Douglas had a personal predilection for unilateral 'blitzkrieg' policy innovation. The significant personality differences were between the prime ministers. Hawke was 13 years older than David Lange. His career in the union movement meant an extensive experience with collective decision making, whereas lawyers Lange and his deputy leader and successor, Geoffrey Palmer, had worked in individualist-based activities. Hawke was trained as an economist, and had worked in quasi-economic positions for most of his life, whereas Lange and Palmer were economic neophytes.

- To these structural factors could be added the different experiences of opposition, arising from the differences in style between the Fraser government and the Muldoon government. Again it was not merely a matter of personalities—patrician Malcolm Fraser versus populist Rob Muldoon—but that disparity captures the policy differences: Fraser leaning to the liberal right, Muldoon adhering to a conservative interventionism. As a rule of thumb, especially in the earlier years, one could predict the policy response of the NZLG by identifying the opposite of what Muldoon would have done. Similarly the ALG consensual style explicitly reversed Fraser's confrontational style.

- The ALP economic policy was the result of its pre-office preparation, involving long and detailed negotiations with the ACTU, begun in the late 1970s. At the 1983 election there was a close understanding between the ACTU and the ALP as to the content of the policy, and a commitment to work together. This co-operation was institutionalised by the summit conferences, plus the informal links between Cabinet ministers and key trade union officials. It led naturally to a consultative style of government. Despite being elected 17 months later in July 1984, the NZLP was much less prepared for office. The replacement of Bill Hayden by Hawke in early 1983 reflected the policy development which the ALP had undertaken in the previous five years. Lange's replacement of Bill Rowling in early 1983 reflected the turmoil in the policy debate within the NZLP. Meanwhile the weakly led FOL had a preference for the traditionalist status quo rather than a modernising strategy. So there was not really any practical possibility of coming to the sort of agreement that the Australians had in the Accord. In any case it was not evident that the FOL could deliver its side of any bargain. There was no NZLP economic policy consensus at the time of the election. The election manifesto, modelled on the 1983 ALP one, was designed to hide the disagreements. But Douglas was not committed to it.

Thus the NZLG was able to introduce much more radical change than its Australian counterpart. Within its six-year term of office it was able to privatise more than the ALG could in ten, institute more microeconomic reforms, and commercialise more of the public sector. In Australia the reform process has been bargained, incrementalist, and slow—vitally influenced by the ALP's partisan coalition,[23] much of it caught up in the interstices of Australian federalism. The ALG was still struggling with labour

Table 8.1: New Zealand and Australia economic performance, 1985–1996

	NZ	Australia	OECD
Inflation Consumer Prices (% p.a.)			
1985	15.4	6.7	5.9
1995	3.8	4.6	5.5
Employment Growth (% p.a.)			
1985–1996	0.7	2.0	1.0
GDP Volume Growth (% p.a.)			
1985–1996	1.3	3.0	2.7
Current Account Deficit (% of GDP)			
Average 1985–1996	3.2	4.5	0.3
Average Labour Productivity Growth (% p.a.)			
Average 1985–1996	0.6	1.0	1.7

OECD (1996). These data do not always correspond to local data.
1996 data projected by OECD

market reform in mid 1990s, which the NZLG had disposed of within three years of gaining office with its 1987 Labour Relations Act. Yet, as Table 8.1 shows, the Australian economy performed better than the New Zealand one.

In summary, except for reducing inflation and the current account deficit, New Zealand does worse than Australia. Indeed, Australia's performance compares favourably with the OECD on the whole. New Zealand's does not. New Zealand's post-war long-run labour productivity increase was about 1.5 percent annually. Yet the increase over the seven years averaged 0.6 percent p.a. compared to the OECD 1.5 percent p.a. The Australian rate, higher than New Zealand's but not as high as the OECD average, may reflect the Accord strategy of increasing employment at the expense of productivity growth.

Why the divergence? The New Zealand reformers, and the Australians who praised them, would predict that the New Zealand economy would perform better than the Australian one since their policies were implemented more quickly and more extensively. Even with a more favourable external environment, New Zealand did worse. How are we to explain this?

New Zealand advocates of the reforms, on the few occasions they have been willing to confront the poor performance of the New Zealand economy, have resorted to two sorts of arguments. The first is that New Zealand was much worse placed than Australia in the early 1980s as a result of Muldoon's interventions. Challenged to provide quantitative evidence of this assertion, they have lapsed into silence. In contrast, there is an equally anecdotal argument that New Zealand was well poised for strong economic growth in the early 1980s without any major reforms. Moreover, deficiencies in the Australian performance might be due to its deteriorating terms of trade—something that did not happen to New Zealand.

A second claim is that New Zealand will perform better than Australia in the future. But the reformers have been promising yet-to-be-attained improved economic performance for a decade. Why should one trust their predictions this time?

Instead, there is the argument that the more corporatist approach of the ALG was more successful than the commercial approach of the NZLP, exactly as the ALP strategists had predicted when they chose it in the early 1980s (and despite the difficulties with a deteriorating external environment). Moreover, there was one crucial benefit from the Australian approach. Suppose a policy proposal is misconceived and does not give the outcome that its advocates promise. What mechanisms are there to sift it out from a competent proposal? The New Zealand approach assumed that the business model used by its Treasury was the uniquely correct solution. Once Treasury and the Minister of Finance advocated a policy, there was only the limited wisdom of the Cabinet to assess its merits. A more consultative approach places a decision into the public domain and thus subjects it to a broader scrutiny. Thus the gains from the blitzkrieg approach in avoiding the power of interest groups were more than offset by the losses from implementing bad decisions. The more consultative approach of the ALG recognised and allowed for the possibility that even its Treasury or Cabinet could make errors.

PART THREE

Case Studies

9

The Health Reforms

UNDOUBTEDLY THERE WAS AT THE END OF THE 1980s A WIDESPREAD perception that there was a problem with the health system, although in retrospect this seems to have been a grumbling rather than a deep discontent. When the reforms were being put in place, the public indicated they were more satisfied with the existing structures than their earlier surveys had shown. Every health system in the world appears to be beset with difficulties, which ought to be a warning to reformers that there are no easy solutions.

National had campaigned in 1990 on the typical Opposition policy of agreeing broadly with the existing system but promising to be more benign. Following the election the spokesperson on health, Don McKinnon, now deputy prime minister, was appointed to the foreign affairs portfolio, and Simon Upton was unexpectedly appointed Minister of Health. Almost certainly four factors set a context for his thinking.

Upton wrote in his Mont Pelerin Society prize-winning essay:

> . . . there are the vicissitudes of ill-health and old age which no one can hope to avoid. These should, whenever possible, be the responsibility of individuals. It may well be desirable to require some form of compulsory insurance to cope with those who would otherwise make no provision and then become a burden at a later stage . . . because a service is funded out of taxation, it does not mean that the government should actually provide the service itself. In many cases it will be possible to have the work put up for competitive tender by the private sector.[1]

The second factor was the negative one of the Royal Commission on Social Policy. It had convincingly demonstrated that the ma-

151

jority of New Zealanders were not enthusiastic about the economic reforms which gathered speed after 1984. Its alternative vision was less convincing—backward-looking, riddled with nostalgia, and almost incoherent. Upton was perfectly entitled to conclude that it offered no alternative to the sort of social policies being proposed by the reformers. The conclusion was right once there was the commitment to radical change. But the fundamental lesson of the Royal Commission was that the public did not want the economic reforms, and they wanted the associated social policies even less.

So, thirdly, Upton turned elsewhere for his health policy thinking. *Unshackling the Hospitals* was in two parts.[2] The Chicago-based accounting firm, Arthur Anderson, purported to find the potential for efficiency improvements of around 30 percent, but it was based as much on wishful thinking and assumption as rigorous analysis.[3] Much of its claimed potential 'productivity' amounted to cost-shifting; that is, switching costs from the public sector to the individual patient, family, and community. The commissioning committee, chaired by Alan Gibbs, a prominent New Right proponent, used the Arthur Anderson findings to assert that a different management regime would obtain the more efficient outcomes. Their report advocated the fashionable separation of funding and provision, with the providers (i.e. hospitals) run on business lines. The Labour government rejected the conclusions.

The fourth major factor in Upton's health reform thinking was his proposed reforms of the public science sector, where similarly there were the separation of funding and provision, contestable funding, and more businesslike management of the public providers as Crown research institutes. Yet Upton was not well suited for a blitzkrieg: he is more Hayekian than the radical engineer the approach requires. The demand for the rapid radicalism probably came from the Minister of Finance, Ruth Richardson, a close colleague of Upton. As well as having a radical New Right ideological commitment, no doubt fortified by her close association with Gibbs, Richardson faced a fiscal problem, like every one of her predecessors. So did her ministry, Treasury. The New Zealand government budget had gone into severe fiscal stress in the late 1970s, when the budget deficit stayed obstinately above the sustainable level where debt servicing grows no faster than the capacity to tax.

Public spending on health, at 14.0 percent of net financial expenditure in 1993/94, is a significant part of fiscal outlays. It was claimed, wrongly, that the volume of spending on public health was rising. The mistake arose in a Treasury paper which deflated the nominal spending with the wrong price index, failing to compare apples with apples, and then using a period which maximised the size of the error.[4] The faulty Treasury figures had misled Labour ministers into accepting cuts in public spending. Upton quoted the incorrect figures frequently, both in opposition and in government.[5] They were used to reinforce the thesis that the health sector was inefficient, since it appeared that although resources had been poured into the sector, outcomes had not markedly improved.

Treasury seems to have had two major objectives. The first amounted to shifting the cost of health from the government to the individual via some form of user-pays. Aside from any ideological merits—disguised as a claim for efficiency improvements—the effect of any cost shifting would be to reduce fiscal stress, as the government's exposure to funding health could be reduced. Practically the mechanism involves shifting the burden onto private households, especially those of the sick. The other Treasury concern was to reduce its management of resources by privatisation. Again this was partly ideological, but privatisation can reduce fiscal stress by shifting cost blowouts into the private sector.

SURVEYING THE BATTLEFIELD

Consider the terrain over which a health blitzkrieg would take place. On the right front of the campaigner would be high mountains commanded by the formidable medical profession, led by the New Zealand Medical Association (NZMA), with a long history of successfully resisting encroachment on its territory.

On the left front was the vast, disorganised population—the sick, the potentially sick, their family and friends, everyone. There were a few villages of systematic organisation: public health sector workers' unions, charitable organisations lobbying in the health area, the pressure groups for specific public policies. The difficulty of achieving any reform through a left flanking of the doctors was that the terrain is swampy, and a campaign needs the co-operation of the natives to find a path and help repel attack from the medics. But like its predecessor, National was in no mood to consult with the public on matters of significance.

In the centre—rolling foothills from mountains to swamp—were the recently established area health boards (AHBs), amalgamating the population-based delivery component of the Department of Health, with the long-established hospital boards. The AHBs had had a long development history, for they were presaged in the 1974 White Paper on Health. Resistance from the medical professions had been such that it had taken a decade and a half of experiment, consultation, and development to implement them fully.

Astonishingly, for that is what a blitzkrieg is all about, the government chose to drive its reforms through the centre, eliminating the AHBs. It passed legislation to abolish the (two-thirds) elected boards—an extraordinary constitutional innovation more characteristic of dictatorships, but one which had the advantage of erasing overnight the one institutionalised and well-funded group with official moral authority who could have resisted the reforms. The philosopher-kings showed their contempt for democracy yet again.

Yet in planning its centre strike the government overlooked some key issues. First was the state of its own forces. How committed the Cabinet was to the reforms is unclear. They may have been persuaded by Upton's intellect, but their gut commonsense may have been less certain. Caucus was not at all convinced.

Treasury officials were battle-hardened, fresh from past victories, eager for more. Whether there were enough of them is more problematic: some of the successful commanders had moved into the private sector, so that there was a shortage of experienced leadership. And there were other citadels to be protected, other battles to be waged. The reforms involved the Department (later Ministry) of Health, which for almost two decades had been committed to the development of the AHBs. The Department had neither the troops available nor the enthusiasm for the fight. A third government agency, the Department of the Prime Minister and Cabinet (DPMC), took responsibility for the reforms, while the Department of Health administered the existing system. The result was a cumbersome structure at all levels. Seven ministers were directly involved.

Previous blitzkriegs had effectively used mercenaries, consultants from (typically) the financial sector. Whatever their past performance, this time the consultants were inexperienced, knowing little about the health system if they were from New Zealand, little about New Zealand if they were from overseas (and even then only those who were ideologically acceptable were consulted). A similar problem applied to Treasury officials. It was a bit like taking a well-equipped and victorious army from the deserts of commerce and letting it loose in the health Himalayas.

Indeed, there does not seem to have been sufficient thought about the differences in the terrain for this blitzkrieg. Smashing through the AHBs might be possible in a night, but then the troops were faced with miles of rolling countryside, up and down and up again, with no obvious camping places. Corporatisation of public health provision in under two years was perhaps the most ambitious of all the blitzkriegs.

TO THE GREEN AND WHITE PAPER

In its December 1990 *Economic and Social Initiative* the newly elected National government announced a new health policy, which proved to be very different from that stated in its election manifesto. (The statement's title itself was an indication of a new stance. National was not going to compartmentalise the two policy areas, as Labour had tried.) Although a health services taskforce was then established, it never finally reported, being superseded by the Minister of Health's *Your Health and the Public Health*. Described as a 'statement of government health policy', its nickname 'Green and White Paper' captures some of the ambiguity. Was it a green paper for discussion or was it a white paper of government policy? The greater proportion of green on the cover belied the intent. The major decisions had been taken—matters for consultation were minor. Its summary states that the government

> has made decisions about the future of the health sector. These include
> * separating purchasing from providing;
> * integrating funding for all types of health service;
> * allowing choice among health care plans;
> * separating the funding of public health care from personal health care.
> The government wants there to be a wider debate on . . .

- the definition of core services;
- the future financing of health services.[6]

Whence came the ambiguities and certainties? Probably the Taskforce provided a background. The Minister of Health was primarily responsible for writing the paper. Matters for decision then went to a Cabinet committee chaired by the Prime Minister. The papers then went to Cabinet, more often than not headed 'these papers were received after the deadline [for papers to Cabinet]'. As in Roger Douglas's day, late submission meant Cabinet opposition could not prepare.

The Green and White Paper was tabled as a 1991 Budget paper, the night Parliament passed legislation to replace the majority-elected area health boards with appointed commissioners for public hospitals. The budget also introduced charges for laboratory services and inpatient and outpatient fees.

It could be argued that the user-charge proposals were not connected with the overall health reforms, although this was a government which claimed it was integrating economic and social policy. The public thought the charges and the reforms were connected. After what can only be described as administrative fiasco and public indignation, most of the charges have been withdrawn. But the damage was done. The public had been warned that the reform proposals were radical and—in its judgement—nasty. It was as if a blitzkrieg launched under the cover of darkness had signalled its presence by shooting user-charge flares into the sky.

THE ULTIMATE DESTINATION

The uncertainty about the purpose of the reforms seemed to suggest that they merely had the general aim of improving the health system. But more sinisterly they appeared to be a coherent plan to move towards the privatisation of the public health system—on the supply side via the conversion of providers (especially hospitals) into private businesses, and on the demand side via the conversion of public sector purchasing into private purchasing by user charges and private insurance.

There were parallels with the 1985 Cabinet paper for the corporatisation of state trading activities, which had been sufficiently ambiguous to let a determined and committed group direct the reforms towards their ultimate destination of privatisation. For fundamental to the reforms was the replacement of the AHBs by Crown health enterprises (CHEs), which would be run on a 'business-like basis', and which would 'make adequate provision in their pricing to make a return on assets'—phrases which could have come from the earlier corporatisation program. Once this had been attained, it would be simple to sell the CHEs to private buyers.

Plans to privatise the demand (or purchaser) side were less elaborate. User charges for health care had been introduced and increased. The issue of the major source of funding was to be left to public discussion (with an Orwellian use of the term 'social insurance' to mean private insurance). There were to be 'health care plans' which were to allow a group to take its share of government funding and manage it separately, with the possibility of adding privately to the funds, which could ultimately lead to some sort of 'social' insurance. This proposal may have been the result of compromise in the ministerial committee, arising from a refusal to commit the government to the more radical option of private funding. Certainly it appears ill-thought-through. Not surprisingly the health care plan proposals were later dropped as unworkable, although there remains a residual provision in the legislation.

Despite Upton's earlier writings, it may have seemed paranoiac to argue on such evidence that the ultimate destination was privatisation of health, but as the blitzkrieg moved forward in the light of day, more evidence became available. The so-called 'Danzon' report, *Options for Health Care in New Zealand*, was not a smoking gun either. It had been commissioned by the Business Roundtable, of which Gibbs was a member. The senior author, Patricia Danzon, was an American economist specialising in private insurance who had impeccable right-wing credentials, including a Mont Pelerin fellowship and working at the Hoover Institute. The junior author, Susan Begg, was from CS First Boston, which had a record of general advocacy of privatisation, had benefited as a consultant from the corporatisation and privatisation of various government assets, but had no expertise in the health sector.

The report concludes that 'a private insurance option . . . could be viewed as a final stage towards which a mixed public/ private system could evolve. . . .' An earlier section concluded that 'corporatisation . . . would also be a sensible transition path if more far-reaching reform is contemplated.'[7] Thus it argued for reforms not dissimilar to those being introduced as a step towards the ultimate destination of privatisation. The report had been sent to the Minister of Health. It had neither been published by the Roundtable, nor been seen by most members of the taskforce, so that it had an air of secrecy. The minister could have argued that it did not influence his thinking, but then an extraordinary set of appointments were made.

A key agent in the transition was the National Interim Provider Board (NIPB) located in the DPMC, which was to supervise the establishment of the CHEs. The chairman appointed to the board was Sir Ronald Trotter, chairman of Fletcher Challenge Ltd, which had been an active purchaser of public assets. Trotter, a well-known spokesperson for privatisation, was also chairman of the Business Roundtable at the time of the Danzon report. He had no background in health administration. The NIPB's chief economist was Geoff Schweir, an early advocate of privatisation of state trading activities, with little or no experience in health economics.[8] Its primary consultants were CS First Boston, the sponsors of the Danzon report, again without specialist experience in the health sector. The NIPB hired overseas consultants of a privatisation persuasion, including Danzon. Later it hired Peter Troughton, an ex-Roundtable member who as CEO had been involved in the privatisation of Telecom, again with no background in health administration. This was generic management with a vengeance, with the managers committed to privatisation.

The government never explained why it appointed so many privatisers. Even were it a series of coincidences, and privatisation of the public health system was not the ultimate destination of the government, the steps being taken would make the task simpler for a future government. The parallel with the corporatisation of the state-owned trading enterprises loomed large.

RESISTANCE

The earlier review of the terrain suggested that, except for the medical profession, little effective resistance might be expected. In previous blitzkriegs there had been significant public discontent, but despite attempts to resist there had been little effective opposition. It is not at all clear how the government intended to deal with the doctors. The strategy at first seems to have been one of ignoring them. Significantly, there seems to have been no deliberate attempt to divide the medical profession. The purity of the justification for the reforms—they were in the national interest; resistance was only a matter of vested interest—resulted in a naive political strategy. Surprise and speed were to be the essence of a blitzkrieg: political acumen was not. Unsurprisingly, in the light of their past record, the medical profession proved doughty foes, especially through their union, the NZMA.

There were also sporadic attempts to organise the public into mass movements, but while there was the occasional meeting, march, picket, or petition the actions were the public's protest rather than any real threat to the government. Another centre for resistance developed, which was neither simply a vested interest nor simply a mass movement.

The Coalition for Public Health, in which a number of union and community organisations joined together, was a gift to the media, its spokespeople providing informed commentary on the reforms. As in previous cases, this blitzkrieg was hard for the media to present. The coalition provided a public face, and a face which reflected the concerns of the public. It is outside the scope of this paper to detail the activities of the coalition, but crucially it was backed by the Wellington Health Action Committee (WHAC). Some idea of the breadth of the group can be obtained from the writers in the WHAC publication, *The Health Reforms: A Second Opinion*—retired senior administrators, economists, unionists from the health sector, medical practitioners, workers in the voluntary sector.[9] In some respects the coalition was better served than the government was, since the coalition's advisers had combined a wider and deeper knowledge of the health system. A number of overseas health professionals passed through adding to the depth of the understanding and critique.

Part of the aim of the blitzkrieg seems to have been to replace people well experienced in the health sector with outside business people who were often very ignorant of it. But as the government turned its back on the expertise in the sector, it created a pool of resentment from the redundant and those threatened with redundancy, who were willing to give their energy and their expertise. Those who became redundant were not necessarily the least competent, as is evidenced by many being recruited to positions in overseas health systems. Threats to employees, sometimes explicit, discouraged some protest, but no doubt encouraged underground resistance. (A consultant's report said, 'Don't shelter non-committed employees.'[10])

One other crucial feature was that the coalition, unlike many other campaigns, had some access to funds, initially from unions but later, as it built up credibility, from doctors with a commitment to the public health system. Not that the coalition was well funded. In total it spent over a two-year period the same as the government probably spent every day on its health reforms advice.

The non-party coalition's initial strategy was to discredit the most objectionable aspects of the reforms by offering an alternative which appeared to meet the government's stated intentions without the extreme elements (such as the profit driving of the system). The approach acknowledged the defects of the AHB based system (neutralising the potential criticism that the coalition was merely a front for vested interests), but argued for incremental evolution rather than radical revolution. The minister said that there was not a great gap between his proposals and the alternative strategies, but the dominance of the NIPB and Treasury with their totally different ultimate destination meant that the reforms were not to be deflected.

In summary, the Coalition for Public Health had status from the organisations which supported it, it had expertise from highly competent volunteers, and it had some resources to lobby and debate publicly. That gave it credibility—with the public, with the media, and (grudgingly admitted) with the politicians. The government may have quickly broken through the AHB line, but it unexpectedly met a second one linking the medical heights with the public plains.

THE GOVERNMENT RESPONSE

It is not this chapter's purpose to detail the campaign, nor highlight individual skirmishes, except in so far as they illustrate more general points. Central to understanding the campaign seems to be the government's poor tactics and irresolution.

Tactically it seemed brilliant to promise an 'integration' of primary and secondary health care, especially as it can mean all things to all people. For many general practitioners it means the anathema of being put, directly or indirectly, into an employment relationship similar to a salaried hospital doctor. The government was under the impression that there was widespread medical support for the change, an illusion perhaps partly fostered by the fact that one of the strongest medical advocates of the reforms was Tom Marshall, deputy chairman of the NZMA, and chairman of the General Practitioners' Association (GPA). A rebellion within the ranks had Marshall's team toppled from the GPA and Marshall himself from the NZMA.

The government seemed to be beset with irresolution. The Prime Minister recognised the need for an advertising campaign to get the public on side during the February 1992 Tamaki by-election. National MPs, returning in January 1993 from their Christmas vacation (a traditional period for getting a feel of the public's concerns), demanded a campaign. But nothing was done until May 1993, a couple of months before the new system was to be introduced. By then it was too late.

And it was neutered. Previous blitzkrieg advertising campaigns had been extremely emotional. In response to public protest to what was seen as political advertising, the Auditor-General had rules limiting government-paid commercials to informational content only. Even then aspects of the campaign were criticised by the Advertising Standards Board. The outcome of the $2.5 million campaign was considered, even by an Associate Minister of Health, to be of little value. Despite the NIPB and officials beavering away, there was surprisingly little leadership. It was almost as if the generals thought a blitzkrieg involved them pointing the troops in the right direction, waving them goodbye, and returning to base.

THE BLITZKRIEG FAILURE

Any campaign whose commander is replaced must be judged a failure. In March 1993 the Prime Minister transferred the health portfolio from Upton to Bill Birch, the toughest administrator in the Cabinet. Birch drove the reforms through to the establishment of the CHEs (and the funders, the Regional Health Authorities (RHAs)) on time in July 1993.

In terms of its own goals, even at their most ambiguous, the government had:

- abandoned health care plans (the public stated firmly it wanted no change in public funding);
- abandoned the public health commission;
- abandoned the core health services definition program;
- withdrawn the hospital overnight charges and withdrawn or reduced some other user charges;
- failed to gain significant productivity gains;
- substantially increased public funding (rather than hold it, as hoped), yet various indicators (such as the length of waiting lists) have not improved or have deteriorated;
- increased the exposure of ministers to minor failures in the system (because previously the area health boards had taken responsibility); while
- despite their business goals the CHEs continued to make losses.

The lack of gains is nicely illustrated by the 1996 OECD report on the New Zealand economy. As the CHE chief executives found, funders control providers, and the OECD is funded by the New Zealand and other Treasuries. Even so the OECD commentary finds it difficult to be positive.

> . . . even though the system is in its third year of operation, it is not yet clear how the reforms will ultimately affect health care in New Zealand. It is too early to observe their effects on health outcomes and to discern what impact they will ultimately have on output of the health sector as well as the organisation of output provision.[11]

Despite claims before the reforms of substantial and rapid improvements, justifying the costs of the upheaval, improvements were not discernible. Claims that significant benefits were delayed but would appear in time became a monotonous litany for all the reforms. When the OECD report tried to make an evaluation, it said 'assessment must rely largely on a priori considerations'; that is, the theory on which the reforms was based was going to be used to evaluate the outcomes. The tight prior remained the benchmark, not itself subject to evaluation.

Inevitably over a five-year period there have been some positive improvements (which could have occurred anyway, if policy development had been more incrementalist):

- there has been some separation of purchasing from provision;

- a simple form of budget holding (which can lead to improvements in management of resources) has been introduced in primary care, although there is likely to be resistance to further changes;
- there have been substantial improvements in the balance sheets and accounting systems of the public providers.

Valuable though each is, they hardly justify the turmoil the reforms have caused, nor their expense—estimates range between 2 and 10 percent of a year's Health vote. Yet the fiscal costs have probably not been as great as the political costs. Jim Bolger specifically mentioned the government's health policies as a major reason for the substantial loss of support for National in 1993. National lost a quarter of its 1990 vote.

THE CAMPSITE TODAY

By 1996 it was not the tactics of blitzkrieg so much as trench warfare, where the government relied on its weight and momentum to force the reforms through, co-opting people as they went. But while those health professionals who were left continued to service their patients, few committed themselves to the reform. At one stage the tactic of the 'sap' appeared to be evolving, undermining the public health system by increased funding of the private system. This continues, but has not proved to be as effective as it might have seemed, probably because of the dominance of the public sector in the system, and the commitment of the public to a public system.

If by the 1993 election the health reforms were temporarily camped uneasily on a hillside, under fire from the public, by the 1996 election it was difficult not to discern preparations for a strategic retreat, even if these were overlooked by the OECD report. Bill English, the new National Minister of Crown Health Enterprises, foreshadowed (if his government were returned)

- the reduction of the four RHAs to one;
- the reduction of the number of CHEs to about half (the reforms had split 14 AHBs into 23 CHEs);
- the combining of the portfolios of the Minister of Health and Minister of CHEs.

The major reversals in the 1996 coalition agreement on health policy did not represent a backing down. That had happened already. Meanwhile CHE boards were replacing their rapidly leaving chief executives (over half went within three years) by new ones with clinical experiences.

What went wrong? From one perspective, the model was wrong. The reforms were based on the assumption that health was a generic product, which could be administered by generic managers. Even the CHE boards, packed with businessmen (and the occasional businesswoman) who have little experience of the medical industry, quickly recognised the first point. Less than six months after the appointment of the boards, the Chairman of the Crown Health Enterprise Chairs' Consultative Committee wrote '[t]he CHE group are of the view that the business of providing is not a genuine commercial mode'.[12] This culture clash is not only a recipe for worker demoralisation, poor productivity, and industrial disputes. It overflows into public perception. It was reported that 'Capital Coast Health is short of blood because donors believe their blood will be sold'.[13]

And yet there was a more fundamental problem. It was not just that the account of how the health system worked was irretrievably flawed. For a blitzkrieg to work, the map of the territory must also be accurate. In Roger Douglas's words, 'It is uncertainty, not speed, that endangers the success of structural reform programmes', and 'don't stop until you have completed it'. But what if the plan is wrong?

It is especially ironic that Upton, who so respected Friedrich von Hayek, advocate of the organic growth of institutions, commenced down such a radical and disruptive path. If only he had recalled that sentence of Hayek with which he had concluded his prize-winning essay: 'Least of all shall we preserve democracy or foster its growth if all the power and most of the important decisions rest with an organisation far too big for the common man to survey or comprehend.'[14] Not surprisingly the reforms generated a state of affairs that Alan Maynard, an eminent British health economist describes as 're-disorganisation'.

Effective health reform probably requires an incrementalist approach, involving consultation with the public and the bloodyminded vested interests. Mrs Thatcher tried on a couple of occasions to carry out a major restructuring, and each time backed down in favour of incrementalism: the re-disorganisation task was too large, and the public health system too important to the public to allow an all-out assault to succeed. Health is the part of the welfare state which most touches everyone, including the articulate middle class and the swinging voter. The political power of the medical professions arises not only from their power over life and death but also because they are close to the heart of community and individual aspirations—closer, anyway, than the politicians of the 1980s and 1990s have proved themselves to be.

Appendix: The Fallacy of the Generic Manager

A central notion of the New Zealand reforms of the 1980s and early 1990s was that an able manager was capable of managing any agency in the private or public sector. This has two implications. First, it suggests that all economic activities are broadly the same, or may be treated so for policy purposes, since the required management skills and approaches are not sector-specific. Second, it encourages the replacement of specialist managers, who had typically developed in the sector, with generalists who had not, but who would be loyal to the managerialist philosophy and anxious to impose it on the institution.

It might seem that this issue is marginal, except perhaps to those who were promoted or made redundant as a result. However, the consequences are widespread and potentially destructive. For example, the theory says that the same skills are needed to run a hospital as to manage a brewery, that ultimately the production of health services is not fundamentally different from the production of beer. Put so bluntly, the theory now seems laughable, even absurd, but it is a matter of record that the first chief executive officer of New Zealand's largest Crown health enterprise (CHE) was previously involved in brewery management.

Arguing the fallacy of generic managers is not to argue an uncritical case for specialised managers. It is certainly not an argument for inbred management, where senior managers enter the firm at the bottom level and work their way up, without any other sectoral or firm experience—a successful senior manager is likely to have had a range of experiences in a variety of agencies. Neither does rejection of the fallacy mean that a senior executive should never come from outside the industry. Rather it suggests that if a new manager comes from a sufficiently different industry, he or she will take a considerable time to settle in.

Nor is it denied that there are generic management skills such as those which the MBA, for instance, provides to students. A good MBA graduate should be able to go into almost any junior management position. As the manager progresses, industry-specific skills will be added to the generic ones. The fallacy of generic managers applies to senior managers.

Like most such misconceptions there is just sufficient truth in the fallacy of generic managers to deceive the unwary. A senior manager may be able to move successfully between what appear to be quite different products or firms. As an aside we should not make too much of these shifts. A misunderstanding of their nature led in the 1980s to mergers between firms of very unlike characteristics in the name of 'synergies'. Typically these mergers came unstuck, and the firms—if they survived—later sold the disparate activities.

The fallacy, however, is concerned with a broader issue. Although some products or services have sufficient similarities so that their senior managers will need to have broadly similar skills, many do not. That a foodstuff CEO may make an admirable hardware CEO does not mean that inevitably he or she will make a competent health services CEO.

Moreover, there will always be managers, generic or otherwise, who have the talent to rise above the limitations of their training and background when placed in a new situation. Undoubtedly some of the new managers in the health services have done well. The concern is with the average level of performance, not a few isolated peaks.

THE RISE OF GENERIC MANAGERS

There are a number of economic products and services whose characteristics are so different from the general run of commodities that they have typically been treated quite differently from those conventionally supplied by private enterprise. Indeed the raison d'être of the public service was that its 'outputs' were so different from market ones that they required different management styles.

By the 1980s this view was under attack. The rise of managerialism reminds one that the phenomenon is not peculiar to New Zealand, although the country may well have experienced one of the most intense applications of the theory.[1] When faced with a problem of institutional reform Treasury tended to solve it by converting the institution as closely as possible to a private-enterprise firm. While this may make sense for public enterprises which are functioning in a competitive market with (at least nominally) profit objectives, the extension of the model to traditional social services is more problematic.

Certainly Treasury despaired of the old public service ways, but the selection of the business alternative was a little like awarding the prize to the second singer in a competition after having only heard the first. Few Treasury officials had real experience of private business (if any, it was in the finance sector), so they were attracted to an idea with which they had little familiarity. Ironically, Treasury is one of the few public sector organisations which have not been affected by generic managers. All its senior executives had experience as junior Treasury officials, and few had outside public sector experience, other than perhaps graduate school.

There was a progression. The introduction of business management procedures was begun in those public activities where they were most applicable, and it then spread out to steadily less applicable areas. The return of a National government in 1990 led to managerial reforms in social services sectors, of which the health reforms are a good example.

THE HEALTH REFORMS

The debacle of the health reforms is described in the main chapter. Their underlying premise was that health services were just like any other economic commodity and could be supplied in the same way, and that ideally they should also be funded privately. As Chapter 2 explains, the provision of health services is very different from the supply of standard commodities. The main strengths of normal market transactions simply do not apply to the standard health service exchange.

This elementary point, which explains why there is a specialised subject of health economics, was dismissed by the reformers, who simply ignored it. It was a matter of practice that none of the New Zealand economists hired by the agencies supervising the reforms were experienced health economists. Rather, generic economists with little health economics experience were employed.

The reform units did hire some overseas health economists, carefully selected for their ideological sympathies (while some of the world's top health economists were ignored—most notably Bob Evans of Canada and Alan Maynard of Britain, who were visiting New Zealand on other business). Even so, the overnight consultants did not have enough local knowledge to be useful, while the local ones they interacted with did not know enough to give them key information. For instance, New Zealand has the peculiarity that litigation for medical malpractice is all but prohibited by the accident compensation legislation. Thus, one of the key mechanisms for quality control in a privatised medical system is missing. Yet at no stage did the reformers address the question of quality control in a system becoming more exposed to commercial pressures.

Illustrating the effects of generic professionals by the example of economists is appropriate because the modern economist is often given the role of the ideologist, even high priest, of the managerialist revolution. The debate occurs in terms set by them. But the economists were not the only generic professionals who made elementary mistakes.

The most obvious example was Peter Troughton, the man appointed to head the National Provider Board, who had been chief executive of Telecom New Zealand and who went on to electricity distribution reorganisation in the state of Victoria. Telecommunications and electricity are both network industries, so there may be sufficient overlap for a good manager to move easily between the two. But by no stroke of the imagination is there an overlap with health service providers. Trained as an engineer, the man exuded a charming confidence which soon betrayed a not surprising ignorance. For instance, he confused an intensive care unit with a post-operative recovery unit, a misunderstanding which could be fatal for a person suffering a cardiac arrest.

Troughton claimed that under the reforms there would be

early productivity gains of 20 to 30 percent. Challenged, he said that whenever he had been involved in industry rationalisation he had attained such gains. Systematic measurement of his achievements might find that the gains were somewhat less than claimed, since the conventional measures have tended to look at output per person employed, and fail to allow for the circumstance that redundant employees often became self-employed subcontractors. But in any case the generic manager failed to observe that labour productivity gains in a capital-intensive network industry, such as telecommunications, are a very different matter from those in a labour-intensive service industry, such as health services.

Pressed further, Troughton cited the example of a particular hospital which was already making such gains, so he claimed. The reader will notice the logical flaw that if a hospital was already making such gains under the old regime, then perhaps a new regime was not needed. However, there was no systematic measure of productivity gains to support the claim. Some of this hospital's gains were said to be the result of recent improvements. For instance, the introduction of a preferred medicines list had the effect of cutting the hospital's drug bill by the equivalent of a productivity gain of 1 percent.[2] The advisers in the National Provider Board did not seem unaware that preferred medicine lists had been introduced into leading hospitals a decade earlier. The hospital in question was a laggard, not a leader.

Another claimed performance measure was the substantial reduction in waiting lists at the hospital. This was true, but it was the result of a special grant from central government which enabled the purchase of more inputs. The non-specialists had no institutional memory.

GENERIC MANAGERS

The generic reformers appointed non-specialists to the boards of directors who were to govern the CHEs according to commercial criteria. The government's own list identified less than 5 percent of the board members as having medical health services experience. In turn, the non-specialist directors usually appointed generic managers to be chief executives, who in their turn appointed generic managers to other senior management positions. Many managers who were professionally skilled and trained in the area of health services management lost their jobs. Some were appointed to managerial positions overseas, suggesting that it was not incompetence that led to career termination in New Zealand, but incompatibility with the ideology of generic managerialism. The general perception was that the system of reform was so committed to generic management that it was a disadvantage to have health sector experience.

There is only anecdote to report on the new managers, for despite their claims to emphasise systematic management, and to monitor worker performance, there was surprisingly little effort by the managers to monitor themselves. Anecdote has medical personnel reporting that some of the new management teams did not understand the medical issues with which they were grappling, and were wasting resources as a result. It seems almost certain that ongoing efficiency improvements were delayed because the generic managers had to get up to speed in the peculiarities of their new industry. Sometimes the new managers were taken in by latest fashions, having no criteria by which to judge feasibility. At one stage the enthusiasm favoured heavy investment in information technology, a perception encouraged by the not-so-generic managers of the information technology industry.

An instructive anecdote comes from a meeting which involved presentations by three new CHE chief executives. Anxious to impress the mainly health service audience, the CEOs insisted that they had quality staff with whom they would be working to obtain performance gains. One CEO enthusiastically announced that his task was to get his staff 'to own the problem'. He was promptly asked what he meant by that, since if someone went into a hospital with a medical condition the staff already worked their butts off to resolve it. The new CEO responded by saying 'the problem' was the CHE profit line, and then his voice trailed off for even he realised that his staff would not be overly impressed by the profit outcome (nor that his salary package included a bonus if he met it).

Without question the effective use of resources by clinicians (doctors, nurses, and health technicians) has been one of the persistent problems for at least a quarter of a century. Slowly clinicians began accepting that they have a responsibility to be efficient in their resource use, and that this need not compromise medical ethics. They have been even more reluctant to accept the notion that providing resources to one patient reduces resource availability to others (who perhaps are not even the clinician's patients). The clinicians' reluctance reflects deep, and not easily resolved, ethical questions. The overall profitability of a hospital may have some connection with these questions, but in practice it is tangential and even irrelevant. In the end we have a clash of culture between generic managers focused on profit and clinicians focused on patients, with the commercialisers ineffectually claiming the two objectives are much the same thing.

THE OUTCOME

Evaluation of the reforms is complicated by the knowledge that there would have been changes, including productivity increases, even if the old regime had continued. However, as the main chapter details, the reforms have been far from successful compared to the promises made. For instance, the official estimates of the gains has been revised to an increment of 1 to 2 percent a year, probably about the rate that was occurring before the reforms.

This does not prove that the generic managers failed. It could be argued that the reforms were so ill-conceived that no class of managers could succeed. Even so, there is no evidence that these managers contributed to resolving a difficult situation. But recall that the theory of generic managers was central to the justifications of the reforms. If the generic reformers had not been so seduced by the idea that health services were just like any other economic activity, they would not have been so committed to appointing generic managers.

Moreover, within a couple of years over half of the CEOs of the CHEs left, often citing their reasons as managerial difficulties. They had come to their new jobs expecting to be working in a similar environment to the commercial businesses they knew about. They were soon disillusioned. Ian Frame, when CEO of Canterbury Health, wrote '[the] professional and commercial cultures have come face to face in a way that has not happened before. . . . At present there are serious tensions. . . .'[3] He was optimistic that the tensions between management and the medical staff could be resolved. (He thought the academic medics presented a greater problem.) Ironically, or perhaps inevitably, within six months his CHE had a major industrial dispute with clinicians over work practices (as well as pay rates), and Frame had left.

CONCLUSION

The story told here about managers in the health reforms could be told with similar detail about the changes in a variety of other activities, including education, housing, science, social services, and even the core public service itself. Generic managerialism did not lead to marked improvements in the ability of such agencies to carry out their tasks. Not surprisingly we are seeing a return to older management forms, in so far as the reversal can be made without appearing to be an admission of failure. Nevertheless the language of new managerialism dominates the public discourse, even if its practice is in retreat in some places.

All public sector agencies have a positive impact on the welfare and prospects of New Zealanders. The turmoil of reform, without any evident gains, has meant that those who benefit from the agencies have suffered, as has the public purse. Undoubtedly the health of some New Zealanders has suffered too—yet less than might have been expected. For despite the insecurity and demoralisation provoked by the reforms, the staff have continued to maintain their high standards of performance in health care. One would not expect generic managers to perform as well under such circumstances. Fortunately for the patients, the culture of the health professionals has triumphed, despite the attempt by the new managerialism to override it.

10

Central Government

HAVING SETTLED THE STRATEGY FOR GOVERNMENT TRADING ACTIVITIES
(corporatisation with an ultimate destination of privatisation) by
1987, Treasury turned to the reorganisation of core government
activities, as presaged in its 1987 post-election briefing *Government Management.*[1] The two key resulting statutes were the State
Sector Act of 1988 (SSA), and the Public Finance Act of 1989
(PFA). Each was addressing a number of issues, but their underlying direction was the shifting of core government departments
towards the adoption of commercial practices as far as was possible.

THE PUBLIC FINANCE ACT

Although the SSA preceded the PFA, it is easier to begin with
later act. For our purposes the PFA had two main features. First,
it put the government accounting on to a new basis, which was
largely paralleled by commercial practices, based on 'Generally
Accepted Accounting Practice' (GAAP), set down by a non-gov-
ernment board of the Society of Accountants.

In many ways the new form of financial statements required
by the PFA represented a major step forward, incorporating the
developments in public sector accounting and financial reporting
since the previous Public Finance Act of 1977. At a superficial
level they are easier to read and understand by the layperson.
Government accounting was switched to an accrual method,
which avoided oddities such as the practice of the Ministry of
Works finding it had unspent funds, and purchasing shingle before the end of the financial year, and then selling it back to re-

cover the cash. The new financial statements also require disclosure of contingent liabilities, which means the government will not be able to hide potential costs which may arise from its decisions without telling Parliament, as occurred with many of the Think Big projects.

But there are oddities. For instance, the balance sheet (or, as it is now known, 'statement of financial position') shows a deficit in the Crown Balance, but ignores the sovereign right to tax, which swamps any of the other items in the account. Considering that many countries' tax revenue exceeds 40 percent of GDP, the sovereign right could be valued at least $360b,[2] whereas in June 1995 total reported assets were $54.5b and liabilities $57.6b (a deficit on the reported government balance of $3.1b). The omission is to make the financial statements almost totally meaningless as a measure of the strength of the government's position.

The neglect probably reflects not only that the right to tax is difficult to value (and there are other problematic items—see appendix), but there being no commercial equivalent, the underlying conceptual issues were not addressed. Perhaps it reflects the commercial sector's hostility to the power of a government to tax. Whatever the rights and wrongs, it is clear that it is difficult to give any meaningful interpretation of the Crown Balance other than the arithmetic difference between a certain set of assets and liabilities, valued in a certain way.

A significant feature of the PFA was the change in the arrangements by which the government of the day acquired monies from Parliament. First there was the jargon: ministers sought 'outcomes', while departments delivered 'outputs' 'contracted' by the minister to enable the achievement of desired government outcomes. Ministers would 'purchase' from the departments (strictly it is with the chief executive of the departments, see below) to provide the desired outputs, and Parliament votes the requested funds. One can see in this new arrangement the introduction of a market and commercial notions.

While one may idealise these arrangements, arguing it enhances accountability, the practicalities are rather messy. Consider the finance vote, whose 1995/6 'outcome' was:

> The appropriations in Vote Finance will make an important [sic] contribution to a number of the Government's strategic objectives for the public sector. They will fund policy advice aimed prima-

174

rily at the maintenance and acceleration of economic growth, and a number of strategic objectives in other areas, including enterprise and innovation, external linkages, education and training, social assistance, Treaty claims settlement and health.[3]

One is not overwhelmed with the impression of clear outcomes desired by the Minister of Finance (and in truth his actual desires are more likely to be to get re-elected, make people feel better off, and lead a quiet but respected life). Now look at the first 'output class' of Treasury, 'Policy Advice: General Economic and Fiscal Strategies':

> Provision on the economy, including the government's overall economic and fiscal strategies and macroeconomic forecasting and monitoring.

Well, yes. One is left with the impression that those in Treasury who recommended the conceptual framework of the PFA did not consult with their colleagues as to whether it was practicable in Treasury (any more than those colleagues consulted with other departments on their policy proposals). The hard notion of an output has been reduced to a warm fuzzy, as is true for the many other outputs of all the government departments. How a Parliament or minister is to judge objectively the quantity (let alone quality) of such an output is a mystery. Perhaps it is a façade to give the impression that there was some accountability, or that there was greater accountability than in the past.

How a game is scored affects the way it is played. A system dominated by commercial accounting practices with their emphasis on the measurement of profit is going to reduce the significance of activities which do not make a profit. Not surprisingly government departments were pushed into corporatising and privatising their activities or contracting them out to the private sector. Those which remained were seen as cost centres, with the benefits of what was supplied tending to be neglected.

In 1995/96, Parliament voted $5.8m for the Treasury output class described above. How is one to decide that is the right amount? Prior to the 1989 statute, Parliament had voted an amount to reflect the inputs of the activity: so much for wages and salaries, so much for transport, so much for buildings, so much for miscellaneous expenses, and so on. One had some idea of how many officials were being provided and, quality aside, that gave some idea of the amount of activity. This detailed parliamentary control became less functional with the new responsibilities of chief executives under the SSA (discussed below).

The term 'purchase' explains the fallacy. As Chapter 2 described, when someone purchases bread they have a reasonably clear idea what it is they are obtaining, and they do so in a reasonably competitive market. Neither of these properties apply to the 'purchase' of advice from Treasury. (In regard to the second property, the transaction is between a monopsonistic minister and a monopolist department, for ministers do not have the opportunity to tender to other institutions for the advice they receive using the funds provided for Treasury.) When we purchase bread, we are not greatly concerned about the inputs that went in to make the bread, because the output is reasonably well defined (and competitively delivered). Where it is not, the input and production processes are of far greater interest. For instance, a woman purchasing a dress is likely to examine the material, the stitching, and the cut, even where it is made—as well as looking at the label.

The input approach is not necessarily superior to the output one. Both have defects. What is relevant is the way in which a pseudo-commercial approach was uncritically adopted. While both sides (supply and demand, inputs and outputs) were addressed, the balance was swung to the reduction of the usage of resources at the expense of the provision of service. Under very great pressure because of the stagnation of the economy and the fiscal deficit, the government kept arguing that gains could be made by reducing the resources available to departments, and it cut the available funds. Departments, already under pressure from burgeoning demands often as a result of the economic stagnation, tended to reduce service as a means of coping with the reduced resources available to them. There was no real mechanism for the government to assess this service reduction. Although people felt it, and often indicated their resulting distress to the politicians, there was no effective means for Parliament to evaluate the service cuts either, other than to parade glaring instances. The final section of this chapter examines one dreadful outcome.

THE STATE SECTOR ACT

Chapter 8 reported that the State Sector Act was a blitzkrieg with little consultation. Although the main concern at the time was its impact on the conditions of state sector employment, the treatment of chief executives was even more revolutionary.

The powers of chief executives were increased, giving them the maximum autonomy, responsible to the minister for the 'general conduct of the department', and for the 'efficient, effective and economical management of the activities of the department'. So it was they who signed the contract with the minister, they who decided how to use the funds, and they who made the employment and other input decisions. They were almost business chief executives, although as there was no board of directors—only a busy minister, supplemented a little by the State Service Commission (SSC)—they had even greater power.

One of the ideas behind the change was a separation of policy advice from operations. The minister made policy, the department implemented it. The distinction suited Treasury because it supported their notion one could make policy without detailed knowledge of the operational context, and empowered them relative to other departments. But it resulted in odd outcomes.

The Department of Defence was split into two: a policy-oriented Ministry of Defence, and an operational New Zealand Defence Force. The separation generated some anxiety among the military because, uniquely in the Commonwealth, it involved the constitutional innovation of the transfer of control of resources from a civilian (previously the Secretary of Defence) to a military person (Chief of the Defence Force). Moreover, the Defence Force found it necessary to establish its own internal policy unit, denying the efficacy of the division.

An even greater irony was that the consultants who recommended the change then went on to review Treasury and concluded that the policy–operational split was unnecessary in their case. Whatever the justification, there was—and is—a strong argument for the division of the economic and financial advice service into, say, a Treasury and a Ministry of Finance, as there is in Canberra, to generate systematic competition in the tendering of economic and financial advice. Instead the Treasury monopoly on advice prevailed.

Not surprisingly, in the light of the popularity of the notion of the generic manager, the system of appointment was modified so that those outside the public sector could be more easily appointed, enabling the selection of businessmen (and occasionally businesswomen) with little public sector (or policy advice) experience. These appointments were not always successful, and latterly there has been a reversion to a predominance of appointments from within the public sector. Thus the culture of the public service was undermined.

Another change was to involve the minister in the appointment of a chief executive. To what extent this undermines the traditional notion of an apolitical public service is a question that belongs elsewhere.[4] The point here is that the relationship between a minister and her or his department became quite paradoxical. As a result of the SSA a minister is more responsible for the chief executive, in so far as the minister was involved in the appointment, but the SSA also gives the chief executive more control over the department, and so the minister is less responsible—a paradox underlined by the outcome–output distinction of the PFA. The overall impression is that the ministers promoting the two acts were anxious to reduce their ministerial responsibility. Even the increased use of the term 'accountability' diminished the 'responsibility' of ministers.

The confusion is nicely illustrated by the example discussed in the final section. Following the Cave Creek tragedy, there were calls for the resignation of either the Minister for Conservation or the chief executive of the Department of Conservation. The minister eventually resigned the portfolio (but not from Cabinet), upholding some notion of ministerial responsibility, but even so there were still calls for the Director-General's resignation.

Undoubtedly the two statutes strengthened the chief executives' powers. One consequence is that since the chief executives are personally responsible for the appointment of all staff, including those immediately below them, there can be less willingness by the subordinates to challenge a decision, especially if the chief executive is of an autocratic disposition. The full story of the resignation of the Auditor-General over some alleged financial irregularities is still to be told, but one cannot help wondering whether a more collegial management structure might have picked the problem up earlier.

A second consequence of the chief executive employing staff is that he or she literally became the staff's legal employer, in contrast to the earlier arrangement where the SSC was the employer and there was an integrated public service. The SSC still gets involved in general pay negotiations, ostensibly in a role not unlike the hire advocate in a private sector negotiation. But it acts as a coordinator as well. The state as an employer has not given up the advantages of the monopoly powers of a large employer. Nevertheless, the general approach of the SSA was to put state industrial relations on almost exactly the same basis as private industrial relations. In 1988 that meant the basis set down by the Labour Relations Act of 1987, but the 1991 Employment Contracts Act has no mention of the state sector. As a result of the SSA, employment relations in the state sector come directly under the Act just like any other employment relations.

Yet there is a difference, which the state has been willing to exploit. The setting of remuneration is quite different, even if the PFA seems to imply otherwise. Prior to 1988 the state, frequently a monopsonistic buyer of public servants' labour in markets which are not nearly as responsive to demand and supply pressures as—say—financial markets, accepted that the pay rates should reflect some notion of fairness and equity with private sector rates. The principle was difficult to put into practice, with complicated linkages between private and public pay rates, and claims by each side that their rates lagged behind the other. The combination of the SSA and the PFA nicely abolished all this, by setting a sum inside which the chief executive had to pay staff, and not requiring any parity considerations but merely remuneration of whatever the market will bear.

In effect Treasury and its ministers set the public sector pay rates by allocating the funds for departmental expenditure, four-fifths of which would typically be for remuneration. Chief executives and their employees are told that they can give increases above the rates implicit in the monies voted, but that would have to come from labour increases (i.e. more output per worker) and the reduction of staff numbers. (The system is rather like the wages fund of classical economics where total remuneration is set exogenously, and there is a direct trade-off between numbers employed and the wage rate.) No longer is equity or fairness a consideration in setting public sector remuneration (yet another example of the abandoning of equity discussed in Chapter 3). The new principle is that public sector pay rates will be whatever the government and Treasury can get away with. The result has been that public sector remuneration rates have fallen relative to private sector ones, which themselves were falling in real terms in the early 1990s.

Thus the core public service was put on a 'more businesslike' basis, more likely to be led by a businessperson or generic manager, with its chief executive having the powers of a business leader, with its accounting system and industrial relations more like commercial ones. What did this mean for the efficacy of the department's operations and the culture of the public service? A tragedy in the distant West Coast told much about what had happened in Wellington.

THE DESTRUCTION OF PUBLIC SERVICE CULTURE

In April 1995, a group training to work in the outdoors stood on a badly constructed platform overlooking Cave Creek in the Punakaiki National Park, administered by the Department of Conservation. The platform broke, 14 young people died, and others sustained severe injuries.

It would have been easy to treat the tragedy as an isolated instance, but in the concluding paragraphs of his report, Judge Graeme Noble, wrote:

> Standing back and viewing the evidence objectively, I am left with the overwhelming impression that the many people affected were all let down by faults in the process of government departmental reforms. Society always likes to feel it is progressing, but there are lessons for society in all of this. No government organisation can do its job without adequate resourcing. In my opinion, it is up to governments to ensure that departments charged with carrying out statutory functions for the benefit of the community are provided with sufficient resources to enable them to do so.[5]

The reforms had aimed to break up the culture of the old public sector. They could not do this selectively. Everything had to be destroyed. Thus the practices of the corporatised, and eventually privatised, Ministry of Works and Development in the construction of platforms were not fully transferred to the Department of Conservation.

This failure to transfer practical aspects of the past culture was not unique. Take 'cost shifting', the phenomenon of a business shifting costs from itself to the customer. The health reforms were deliberately set up to encourage cost shifting, not only with the introduction of user pays. The operating culture of the hospitals was changed, so that instead of being focused on the patient they have to act in a businesslike manner. The government promised there would be no cost shifting—but it was an example of the sort of promises which the reformers insisted on making, but never keeping. Consider the easiest form of cost shifting open to a hospital—early discharge, where patients leave the hospital before they are ready. Does it happen? How would we know? A patient has an operation, is discharged early, the burden is borne by patient and family, but it is not recorded. The trick is that the cost is shifted to the individuals and their close friends and families, so the community does not notice. The same thing happens with geriatric care—early discharge, perhaps without any community support. Only the patient and those close to the patient notice.

There are exceptions. Mental patients cannot usually cope by themselves, and often they have had no one close to assist them. So they ended up on the streets, discharged when they should not have been. Because these people are seen as a menace to the community, there was a public outcry, but it was the tip of the iceberg of a much wider phenomenon of early discharge and related cost shifting.

At a meeting in late 1995, a senior administrator in the health sector described the skills needed for the work in his agency. References to knowledge about the health system were notably absent. When questioned about the omission he said that sort of knowledge was unnecessary. One of the audience said: 'It helps to know what you are talking about.' He replied: 'I dispute that.'

For a totally different example, recall the lack of papers to the government mentioning the tax implications of abandoning capital controls on foreign exchange. When the restrictions were terminated, the financial sector went overseas to available tax havens. That is the underlying story of the Winebox inquiry and its allegations of tax fraud. Half-baked policy led to the loss of millions of tax dollars—mainly legally.

Recall the reply of Wyatt Creech, the Minister of Revenue, to Ruth Richardson's claim that he blocked her tax reforms. 'The devil', he said, 'is in the detail.'[6] That truism applies to tax law, to the bolts missing from the platform, to the discharge decisions, to everything. The philosopher-kings ignore the detail.

The traditional culture of the public service, skilled in dealing with such detail, was gutted, to be replaced by something which was more inefficient, failing to provide the service and security that was promised. As the Noble report says, the failure was 'systemic'; that is, it was riddled throughout the system—not just that of platform construction, not just in one department, but through the entire state sector.

Postscript

About the time this book went to press, *The Spirit of Reform* was released. Written by Allen Schick, an eminent US professor of public policy, the report might have been expected to laud uncritically the reforms of core government, given that it was written under conditions which would be expected to give a favourable outcome—terms of reference written by the State Service Commission and the Treasury, who have a self-interest in the report's conclusion; the report writer an overseas visitor on fleeting visits; the confining of those consulted to insiders, largely excluding academics, dissenters, and those outside Wellington; and a reliance upon anecdote. But Schick was able to overcome these handicaps, and produce a report critical of many aspects of the reforms.

He described the reform's concepts as 'avant garde' (p. 14) and 'novel' (p. 15), while the Treasury post-election briefing *Government Management* was 'extraordinary' (p. 18). Such adjectives belie the report's measured tone, and its careful—although not always easy to follow—arguments. The central theme is that the reforms were 'influenced by two overlapping but distinctive sets of ideas, one derived from the vast literature on managerialism, the other from the frontiers of economics. Managerial reform is grounded on a simple principle: managers cannot be held responsible for results unless they have freedom to act. . . . The new institutional economics is grounded on a very old idea: people act in their own self-interest' (pp. 15, 17). It was the latter that the 1987 Treasury post-election briefing emphasised, but '[c]learly different conclusions might be drawn if the brief were argued from different premises' (p. 18).

Schick is sympathetic to managerialism, but his vision is not that public sector managers are driven by private sector principles. The alternative, contractualism, is the more

commercialist approach, which undermines public managerialism, for it 'may diminish public-regarding values and
behaviour in government', including values such as 'the trust
that comes from serving others, the sense of obligation that
overrides personal interest, the professional commitment to do
one's best, the pride associated with working in an esteemed
organisation, and the stake one acquires from making a career
in the Public Service' (p. 25).

Contractualism also weakens the collective interest, for a third
party is difficult to fit into a bilateral deal between a purchaser
and a provider. Schick reminds us of Edmund Burke's challenge
to his local electorate that his obligation was to the public good
as he saw it, not just to serve as their agent. The reader is left
wondering, as Schick intends, where the public good belongs in
a bilateral contract.

The report also expresses doubts about the efficacy of the out-
come/output distinction, the ownership/purchaser distinction,
the policy/operations distinction, and the complete exclusion of
inputs from the purchaser agreement. Contractualism, it argues,
breeds high transactions costs. Moreover 'there is . . . more pressure for conformity and group-think' in the public service (p. 7).
Schick also writes that he is 'troubled by the concept of split-
personality government that has influenced financial and other
reforms practices' (p. 72). He praises the accountability—'an im-
personal quality, dependent . . . on contractual duties and informational flows'—required under the reforms, but distinguishes it
from responsibility—'a personal quality that comes from one's
professional ethic, a commitment to do one's best, a sense of public service' (p. 84).

The above is sufficient to show that many of the report's
themes and criticisms will be found elsewhere in this book, although sometimes in less detail. However, the main reason for
adding this postscript is not just to express regret that the report
was not available earlier in order to have its findings integrated
into the text, but to observe that it may well be a watershed in the
process of government sector reform and management. In the
past it was possible to ignore the growing difficulties in the public sector and the criticisms of domestic dissenters, while the reformers glowed in a foreign adulation based on a superficial
understanding as to what had occurred. *The Spirit of Reform* challenges the public sector managers. Not only are the reforms un-

finished, but many were ill-conceived and will result in a steadily deteriorating public service performance unless major initiatives are taken to address the basic structural failures that Schick has identified.

Appendix: The Heritage Assets

This appendix is different from many other parts of the book, not only because of its length, but also because it arose out of a policy problem posed to the author, and thus the discussion has a more normative flavour.[1]

Consider the treatment of archives and other heritage assets in the Financial Statements of the Government of New Zealand (FSGNZ, a.k.a. the 'Public Account'). Its Statement of Financial Position (SFP) for 30 June 1995 is shown in Table 10.1.[2] In the past the SFP was called 'the balance sheet'. It lists the assets and liabilities of the Crown.

In one sense the asset component of the SFP is no more than a list of all the assets which the Crown owns. Itemising every possession would lead to an unwieldy and weighty report. To make the exercise tractable, the assets are summarised into groups, and the market value of all the items in the group is reported. In one way any valuation is arbitrary (a point acknowledged in the FSGNZ as '[t]here are difficulties associated with obtaining objective valuation for certain of the Crown's assets').[3] How is the public account to value the Tongariro National Park— gifted to the nation by the Tuwharetoa iwi—or the manuscript of the Tiriti o Waitangi held by the National Archives? In another way this is just a mechanism for summarising the inventory of assets. If so, it does not matter greatly how such items are measured, providing they are done so systematically, although from other perspectives arbitrarily.

Many of the heritage assets are included in the 'Physical Assets' row of the SFP. The accompanying note identifies a subgroup of 'other assets' worth $2171m in June 1995, of which $850m is for the conservation estate, $765m for the archives in National Archives (including the Tiriti o Waitangi at $26m), and $556m for the stock of the National and Parliamentary Libraries. Note this does not include the buildings or equipment, which appear elsewhere in the SFP. Other heritage assets, such the collections of the Museum of New Zealand and heritage buildings, also appear elsewhere, indicating that there is no consistent treatment of heritage assets.

Table 10.1: Statement of financial position of the government of New Zealand, 30 June 1995

	$m
ASSETS	
Cash and bank balances	210
Marketable securities and deposit	6,523
Advances	4,782
Receivables	4,453
Inventories	326
SOEs and Crown entities	16,420
Other investments	223
Physical assets	13,432
Commercial forests	646
State highways	7,454
Intangible assets	18
TOTAL ASSETS	**54,487**
LIABILITIES	
Payables and provisions	3,824
Currency issued	1,620
Borrowings	44,096
Pension liabilities	8,106
TOTAL LIABILITIES	**57,646**
TOTAL ASSETS LESS TOTAL LIABILITIES	**(3,159)**

Approached in this way, the public account's valuation of heritage assets has no special meaning or significance. However, within the SFP there are assets whose valuation has considerable commercial significance. For instance, other lines in the account deal with cash and with state-owned enterprises (SOEs), which may be privatised for cash. Now there may be practical economic considerations why some SOEs should not be sold. (For instance, the electricity system amounts to a monopoly, which is arguably better in government ownership.) However, the principle of not selling public monopolies is a very different one from that of selling a heritage item such as a national park or the manuscript of the Tiriti o Waitangi.

Yet the valuations of heritage assets appear to have the same status as those of the commercial assets, a circumstance which leaves open the possibility that heritage assets could be treated as commercial assets and even privatised. In early 1995 a Treasury paper recommended that consideration be given to disposing of what it called the 'non-New Zealand' material of the Alexander Turnbull Library, which meant selling the Milton and Bible collections, among other things.[4] In response to the additional funding requirements for the Department of Conservation, the need for which became evident as a result of the Cave Creek tragedy, Treasury recommended that the funding should come partly from the disposal of some of the conservation estate.

On occasions there may be a case for sale or exchange of heritage assets. For instance, it may be that some low-quality land in the conservation estate would be exchanged for some high-quality land. What should drive such changes is better stewardship of the heritage estate, not the commercial considerations which dominated Treasury thinking.

So we might wonder whether heritage assets should be treated differently from the more commercial ones, protecting them from pressures for inappropriate privatisation. The answer to this question does not lie in the FSGNZ or even the Public Finance Act. Rather, the way the ownership of assets is organised determines the way they are presented in the balance sheet.

Consider the curiosity of the ownership of the national archives as implicit in the FSGNZ. For every government asset there is a department or other agency responsible for its management. As far as the FSGNZ are concerned, the relevant department in the case of national archives, the conservation estate, the collections of the National Library, and heritage buildings, appears to be Treasury. In contrast, the collections in the Museum of New Zealand are the responsibility of a board (a Crown entity), and appear in a different row of the SFP, but there is no intermediary agent between the Crown (advised by Treasury) and the nation's archives. Legally, as far as the FSGNZ seems to be concerned, the National Archives is not responsible for the archives in its possession. An even odder case is that the trustees of the National Library are not responsible, as far as the FSGNZ are concerned, for the books of the National Library.[5]

These anomalies seem to have arisen out of the various pieces of legislation which cover the different activities. It is no surprise that the 1957 Archives Act does not co-ordinate well with the public sector organisation of the 1988 State Sector Act and the 1989 Public Finance Act. Over time the anomalies will be resolved, but there is a need to provide guidelines.

Who should be responsible for heritage assets? One answer might be the departments which manage them, but that is to confuse the role of manager with that of trustee. The basic trustee of these assets is Parliament. However it is impracticable, and probably inappropriate, for the members of Parliament to carry out their trusteeship role directly. This suggests that Parliament—not the government—should appoint boards of trustees for its heritage assets. The trustees would be selected for their expertise and integrity rather than to reflect interest groups, but Parliament might well wish to consult with the public before making the appointments.

The boards would meet occasionally and review the state of the assets and the adequacy of their management, reporting annually to Parliament. They would have a special duty to protect the integrity of the heritage assets for which they were responsible. This would mean they—not Treasury—would recommend any disposition of an asset.

The result would be that the Department of Conservation would continue to manage the conservation estate, National Archives would continue to manage the nation's archives, the National Library would continue to manage the stock of books and manuscripts, the Museum of New Zealand would continue to manage its collections, but in each case the ownership would be with another Crown entity. In the FSGNZ the assets would be identified as 'restricted assets', distinguishing them from commercial ones.

Here is a set of principles which might serve to implement the proposal for public heritage assets.

1. Public heritage assets are those assets owned directly or indi-

rectly by the Crown which are preserved and conserved, and because of their cultural, historical, and or environmental significance, have restrictions on their use, on their transformation, and on their disposal. As a general rule they may not be alienated (i.e. privatised). Thus they are not in practice treated in normal commercial ways.

2. The public heritage assets include, among other things—
   (i) archives;
   (ii) books, manuscripts, and other artefacts of the Alexander Turnbull Collection;
   (iii) collections of artefacts and paintings of the Museum of New Zealand;
   (iv) the conservation estate;
   (v) the collections of the National Library;
   (vi) heritage buildings;
   (vii) other gifts in perpetuity to the Crown and people of New Zealand.

3. For management purposes, public heritage assets with similar characteristics would be grouped together, each under the supervision of a separate trust.

4. Each trust would have its own board of trustees.

5. Membership of each board of trustees would be appointed by Parliament.

6. Each board of trustees would report annually to Parliament on the state of the public heritage assets for which they have responsibility, including the adequacy of their management.

7. Public heritage assets would be identified in the government's financial statements as 'restricted assets', thereby recognising the political, moral, cultural, and legal limitations on the right of government to alienate these assets.

8. Local government would be expected to place their restricted assets (which are also heritage assets) into a parallel trusteeship arrangement.

11

Local Government

LOCAL GOVERNMENT PRECEDED NATIONAL GOVERNMENT IN NEW ZEALAND.
Pre-contact Maori had no national organisations, but their iwi
governed the districts of New Zealand. As settler government was
imposed, iwi governance was swept aside. It was not to be the
last time that central government was dismissive of local government. The 1852 constitution had provided for provincial government. But increasingly centralised concerns prevailed (not least to
subdue Maori government), and in 1876 the provinces were also
abolished. A system of local government based on counties, bor-
oughs, and cities was substituted, which for over one hundred
years operated at the local level, as much as central government
would allow.

Over time the boundaries became increasingly antiquated, but
various attempts to reform them failed because of the pressures
of local parochialism (but also because the functions of local government were so limited by central government that there was
little to be gained from a more rational structure).[1] From 1987
the Labour government reformed the structure, reducing the
plethora of local agencies to 12 regional councils and 74 territorial authorities, and 6 special authorities, while reforming their
functions.

The reform might have been used as an opportunity to enable
local government to be a more responsive and creative agency in
the governance of the local communities. Instead central government continued to control and restrict local government. Fearful
of an outbreak of local democracy and the potential challenge to
their vision, the philosopher-kings forced the local bodies into
their commercialist prescriptions. And since their theories had no
role for communities, only individuals, they had little time for

189

local governance. (Chapter 12 describes how in their thinking on core education policy, the fundamental unit was the individual and family.) Their ideal for governmental structures had been set out by the reforms of central government, and the reformers could not countenance local communities rejecting that.

This chapter describes the reforms, and illustrates how they were used to reduce democracy in local government by the example of the pressure to corporatise and privatise electricity supply authorities. Since these are business enterprises, they strictly do not come into this study. However, they nicely illustrate the principle that communities use public ownership as a symbol of their collective desires. Because the tight prior rejects such a phenomenon, it could not be allowed for in policy. Instead the philosopher-kings used central government's power to impose their theories on local government and the communities they represented.

THE TENSION BETWEEN CENTRAL AND LOCAL GOVERNMENT

While central government needs some sort of system of local administration, it also is antipathetic to it. There are basic activities which are required to be done in localities. Central government delivery is impractical in such things as the 3Rs (roads, rats, and rubbish) and so those activities are devolved to some local agency. They could be administered by the prefecture system that has prevailed in France, in which a central government appointee has considerable authority, unchecked by the local community. But New Zealand's political ancestry lies in Britain, where there is a more robust tradition of local government democracy (despite the Thatcher government's attempts to stifle it).

In any case an elected level between the local administration and the central government protects the centre from public disquiet. This was well illustrated when the (majority) elected area health boards were abolished, and ministers of health found themselves under public pressure for every medical failure because there was no one else to appeal to.

If local government is providing only basic services—as was broadly the case in most of the smaller counties—the tension could be ignored by giving a little discretion to the locally elected. However, in the case of the larger counties and, especially, the urban centres, there is a demand for other local services which cannot be so easily disregarded: it is difficult for central government to provide cultural and leisure activities to a locality; the provision of the basic services becomes more complex as population densities rise (e.g. the balance between motorways and public transport); protection of the environment becomes more difficult and a larger local concern; land planning issues become more disputed. Leaving the urban areas in highly fragmented units—Auckland had 34 local bodies in 1987—did not resolve these tensions, but added vigorous disputes between local government authorities. As in the case of unions, central government legislation set an inefficient configuration but offered little in the way of resolution.

Local democracy is a threat to central governance of an authoritarian kind. National politicians could live with the politics of the minimalist government of its friends and relations in the counties, but were challenged by democratically vibrant cities governed by Labour or by the more liberal urban wing of the National party. Labour politicians were not only contemptuous of the squires of the shires, but their own kind in the cities were a potential threat to their national authority. Some politicians had come through from local government. But even for them it was largely a preliminary to their national political ambitions, rather than a local commitment.

The bureaucrats in the central government reinforced this view. First, they have less involvement with local government, which nevertheless can reduce the central bureaucrats' power. In addition, many Wellington bureaucrats considered local government inefficient. Some were: it was difficult to have an effective administration of the borough of Naseby with less than 200 souls, or the smallest non-island county, Wairewa, with less than 700. Unfortunately, one of the least competent local authorities covers the area where most central government administrators work and reside. There is a practical reason for this. Good public administrators in Wellington have greater career opportunities in central government, so there is a constant drain of quality management from the local government. The local hospital board and university face the same problem. Many central government understandings of the working of such institutions across the nation are a projection of the unsatisfactory performance of the local

Wellington ones.

The result of these pressures was a system of local government which was not well organised and often inefficient.

THE 1988 REFORMS

Michael Bassett, Minister of Local Government from 1984 to 1989, was a past Auckland local body politician. Well aware of the irrationality of the local body structure, he used the December 1987 economic package to introduce the most radical restructuring of local government since 1876. Presumably he was not responsible for the collective Cabinet decision to announce the whole package after Parliament went into its 1987 Christmas recess, but the decision was symbolic of the general unwillingness to consult.

The nation can be well satisfied with the resulting structure of 74 territorial authorities and 12 regional councils. Because of the variety of tasks involved, and the geography and population density, there will never be a perfect local body configuration. Some of the district councils still look tiny (the smallest is Kaikoura at around 4000 people, although there were about 60 smaller territorial authorities before the reforms), while the requirement that the regions should generally conform to the river catchments left some odd arrangements (notably the regional centre for both Taumarunui and Pahiatua is Palmerston North). The Maori were especially angered since their iwi interests were ignored. Some communities resented being swallowed up into much larger local authorities. There was some tinkering in the early 1990s, but no major changes to the structure.

However the reforms did not stop at structure, but included redefining functions, the principles of which were as follows:

- functions were to be performed only where net benefits exceeded those of other options (this was later dropped);
- operational efficiencies were a priority;
- commercial, regulatory, and service delivery functions were to be separated managerially;
- there was to be transparency of trade-offs among objectives; and
- clear and strong mechanisms of accountability were required.[2]

For this chapter's purposes only a couple of comments are necessary. First, the principles were imposed with little consultation. Second, they reflect the familiar characteristic of government policy of the period—they appear very general, and perhaps unexceptional, but their underlying agenda was a commercialist one.

And so the new local authorities were pushed along now familiar lines. The chief executive became much more powerful—more like the French prefect—perhaps more powerful than the chief executive of a government agency, because he or she reports to an entire council rather than a minister. Corporatisation, privatisation, and user charges increased. Under pressure to reduce rates, especially from business ratepayers (whose significance had been increased by the general direction of the reforms), greater attention was paid to activities as cost centres, rather than services to be provided to the population. As in the case of central government services, this imbalance is especially problematic where the output (or outcome) is not easily defined as in such cases as libraries, recreation activities, cultural activities, and environmental services. Thus each tends to get squeezed in order to reduce costs (and rates) but at the cost of reduced service. User charges may be also increased.

Local government reform was a blitzkrieg across a very wide front. Not only were territorial authorities addressed, but so were harbour boards, public transport, and electricity supply authorities (discussed in the next section). To change the metaphor, the success was like a landslide. Central government merely had to move some rocks at the top of the scree—to change the legislation—and the landslide was under way. There was some resistance, but before discussing it an example may be useful.

ELECTRICITY SUPPLY AUTHORITIES

The advantage of considering electricity supply authorities (ESAs) is that despite their being business enterprises, and therefore largely outside the main themes of the study, they are nationwide and prominent, and there is a reasonable amount of information about them. If, for instance, we were to discuss local libraries we would soon be reduced to relying on anecdote for want of comprehensive information.

Given a national electricity grid—currently owned by a state-owned enterprise, Transpower, and mainly supplied by other state-owned enterprises—each locality needs a network to distribute electricity to its households, businesses, and other consumers. Historically there had developed around 60 supply authorities, each typically servicing a small area. Some were power boards, independent entities governed by boards of trustees elected triennially. The rest—typically in urban centres—were usually owned by the local councils. The largest by area in Southland supplied 28,740 ha, the smallest a mere 30 ha of the Riccarton Borough. (The Auckland Electric Power Board supplied 3426GWh in 1986/87, while the Bluff Borough Council only 17GWh.) Each ESA had a monopoly within specified boundaries—which could be as irrational as the territorial ones—and no cross-boundary competition was permitted. Having a monopoly encouraged the practice of charging business consumers more than household consumers (who directly or indirectly elected the directors of the ESAs). Municipal electricity departments (MEDs), owned by the local councils, also tended to charge higher overall prices, using the additional revenue to subsidise the rates or other local activities.

The reforms began by privatising the power boards, usually giving shares to the electors or consumers. In the case of MEDs that was not an option. But having been caught in the GST net and the 1987 requirement that any profits were subject to income tax, local body ownership became less financially attractive. In 1988 the prohibition on cross-boundary competition was removed.

In 1989 further measures were taken to increase the level of competition between ESAs. But the degree to which their supply networks can actually compete is somewhat limited. After an investigation of the merger between neighbouring Power Direct of the Hutt Valley and Capital Power of Wellington, the Commerce Commission judged that the two ESA networks were not able to compete effectively against one another, and approved the merger. This is perhaps not surprising given that the cost of the network is about 3 percent of the total of power, so that the margins for competition are small.

Other provisions allowed, in effect, other agencies to 'hire' the network to supply electricity customers (i.e. outside the agency's region), so there is more competition in the supply of electricity than in the local network itself. However the ESAs' distribution networks were, and are, natural monopolies except in some marginal circumstances. It is unlikely that most consumers will have the choice of more than one cable supplying their needs.

Such research evidence as there is—and there is not a lot—suggests that publicly owned natural monopolies can be more efficient and have lower prices than privately owned ones. This may be because the publicly accountable management is under greater pressure to keep costs and prices down, which can be an effective substitute for the lack of competition.[3] Certainly the evidence does not unequivocally favour private ownership. The issue can be avoided by pretending the natural monopoly is open to competition—as the philosopher-kings frequently did.

Ingeniously, the reforms created structures designed to precipitate a change to private ownership. Many ESAs are no longer in public ownership, either because territorial owners sold their ownership to private companies, or because the consumer shareholders sold out to private companies. This allowed amalgamation, and throughout the mid-1990s the financial sector kept itself busy (and renumerated) trading and merging the various companies. Ostensibly this was occurring because of the threat of competition, although there were probably gains to be made from the economies of scale of amalgamation—at least for neighbouring ESAs (although some mergers did not involve contiguous boundaries). The exercise was a typical financial market speculative boom, in which claims were made—often based on unconvincing analysis or quantification—but in hindsight rarely delivered. At the time of writing the merger boom is not over, although the concomitant rise in electricity charges to consumers seems to be under way. (This issue is complicated by 'rebalancing', in which charges to businesses and households were realigned to bring their ratio closer to economic costs, rather than the overcharging of businesses to undercharge households, i.e. electors.)

This is not to argue that there was no choice in the treatment of trading assets as the tale of the two cities of Wellington and Christchurch illustrates. To cut a complicated story short, the Wellington City Council first sold a minority interest in its ESA, Capital Power, and then its majority share, to a Canadian corporation, Trans Alta, which merged the company with the neighbouring Power Direct, which it already largely owned. The case for the sale and merger was not a compelling one, even to the point that contradictory arguments were used at various points. (It was argued that the merger would prevent cross-boundary competition from Power Direct, but to get the Commerce Commission to agree to the merger it had been demonstrated that cross-boundary competition would be minimal.) Probably a majority of Wellingtonians objected to the sale. A citizens' jury had studied the issue and concluded in favour of retaining public ownership. An opinion poll had supported them. Yet the council proceeded with the privatisation.

In contrast, the Christchurch City Council continues to have a substantial shareholding in three major city assets: 65 percent of Port Lyttelton, 75 percent of Christchurch Airport, and 87 percent of Southpower, the local equivalent of Capital Power. (The remaining shares reflect the interests of other local authorities.) David Close, the chairman of Christchurch City Holdings Ltd, the holding company in which they were placed, describes the trading enterprises as 'efficient, socially responsible, and profitable'. The chairman of Southpower thought that its electricity prices would have been 10 percent higher if the company had been privatised. Of the large urban ESAs, Southpower offered the lowest residential charges, with the exception of the summertime rate of the Dunedin ESA (perhaps because it owns a power station). Energy Direct was nearly the highest, and Capital Power in the middle.[4]

Significantly, the sort of pressures to which Wellington had succumbed the Christchurch City Council had seen coming, and had planned an alternative. The trading enterprises operated commercially, subject to a annual contract with the holding company, which set down the required financial, community, and energy conservation objectives. Why was the Wellington City Council not so far-sighted? Why had the central government not made a similar arrangement in the 1980s when the state-owned enterprises were corporatised? The explanation is that the central government corporatisation was designed as a step to privat-isation, not as a means of retaining public ownership.

Perhaps the Wellington City Council had a similar agenda, although its councillors would deny that. Perhaps the aforementioned inefficiency of the council administration was also relevant, but a crucial point was the nature of the communities and of their community governance. A well-known study of economic development and civic traditions asks why some parts of Italy developed more successfully than others.[5] The book concludes that economic success was associated with a long tradition of civic community. The careful argument explores other possible explanations but finds them to have insufficient explanatory power. Nor can successful economic performance explain the superior civic virtue. The patterns of social co-operation based on tolerance, trust, and widespread norms of active citizen participation go back to the thirteenth century, preceding the economic development.

The implication is that, after allowing for differences in resources, those regions with greater civic virtue will perform better than those with less. At which point one might wonder to what extent New Zealand once had a culture of civic community, and to what extent it has been undermined in the last decade.

What the analysis suggests is that the city with the greater civic-mindedness will produce the better outcome for its ESA. There is evidence to suggest that Christchurch is the superior of the two. A 1996 survey reported in *Consumer* found the Christchurch City Council the most popular among local authorities, and the Wellington City Council the least popular.[6] In 1993 Christchurch was a co-winner of the prestigious 1993 international Berkelsmann Prize for achievement in local government. Canterbury was one of the most successful nineteenth-century provinces, and the Christchurch City Council has continued that tradition. Welling-ton citizens are torn between local and central government—until the early 1990s they did not even have a decent civic centre. Each weekday morning 50,000-odd people cross the Wellington city boundaries to go to work, so that the day population differs from the night one. Its community has not the same traditions of active citizen participation, often getting diverted to national issues—so easy to do in the capital city.

Suppose the philosopher-kings are correct and private enterprise is more efficient and will result in lower prices in the long run. Harry Johnson, a Chicago school economist, pointed out that people may yet be willing to accept lower material welfare in exchange for expressions of nationhood.[7] Almost certainly it was this vision that the Christchurch and Wellington citizens who favoured public ownership had in mind. Public assets are expressions of their community. So even were the philosopher-kings correct when they claimed that private businesses were more efficient than public ones (and, recall, there is no overwhelming evidence that they are), communities which promote civic virtue by public ownership may still be better off. The reformers cannot deal with this point, because they have no account of community, or of humans as community animals. Their policies, focusing on the isolated human being, not only fail to support communities, but have tended to destroy them.

Civic virtue is expressed not only by local government service. Participating in voluntary activities for non-personal and community ends is another means. Historically, New Zealand has had a high rate of such community involvement, but it too came under pressure from commercialisation. Voluntary agencies, which depend on community support together with public funding, found themselves in severe tension, torn between commercial and community philosophies, following the tightening of the application of state funds in line with commercial principles. The resulting adjustments included pressures within some agencies to, in effect, corporatise themselves and to create a cadre of paid staff with commercial aspirations and remuneration. Volunteers responded by withdrawing, leaving the organisations of professional staff with insufficient voluntary labour and falling private donations. The government did not increase public funding to offset the declines. Indeed, the funding was more likely to be reduced. The result has been inferior services to those who depend on assistance from the organisations—often the sick, the poor, or those on the margins of society.[8]

WHERE TO?

As this is written, the speculative boom of trading shares in the ESAs has not fully worked its way through. The indications are that the financial sector will then turn to the privatisation of the water supply, another natural monopoly. One may expect further community resistance—already there is a reluctance to accept water meters in many parts of the country, partly because this is seen as a first step to privatisation. Mrs Thatcher's government, as contemptuous of local government as has been New Zealand's, privatised the nation's water supply. It is no irony that the attempt to impose an unpopular local poll tax was one of the reasons for her downfall.

There was resistance to the local government privatisation in New Zealand too. Some hit the national media. The successful protest against the privatisation of the Ports of Auckland was led by a talkback host, Pam Corkery, who in 1996 became an Alliance MP. The Alliance's election to the Auckland Regional Trust on a no-privatisation manifesto in 1992 stopped other asset sales. Much of the resistance which occurred at the local level, led by elected councillors among others, was not reported nationally. Christchurch City Council is not unique. Other citizens protested against changes, thus enhancing their communities—the civic virtue. Yet central government remains reluctant to harness such citizen power. It may do so by default.

For the local level of government may have to play a more important role in the governance of the New Zealand of the future. It seems likely that the new electoral regime of Mixed-Member-Proportional representation will slow down the ability of the central government to take decisions. It may be that the policy implementation gap can in part be filled at the local level—presumably best by communities of high civic virtue.

12

Core Education

IN THE EARLY 1980s THE MINISTER OF EDUCATION, MERVYN WELLINGTON, decreed that schools would not implement *Growing, Sharing, Learning* (the 'Johnson' report), apparently because of its recommendations on sex education. Later he required each school to purchase a New Zealand flag to be flown on appropriate occasions. Whatever the correctness of such decisions, they illustrate the fundamental policy issue of how much control of the core educational system should be at the centre (in these examples, directed by the minister), and how much independence those running the schools should have. What happened to the core (or compulsory) education system in the 1980s and 1990s is a complex story, yet to be told. Here we focus on the centralisation–decentralisation tension, and its relation to the commercialisation of the core education system.

As the previous chapter elaborated, New Zealand governance has been organised in a centralised way, partly because of the small population, but also because the historic patterns served the practical needs of the nineteenth century and the current needs of national politicians and administrators. However, in the case of education, there was a further factor which had impelled central control. From the late 1930s, when Peter Fraser became Minister and Clarence Beeby became Director-General of Education, the centre had operated to generate a progressive education for the children, one which aimed to give a kind of equality of opportunity:

> The government's objective, broadly expressed, is that every person, whatever [her or] his level of academic ability, whether he [or she] be rich or poor, whether he [or she] live in country or

town, has a right, as a citizen, to a free education of the kind for which he [or she] is best fitted, and to the fullest extent of [her or] his power.[1]

Pursuing this goal during the following half-century, the central administrators regarded themselves as more enlightened than the parents of the children—and even than the teachers. By controlling the curriculum and other aspects of schooling, the centre's values could be transmitted to the children, bypassing parents and the more conservative teachers. Put this way, the centre appears to have been very authoritarian. In a way it was. But many of the values it promoted were anti-authoritarian, especially in the primary school. The creative activity one can observe in the primary classrooms is still a joy to behold. Another major achievement was a systematic attack on racism and the promotion in the children of more tolerant attitudes to diversity. Yet the same centralised system gave more conservative ministers, such as Wellington, the same powers to promote different values.

Moreover, by the 1980s the parents of the children in the education system had gone through it themselves a generation earlier. Some children were the third generation of their family to go through the Beeby–Fraser system. In so far as it had been a success, the parents could claim the right to have greater control over their children's education. This demand was not confined to successful middle-class parents, for the Maori argued that their children would flourish better in an educational environment which reflected Maori culture and aspirations. They began building a separate stream of pre-school kohanga reo, core-school kura kaupapa, and post-school wananga.

The issue of fairness also continued to trouble educationalists. Differences of attainment by gender, socio-economic status, race and cultural background, disability, and rural or urban location remained evident, despite half a century of effort to abolish them.[2] The poor attainment of the Maori has been especially a matter of concern.[3] There were persistent criticisms by educationalists drawing attention to these failures—criticisms acknowledged by those at the centre.[4] But as in the case of the pro-public health critiques of the health system, which kept drawing attention to waiting lists, the critics of the education system, committed though they were to a public education system, were in fact undermining public confidence in it.

Neither of these points would have mattered so much had the public policy context of benign centralism been secure. What the critics had not sufficiently noticed was that in the mid 1980s the commercialisers were beginning to address what appeared to be a related problem. They used the term 'decentralisation' too, but it had a rather different meaning, referring to individuals and their families, rather than communities.[5]

PICOT AND GOVERNMENT MANAGEMENT

Two reports introduced these concerns into the late 1980s reforms. The first was the Picot report, developed out of a push by Roger Douglas in mid 1987 to reform the social services. The Cabinet had avoided this by establishing three committees to review the administration of the three main providers of social services.[6] (The health one led to the Gibbs report—Chapter 9.) The committees were to report, conveniently, after the 1987 election.

The Taskforce to Review Education Administration reported in April 1988 with *Administering for Excellence.*[7] It found that 'the present administrative structure is over-centralised and made overly complex by having too many decision points', and proposed that 'individual learning institutions [should] be the basic unit of educational administration' and that the 'running of the learning institutions should be a partnership between the teaching staff (the professionals) and the community', The report's proposals eventually evolved into *Tomorrow's Schools,*[8] and a new educational structure. But there was a cross-cutting report which complicated the outcome.

Attached to *Government Management*, the main 1987 Treasury post-election briefing, was a second volume subtitled *Educational Issues.*[9] Including the sections in the first volume, Treasury had devoted 40 percent of their briefing to education, far out of its apparent importance in overall government. Whatever the reason for this imbalance, it warned the education community that Treasury was deeply committed to transforming education.

The analysis is couched in the narrow language of the economics of education, with a Chicago school bias. A decade later the briefing reads much like an uneven attempt by awkward adolescents with a commerce background to grasp a vast, unfamiliar, amorphous, and complex activity using the rather limited range of intellectual tools they had obtained for other purposes.

Educationalists expressed outrage, becoming among the strongest resisters to the commercialisation reforms. The outcry against the report must have surprised Treasury. After all, for almost three decades educationalists—like the lobbyists in other sectors such as tertiary education (Chapter 13) or science research (Chapter 14)—had been justifying additional spending on the education system on the basis that it contributed to economic growth. All Treasury seemed to be doing was adopting this perspective, and pushing it to its ultimate logic, albeit using an unfamiliar theory of economic growth, in which the public sector took few initiatives other than to provide favourable conditions for private sector initiatives. Why then the outcry?

First, there does not appear to have been any consultation, so that the briefing was seen as an attempt by Treasury to use its privileged position to dominate education policy. Second, Treasury appeared to have only a tenuous grasp of the existing debate or, to put the issue more positively, it wanted to raise its own concerns, which were of less interest elsewhere. A peculiarity of Treasury-speak is that it operates at a level of abstraction which ignores the concrete reality of people living in the economy (or, in this case, learning in the education sector). The non-economist, unused to reading economic articles where it is impossible to see or feel any connection with a tangible reality, finds somewhat uncomfortable this reification of the abstract into what purports to be a material reality.

One of the problems of the various social sciences is that these days each tends to be isolated and uncomprehending of other social sciences, yet its practitioners are willing to invade others' territories—often with an arrogance matched by a comparable degree of ignorance. Economists will rail against political scientists, say, who they claim misrepresent economics, and yet the same economists will misrepresent political studies. By treating education as a commercial investment activity Treasury were proposing the commodification of education, yet there is no hint that they were aware that this might be contentious, or why it might be so.[10] Their conclusions—although they offended educationalists—appeared bland:

[P]ublic expenditure on education may be regarded as largely an investment in the future for and on behalf of rising generations. . . . There appears to be little in the present structure of provision to counter the general costs to Government's role or to keep its intervention well focused on the purposes of that intervention. . . . With a starting point in the family as the primary source of education and a policy to build from that, a stronger overall educational environment can be constructed for all children and young people.[11]

The text seemed to imply a somewhat more detailed policy agenda than was explicit. For instance, there is no specific proposal to increase user charges for education, although the drift of the argument was in that direction. This was not just a matter of tertiary education, for the last sentence quoted above—which, as it happens, is also the last sentence of the document—could be interpreted to favour vouchers, or even user charges, for core education. From this perspective the document looked suspiciously like some of the earlier commer-cialist policy proposals, where politicians would be seduced into adopting what appeared to be general uncontroversial principles, and subsequently find the principles being implemented in ways they neither foresaw nor desired. On the other hand, it might be argued that—given the indications that Labour was shifting towards the devolution policies which would be adopted in *Tomorrow's Schools* while National's education spokesperson, Ruth Richardson, was advocating vouchers—the 1987 Treasury was placing a bob each way.

TOMORROW'S SCHOOLS

In August 1988 the Minister of Education, David Lange, who had taken the portfolio himself after the 1987 election, published *Tomorrow's Schools: The Reform of Education Administration in New Zealand*, following 20,000 responses to the Picot Report. 'Much of [*Tomorrow's Schools*] is an affirmation of the Picot proposals. There are some additions in detail. In some areas the Government has chosen to depart from the taskforce's recommendations.' The proposal's aims were a 'more immediate delivery of resources to schools, more parental and community involvement, and greater teacher responsibility'. The report's summary appears in an accompanying box. (The consequent transfer of many educational advice service workers from salaried positions to being contract workers was less evident.)

The Principal Features of Tomorrow's Schools

The reform of education administration is based on the following principal features:

Institutions will be the basic 'building block' of education administration, with control over their educational resources to use as they determine, within overall guidelines for education set by the state.

The running of the institution will be a partnership between the professionals and the particular community in which it is located. The mechanism for such a partnership will be a board of trustees.

Each institution will set its own objectives, within the overall national guidelines set by the state. These objectives will reflect the particular needs of the community in which the institution is located, and will be clearly set out in a 'charter' drawn up by the institution. This charter will act as a contract between the community and the institution, and the institution and the state.

Institutions will be accountable, through a nationally established Review and Audit Agency [now called the 'Education Review Office'], for the government funds spent on education and for meeting the objectives set out in their charters. This agency will carry out regular reviews of every institution.

Institutions will be free to purchase services from a range of suppliers.

Community education forums will be set up to act as a place of debate and a voice for all those who wish to air their concerns whether students, parents, teachers, managers or education administrators.

A Ministry of Education will be established to provide policy advice to the Minister, to administer property, and to handle financial flows and operational activities.

An independent Parent Advocacy Council will be established. This council will promote the interests of parents generally and will, in particular, provide assistance and support to parents who are dissatisfied with existing arrangements to the extent that they wish to set up their own school.

Groups of parents representing at least 21 children will be able to withdraw from existing arrangements and set up their own institution, provided that they meet the national guidelines for education.

The aim was to devolve power from the centre to the teaching institutions. The outcome was a little different. In addition to the policy-making Ministry of Education and the evaluating Education Review Office (ERO), there was also established a New Zealand Qualifications Authority (NZQA), an Educational Training and Services Agency, and a Careers Service as separate Crown entities. (The Parental Advocacy Council was disestablished in October 1991.) The ironic effect of this was in some ways to increase the power of the centre, yet responsibility was shifted to the schools.

Lange was adamant that the proposals were opposed to the Treasury agenda, and indeed saw the devolution of school management as empowering (not his word) communities to resist Treasury and New Right ideas.[12] But there were doubts about the intentions among much of the educational community, understandably given the government's past record. Yet even if Lange was sincere, Treasury's *Government Management* pervaded all public policy in the period, not least in the contextual legislation of the State Sector Act and the Public Finance Act (PFA). So head teachers became chief executives of these institutions, although the finance provisions of the PFA applied rather imperfectly at the school level.

WHAT DID DECENTRALISATION MEAN?

The language of Picot and *Tomorrow's Schools* about 'community responsibility' can be contrasted with that of the Treasury post-election briefing, which emphasised 'family responsibility'. In the future the minister might have less responsibility for sex education and the degree of nationalism in each schools. But there could be a conflict between the interests of the parents of a child and that of the community (as represented by the School Trust Board) on such matters, or indeed on others. This would partly be determined by the centre, which retained the right and the mechanisms (such as ERO and NZQA) to intervene.

At the same time, school zoning was abandoned, and parents were given the right to choose other schools if they wished, so that the notion of 'community of location' was compromised. The logic of this latter change, and indeed of the reforms as a whole, was that schools would compete for students, and the logic of this was that schools themselves would have perceived differences, in their charters and in the way they operate. What then was to prevent the inequality increasing between schools? A perfectly adequate school in lower suburbia might lose some of its pupils—most likely its pupils with the most educationally committed parents—in favour of a school in a higher-status suburb, as parents chose to avoid perceived stigmas for their children. Because their physical size was fixed, and there was now an excess of demand for places, the selection process of higher-status schools could favour those children with characteristics that would reinforce the high status. Children now had no right even to go to the school nearest to them. The ease of exit over voice could cause severe inequality of educational opportunity, just as medical insurance—as Geoff Fougere argued—would undermine the objectives of the public health service.[13]

Other competitive responses were allowed to schools, all of which exacerbate inequality. Some schools began to improve their relations with businesses as a means of increasing resources available to them (with the concern that this might distort the education—an even more acute issue in tertiary institutions). Schools facing weak demand relative to their capacity were encouraged to recruit fee-paying overseas students (and some became over-dependent on those fees). Schools could increase the resources available to them by higher fees (assuming parents were willing and able to pay them). There had been elements of these in the old system, but the new one unleashed the process of cumulative causation. In a way, given the increasing abandonment of equity, this was not the policy priority it had been of old, but it deeply worried the educationalists and many parents.

The election of the National government, and the appointment of Lockwood Smith as its Minister of Education, reinforced the pressures towards commercialisation. National had abandoned the overt voucher approach which would have given students equal access to private schools using public funding, but a minor shift was the public purchase of places in private schools for selected students. A more insidious proposal, which could ultimately bring about the eventual disappearance of a publicly funded and provided education system, was bulk funding.

Presumably because of the strength of the teacher unions, schools funding remained partly on the pre-PFA input basis of having the teacher salaries paid from the centre. The bulk-funding alternative was to have the school receive a lump sum, out of which it would pay teacher salaries and other expenses.

This is more consistent with the PFA. It also makes it possible to reduce the funding of schools by a laggard increasing of the amount paid, forcing boards to seek alternative sources of finance such as higher fees from parents (after such expedients as depressing teachers' salaries had been exhausted). This is exactly what is happening to tertiary institutions. The government no longer sets fees. But by refusing to increase bulk funding in line with rising costs it forces the institutions to increase their fees.

Smith tried to impose bulk funding on the core education service. When the teacher unions fiercely resisted, he introduced a scheme by which schools could opt in, offering incentives to do so. (The paranoiac would immediately see that although in the short term a school would be better off, once sufficient schools had joined to enable bulk funding to be made compulsory, the squeezing of bulk funding would begin.) Some schools joined the scheme. At the time of writing there is a stand-off, but the two systems cannot continue in parallel. Perhaps the replacement as Minister of Education of the ideological Smith by the pragmatic Wyatt Creech was a signal that the National government was retreating.

It is a matter of record that the principal resistance came from the teachers' unions, although they were usually supported by parents, trustees, and other educationalists. It is understandable that teachers do not want locally determined conditions of service and are uneasy about too great a local input into their recruitment and management. On the other hand many would say they are too economically and educationally powerful, and the sector faces producer capture (the parallel has been argued about doctors and nurses in the health service sector). But teachers would point out that they mediate between state and child, and parent and child, on educational and other matters.

Parents are not well informed about the educational choices, because the transaction does not have the standard conditions described in Chapter 2. If it did, there would be no need for the ERO or NZQA. The non-standard conditions are what give the producers their power in the education and health sectors. Pretending the conditions are otherwise does not resolve the problem.

However, in the shorter term there may be an even more serious problem. Can the boards of trustees and the schools' chief executives (once headmasters and headmistresses) cope with the administrative pressures they face?

The auguries are not good. While there was considerable enthusiasm for election to the boards on the first occasion, three years later there was evident reluctance, and some boards did not even obtain enough nominations to fill all positions. Similarly, head teachers of schools are announcing their retirement, like chief executives of Crown health enterprises, disillusioned with the tasks required of them. The difference is that in this case they are increasingly required to be generic mangers, although they entered teaching as specialist professional educators. And in any case both trustees and boards are finding themselves under-resourced to do the tasks required of them.

Perhaps, even more ominously, they may not have the skills either. The PFA places a demand for considerable financial management skills, which most schools do not have and cannot afford to hire. The impression is that theft and fraud are running at a higher rate than in the past—not surprisingly, given the greater opportunities.

With hindsight it is becoming evident that the administrative costs of the old centralised educational system were lower than those of the more decentralised system. Educational institutions experience economies of scale. Most schools would seem to be below the minimum size for administrative efficiency. Hopes that decentralisation would generate a hands-on managerial efficiency and save resources have vaporised. Only those who see that decentralisation makes it easier to increase user charges and re-duce public, if not total, costs are likely to be happy with the outcome.

There will be a continuing push by a commercialist minority to increase the degree of decentralisation, as presaged by that last sentence of the Treasury report on education, and by the proponents for vouchers. However some re-centralisation of the education system is more likely, although it is unlikely to return to the degree that Wellington—the education minister or the centre of government—exercised in the past.

But fundamental questions remain unresolved. Who is to control core education—the state, the community, teachers, parents, or the market? Who is to fund it—central government via tax revenues, or parents via user-pays? And who is to provide the services—government agencies, or private corporations and trusts? Those who have simple answers are philosopher-kings, or have not understood the questions. Sometimes they belong to both categories.

13

The Tertiary Education Reforms

THE VISION OF THE WATTS REPORT, PREPARED BY A COMMITTEE appointed by vice-chancellors in 1986, centred on the role of universities as 'a major engine of economic growth'.[1] That had two important consequences. The first is that by committing the universities so heavily to economic growth, the style of the universities would be affected greatly by the choice of the style of economic growth. Since economic policy was based on commercialism, inevitably the universities would be drawn in that direction, even in the way they function internally. But, second, if the role of the universities were to become subservient to the economic strategy, other roles would be diminished. The Watts report describes the universities as 'social and cultural asset[s]', but it is a picture of a heritage building retained as a façade in a business district. Contrast James FitzGerald, Canterbury's first provincial superintendent (and a university graduate), who said in his inaugural address in 1852:

> There is something to my mind awful in the prospect of the great mass of the community rapidly increasing in wealth and power without that moral refinement which fits them to enjoy the one or that intellectual cultivation which enables them to use the other.

Commerce is not an end in itself. Universities produce 'merit goods' in addition to the direct economic benefits. Economic growth is not an end in itself, but a means to a higher end.

The quality of the Watts report may be illustrated by its conclusion from one of the six selected subject areas. The economics subject assessment is chosen because it is a subject the writer knows something about, and economics is central to the issues of the present study. The review concludes:

> Overall our assessment is that economic departments are doing creditably well in difficult circumstances at undergraduate levels but are weak at the graduate level. Flexibility of salaries, greater support for graduate students and a recognition by employers of the value of further professional education are needed.[2]

The summary does not fully capture the trifling analysis that goes before, but a couple of points are noteworthy. First, there is no mention in the summary—and little in the text—of the quantity and quality of economics research. All that is stated is that 'in general the level of research in New Zealand departments is similar to that attained in Australia'. In fact, as Erkin Bairam has shown, economics research was weak, in many departments almost non-existent, and certainly not comparable to that in Australia.[3] Second, there is no reference to any public responsibilities of economists. By excluding those, and serious consideration of research, the activities of university economists are defined solely in terms of teaching—a fatal mistake to be repeated in the Hawke report (below).

Note how the Watts report on university economics says that if only they had more resources, or if only they had better internal management, then things would be better. This is a theme throughout the Watts report. Rarely a page goes by in the Watts report without some statement or hint that can be summarised as 'we need more money'. While economic stagnation was limiting fiscal generosity, and increasing student numbers was pressing on available resources, the begging bowl remained present.

Funding from private sources, especially student fees, offered a ready solution. It is difficult to explain the enthusiasm for fees among some university staff unless it came from the view that privately paid fees would reduce the universities' dependence upon government funding, giving them some freedom of manoeuvre. Certainly Treasury saw the attractions of a commercialist solution.

STRATEGIES FOR REFORM

One of the principles of the reforms of the 1980s was that an institution cannot (or will not) voluntarily reform itself. Perhaps the

Watts report demonstrated the principle. It was complacent about university performance, and sought a resolution of all problems from increases in government expenditure.

However, if the universities were failing in internal management, one is not only entitled to ask why, but also to conclude that a likely consequence of this failing management would be inefficient use of resources. More generally, faced in the prevailing conditions of economic stagnation, there developed a view that organisational reform could lead to productivity gains which would resolve the shortage of public resources. There was extraordinarily little evidence for the truth of this notion. Yet the argument was used repeatedly to justify reforms.

One feature of the central reforms was that the reformers were loath to interfere in the internal reorganisation of organisations. Rather, their strategy was to change the external environment, so that pressures would be generated which would force an organisation to reform. The procedure had been reasonably successful in the corporatisation of the state-owned enterprises. Not all of these changes could be easily applied to tertiary institutions. For this competitive approach to work at least five conditions need to be present:

1. Sufficient of the institution is opened up to competition. If only the fringes are, the core is likely to remain unreformed, and not be under the same pressure to seek efficiency.
2. There have to be sufficient competitive alternatives.
3. There has to be reasonably good freedom of entry.
4. The components being supplied to the public have to be reasonably independent of one another. Otherwise the firm can shift its costs for competitive advantage.
5. There are well-defined products and customers.

In the light of such a list, using competition on universities as a means of comprehensively reforming them does not appear promising.

1. To open up the entire university to the market would involve students paying full fees, with a similar approach for research, and for the public and heritage roles.
2. In most localities there is only one local university and, where there are more, they rarely offer competing courses.

3. While from some perspectives—especially training—there may be a degree of competition, thus far no new university has been established.
4. The components of the output of a university cannot be readily decomposed.
5. The precise services a university supplies and the customers it serves are not easily defined.

Given that the standard conditions for competition do not apply, what is public policy to do? It would be easy to ignore competition altogether, but what is the alternative—the complacency of the Watts report?

THE HAWKE REPORT[4]

By the end of 1987 there were a plethora of reports on various activities of the tertiary sector, which Butterworth and Tarling describe as containing 'unexamined assumptions, ill-chosen data, hasty and unfocused argument and conclusion'.[5] A university professor did little better.

The key second recommendation of the Hawke report argues 'that distinctions between education and training should be avoided'. The decision to collapse education and training into a single concept was crucial to the report's recommendations. Was the report's writer aware of the distinction made in the 1925 (Reichel–Tate) Royal Commission on Universities which commented that the University of New Zealand 'offers unrivalled facilities for gaining university degrees but . . . is less successful in providing university education'?[6] Degrees are qualifications, often used for vocational enhancement. Education involves a wider achievement.

There is a 'merit good' element in the output of a university. Merit goods are central in education because they set the shape of a society. Commercialisers argue that democracy is better because it gives a higher economic welfare. (Presumably, if it were shown that it didn't, they would become authoritarians.) A democrat argues that democracy is a merit good in itself. Enlightenment is another merit good, which complicates educational policy because, as John Stuart Mill argued, the unenlightened will be unaware of its merits.

Having discarded the educational component of a university, the Hawke report was able to resolve the problem of any distinctiveness in the university system by ignoring it. Instead, the report focused on the training role of university and other tertiary institutions of formal education.

Moreover, if universities are primarily training institutions, post-compulsory education takes another step towards commercialisation. Not surprisingly, the issue of funding went down that path. The Hawke report recommended 'that a system of student fees and government loans similar to that recommended in Australia by the Wran Committee should be adopted . . .'[7] The government was ineluctably moving in that direction.

GOVERNMENT MANAGEMENT AND REFORM

The Hawke report was not intended to be a public document. Indeed, it has some of the characteristics of a part of a blitzkrieg. Once the report was forced out into the public, the policy battle became more like trench warfare, although initially there was surprisingly little resistance. It is not clear why. That Hawke, a university teacher, proposed such reforms might suggest there was substantial support within the university for changes in these directions. The universities did little to demonstrate otherwise. For instance, only two universities successfully took the government to court over some aspects of the reforms, while the remainder stood aside.

To capture the astonishing breadth and depths of the reforms, consider a country in which the governance of the university system is characterised by the following features:

1. The appointment of the senior academic (the vice-chancellor) required approval by the Cabinet or a Cabinet committee.
2. The public funding of the teaching activities of each university was directly determined by the government.
3. The content of each university course was increasingly determined by a government appointed agency.
4. Public policy did not distinguish between a liberal education and vocational training.
5. The research funding and content of each university was de-

termined by government agencies.

6. The board of governance of each university consisted pre-dominantly of government appointed persons.

In the 1960s, for instance, a university system with such fea-tures would have been characterised part of an authoritarian or proto-authoritarian regime in a totalitarian state. Yet in the 1990s the New Zealand university system shifted in that direction, after fighting off strong pressures to shift it all the way.

1. The appointment of a vice-chancellor has to be approved by a Cabinet committee.
2. There is no University Grants Committee or its equivalent.
3. Course approval by a government appointed qualification au-thority had been rejected. (A subcommittee of the New Zealand Vice-chancellors' committee does it instead.)
4. The Hawke report, on which the reforms were founded, spe-cifically said there should be no distinction between education and vocational training.
5. Increasingly, research funding is controlled by the Foundation for Research, Science and Technology and other directly ap-pointed government agencies.
6. At the time of writing there were pressures to eliminate faculty and student representatives from university councils, as a part of the 'ownership' reorganisation (see Appendix).

In summary, the New Zealand university system came increas-ingly under the direct control of the government. By the measures of the 1960s, the governance of New Zealand shifted towards the sort of control that in those days we would have called fascist.

This is not to say that government of New Zealand is—or the individuals (politicians, advisers, acolytes) in it are—totalitarian. It would be easier to discuss these issues and deal with them if they were. But by their ignorance and naivety the philosopher-kings prepared the way for totalitarianism. If authoritarians were ever to take over the government, they would find it easy to impose their ideology in teaching and research and to repress dissidents.

It is not enough to say that academic freedom in New Zealand is guaranteed by law. Most totalitarian states have such laws. A statute does not protect the universities from authoritarian inter-ference by a central government.

It appears that, without thought for the constitutional and democratic implications, the Labour government adopted a restricted vision of the set of acceptable institutions. At one extreme were market-driven privately owned businesses. At the other were government agencies accountable directly to ministers and Treasury. There was no place for institutions in intermediate positions. Thus the policy was to privatise government-owned businesses, and to shift the universities under direct political surveillance.

The arrangement arose from the tension between accountability and decentralisation. As Treasury saw it, the more distant an activity got from the direct control of government, the less sure the government could be that the funds would be spent in the way that was intended.

The concern here is with 'capture', where an institution is run in the interests of the some of those who work in it rather than of those whom it is ostensibly intended to serve. This particular problem does not seem to be significant—at least for the government—if the activity involves only private commerce, in which only the transactors' own money (and not the state's) is involved. Hence the policy logic of commercialism, which argues that as far as possible institutions should be run as private businesses. Contrariwise, where that was not possible, the logic seemed to be tight government control to ensure accountability, especially for expenditure of the public monies.

Geoffrey Palmer, the Prime Minister, and Phil Goff, the Minister of Education, appear to have adopted this framework. Why they did so is something for them to explain. The Butterworth–Tarling account is of the two as a pair of latter-day Procrustes, forcing the universities into the same bed as schools, kindergartens, and departments of state.

Now, the universities can be freed from this oppressive state involvement in so far as their revenue comes from non-state sources—user pays—especially if universities have been reduced to training establishments. This suggests that students paying fees will give the universities some independence. Combined with relief to the public account, the option has its attractions to the public policy maker.

The Labour government accepted a Hawke-type proposal of higher fees and student loans which would be paid back as the graduate earned income, perhaps because it was thought this would make possible the spreading of the limited funds across more students. This was at a time when the government was in severe funding difficulties—revenue was not increasing in real terms because of the economic stagnation, there were burgeoning pressures for further spending, and there was the need to reduce the deficit. These issues loomed even larger in the controversy which surrounded the Todd report.

THE TODD REPORT[8]

In August 1993 the National Minister of Education established the Todd committee, whose terms of reference were to advise the government 'on the appropriate proportion of public and private contributions to tertiary education'. However, the primary concern was to be the level of student contributions, rather than some wider agenda.

The fiscal context in which the deliberations took place is revealed in the 1993 Treasury pre-election report. Public funding per student was planned to fall around 2.3 percent p.a. in real terms. Whatever the merits of this cut in funding for the fiscal position, it would put further pressure on the tertiary institutions. The implication was that student fees would rise.

The Todd Committee was split over the appropriate level of student fees. Four members supported Option A, which would have lifted the average student fee to 25 percent of average tertiary costs per student (compared to 20 percent at the time), and four supported Option B, which would have raised the ratio to 50 percent, but offered increased support to Maori and low-income people as an offset. Two committee members rejected both options, favouring the status quo or even lower fees.

To explain Option B—the high-fee alternative—we need to go back to the commercialist approach to policy in which by a sleight of hand the university's education activities were converted into mere tertiary training. Human capital theory treats expenditure on education as if it is an investment that enhances the student's earning power in the long run. The commercial logic, then, is that people make private investment decisions about their education on the basis of the return their decisions obtain. The best outcome is if they make the decision themselves, taking all spending and returns into consideration. There should be no public subsidies to distort their decisions. The

Todd report pursues the human capital model as its integrating idea.

Does it matter if the return on education is low? There is a tricky point here. If the return of tertiary training is low, then people will not invest in it, but do other things with their time and money. That would—so the approach would argue—be a better allocation of resources, and ultimately the economy would be better off.

Many would think that a surprising result, because they see tertiary education having a broader impact on the economy, even if we ignore the merit good qualities FitzGerald drew attention to over a century ago. Economists have been unable to identify the relation between university activities and economic growth with any precision. Perhaps many of the benefits from tertiary training are captured by producers in higher productivity and lower costs, or by consumers in lower prices and new products, rather than by the graduates themselves obtaining a higher income as a result of the education and training they have undertaken. Perhaps not, and all the long-run benefit goes to the student in higher income. We just do not know. However, in so far as these former effects exist—economists call them 'externalities'—they invalidate the conclusion drawn from the commercialist analysis that if there is no private return on getting tertiary training, then it is not in the nation's interest to proceed with it.

There is a complication to human capital theory. Consider what we might call 'human cattle theory'. Suppose a bovine student went to university, obtained a degree, and as a result of that degree enhanced her subsequent earning power in terms of higher milk production. The tax liability of this cow would differ from that of a human student. The costs of obtaining the degree would be tax-deductible. Since in her student years she would make a loss from her training expenses, and from the costs of being fed, watered, and housed, there would build up a tax credit over the years during which she obtained her qualification. Thus immediately out of university the cow would pay no tax on her earnings, until the tax credit was exhausted. This happens for real cattle, but not for human students. Surely, according to human capital theory, expenses incurred in obtaining the capital increment should be deducted for tax purposes?

There is another difference between cattle and students. Farmers are able to raise a higher proportion of the value of the beast as a loan from the private financial system than human students can raise on their human capital. Why? Bankers can own cattle, but because of anti-slavery laws they cannot own people. This restriction represents an important distortion in the labour market, which severely limits the usefulness of human capital theory. There is much to be learned from the human capital model as an intellectual exercise, and it has some relevance to the policy issues. But to concentrate on the approach without a robust understanding of its limitations is likely to play into the hands of the commercialisers and privatisers. In summary, the human cattle theory demonstrates there are serious limitations to the human capital theory. Perhaps the application of human capital theory contains a bit of bull.

ALTERNATIVES TO THE TODD REPORT

Any alternative need not entirely abandon human capital theory or the commercialist analysis. Each provides useful insights to such issues as the utilisation of resources, the regulation of institutions, and the way people behave in economic situations. But making use of an approach is not to adopt it uncritically and wholeheartedly.

When I was reviewing the classic Fraser–Beeby statement on educational opportunity and the goals of the education system, I puzzled over the following. Why should some education—such as primary and secondary schooling—be provided without charge, while for other levels there are fees (pre-school and tertiary education)?

Despite its universalism, the statement has also to be read in an historical context. With one exception, the full text refers only to primary and secondary education. The tenor of the argument is that secondary education should be as readily available as primary education. The Fraser–Beeby statement seemed to be saying that each New Zealander had an educational entitlement—a right to obtain a certain education. Up to 1940 it was only to primary schooling, but henceforth it would be secondary schooling. In a later age a society might want to extend that entitlement. How much to extend it by will be a function of the age and national circumstances as well as of the personal situation and circumstances of the individual involved.

Fraser and Beeby would certainly say that today every pre-schooler had a right to appropriate pre-school education. What would they say about tertiary education? My guess is that they would have expected—in today's circumstances—that an appropriate free education would have been, say, three full-time years after secondary school.

Let us tackle the issue from a slightly different perspective, by coming to it from the commercialist end. If the Todd committee argued that tertiary students should pay 25 or 50 percent of the cost of their tertiary training, is it not equally logical to apply this rule to primary and secondary schooling as well? Lockwood Smith, the Minister of Education, when asked why he favoured charging for tertiary training but not secondary schooling, replied that secondary schooling was compulsory. That is not entirely true: after the age of 17, a student has the choice of staying on or leaving. Similarly, parents are not obliged to send a child to primary school before the age of 7. Perhaps school students outside the 7–17 age range may one day be charged full fees.

A distinction one might make between secondary and tertiary education is that the student has a much greater degree of choice at the tertiary level. This is not just whether they go or not, but also which institutions to attend and which courses to take. In practical terms, this suggests that some sort of student charge at tertiary level might be appropriate, so that students will take resource consequences into account when they are making their decisions.

But how high should such a charge be? The commercialist response is 100 percent. However, a rate a little below the current 20 percent gives the government a fair return on its investment in tertiary education. (Many rich countries charge considerably less than 20 percent.) There is an interesting philosophical twist to this approach. It allocates the benefits from tertiary education to those involved, keeping only enough back for the state to pay for its investment. In contrast, the high-fee approach allocates the benefits from tertiary education to the state, keeping only enough back for the students to pay for their investment. Thus the commercialisers are centralists exploiting the state monopoly, while the alternative approach of the state merely covering its investment outlays is closer to a minimalist state and a maximalist private sector.

Human capital markets work most imperfectly—much more imperfectly than financial ones. A resolution of the imperfection is for the state to fund tertiary education, at least in part, because it has the monopoly power to tax, and hence to recover its investment. However, should the state try to maximise the return on its investment, minimising the return to the person, or should it take a fair return? Putting it this way, we are close to questions that are at the heart of a liberal democracy. The state, it can be argued, should use any monopoly powers it may have beneficently rather than for the state's benefit, and hence should not exploit potential university graduates. In summary, an entitlement approach to tertiary education would provide that all citizens have a right to a certain amount of low-cost education after they have finished their secondary schooling. The state contribution to the training costs should not be less than the return it will, on average, obtain from the elevated earnings and tax revenue from the training.

CONCLUSION

The argument has been that the principle of commercialism has been applied to the universities, but at the expense of the central non-commercial objectives which are at the heart of the activities of a genuine university. This is not to reject all aspects of the commercialist approach. Some of its elements are valuable for understanding how tertiary training works and developing policy prescriptions. But it is a limited approach, and it needs to be imbedded in a broader framework.

The tertiary education debate has accepted large parts of the commercialist model. It is extremely rare to see the underlying principles of the model challenged. Rather, the model tends to be modified by the addition of other aspects, such as equity. Yet, as this chapter has illustrated, the economic theory underpinning the commercialist model can be directly challenged, using good economic analysis.

Why was the commercialist model so popular among policy makers? Butterworth and Tarling present a picture in which ideologues captured the policy high ground and imposed their will. But it should be acknowledged that the approach did pragmatically face up to issues that the universities had avoided, such as internal reform and fiscal pressures.

Curiously, those who would reform the university system in a commercialist direction—Treasury and other officials, the main ministers involved, and most of the Cabinet—were themselves university graduates, mainly from New Zealand universities. Thus the failure to see the distinctive role of a university in a democratic society, to distinguish education from training, or to recognise educational entitlements, came from alumni of New Zealand universities.

Butterworth and Tarling describe the Fourth Labour government as anti-intellectual, but there is an alternative explanation that focuses on policy rather than personality. Collectively the government adopted a policy of commercialism, and that policy was fundamentally anti-intellectual because it pursues no higher goal than material prosperity. As FitzGerald reminds us, material prosperity is no mean achievement, but it is not the ultimate goal of civilisation.

The tertiary sector reforms remain incomplete. The situation—partial commercialisation—is inherently unstable. The universities have successfully resisted some of the encroachments on academic freedom, and may yet reverse some others. But their long-term funding arrangements remain unresolved. The balance between public, student, and business contributions would appear especially unstable. Similarly the balance between research and teaching is unresolved. Do universities do research, or do they just train potential researchers?

In the interim New Zealand universities might reflect that they failed miserably to inculcate into their graduates the values they claim to stand for—not the Watts report objectives of the universities' role in a knowledge-based society and an international economy, but those of liberal education, with an accompanying training element, contributing not only to the commercial ends of society but to its wider ends too. One cannot help wondering whether perhaps, as the Reichel–Tate report shrewdly assessed seventy years ago, New Zealand's university system is still dominated by the awarding of degrees and is still failing in its provision of education.

Appendix: A Question of Ownership

In 1995 the New Zealand Vice-Chancellors' Committee commissioned Graham Scott, a retired Treasury secretary, to write a 'thoughtful essay' concentrating on the ownership issue and the related topic of governance. His response (written with Simon Smelt, an ex-Treasury official who had been involved in some of the Treasury papers discussed elsewhere in the book) is yet another example of the commercialist approach.[1] It is explored here because it raises interesting questions as to the nature of 'ownership' in the public sector.

Surprisingly perhaps, the concept of 'ownership' is not usually defined in most economic dictionaries. A standard notion from the law and economic literature is that ownership involves the right to use, to transform, and to alienate (i.e. sell the rights to another party). Very often the putative owner has only some of these rights. For instance, a land owner might be restricted in the use of the land by planning laws, and in the transformation of the building by the heritage laws, while there may be some caveat on the title which prevents its sale (e.g. if it must be left to the eldest son).

However the New Zealand government has a definition: 'ownership interest . . . means a person controls all the uses and potential uses of a resource (subject to contractual obligations, such as leases, and any overriding laws and regulations).'[2] As the source indicates, the meaning was established as a part of the Crown's negotiations with the Maori over Treaty of Waitangi claims. This definition, plus those for 'use interest', 'value interest', and 'regulatory interest', are required to distinguish some of the complications of the various classical Maori property rights. The Crown's definition of 'ownership' is an encompassing one, not too different in spirit from that of the one based on the law and economics literature.

Now the Scott–Smelt report does not define ownership, but merely introduces the notion of 'ownership interest', although it does say that 'with regard to its ownership interests, [the report's] emphasis is primarily on containing the financial risk of the Crown and improving performance'.[3] We saw this vagueness in other reports, where sometimes it reflected a lack of rigour, sometimes a hidden agenda. Presumably, until the writers are more explicit, we must assume that by 'ownership' they mean the total control of the above Crown definition.

The report arose out of a long dispute between the government and the universities over the proposal to place a capital charge on the physical and financial assets of the universities, as is done for other government agencies. (The universities had argued—among other things—that there was some ambiguity as to whether their assets were owned by the government.) It is the ownership of these disputed assets, and the consequences of that ownership, that the Scott–Smelt report focused on. In doing so, they define the university in terms of the balance sheet in which those assets appear.

THE HEALTH SECTOR'S ASSETS

The experience of the health sector warns against a focus on financial balance sheets. During the debate on the possible range of reforms it was argued that the area health boards should corporatise their properties (the land and the physical buildings of the hospital) by placing them into a limited liability company which would be run on commercial lines including, no doubt, long-term lease of some or all of them back to the boards (although the boards would be free to lease from other property owners too).[4]

There were a number of subtle notions behind this proposal, one of which is particularly relevant to the universities. A health service is not the same thing as the properties which it occupies. In practice the buildings are a means to an end, even though often in the public perception those properties define the health service. Separating the two notions will be a long-term process, but until the public, the politicians, and the public servants can readily distinguish service delivery from buildings, health policy is going to be distorted. In the old regime secondary health-care services were dominated by the hospital building program, often at great cost to the taxpayer and with inefficiency of service delivery. Separating the property activities of the area health board from the service delivery, and requiring them to be run on commercial, rather than sentimental, principles would have addressed both these issues.

Ironically, the implemented health reforms have probably worsened the service delivery aspect. Certainly now the CHE (hospital) properties are run on more commercial principles, but they continue to dominate the balance sheet of the CHEs, concentrating the mind of the board members (who have very little expertise in health care anyway) on the physical assets and not on service delivery.

Conceptually, it is quite easy to envisage a secondary health-care service delivery system in which property plays a minor role. Most people would characterise their primary health-care service by the people they interact with—the nurses and general practitioners. Certainly they are housed, but the surgery or clinic is not typically the image that comes to mind. The video image of secondary care is frequently the hospital building.

THE UNIVERSITY BALANCE SHEET

Similarly the university is not the same thing as the buildings it occupies. Plato's Academy at Athens, which has had an influence on the political vision underlying the commercialist strategy, did not have any buildings of its own. While it may be impracticable in today's conditions to have a university without some buildings, the policies towards the buildings should not dominate university policy, just as we should not confuse the buildings of a hospital with secondary health care. Nevertheless, the Scott–Smelt report is riddled with this confusion.

Suppose we try to construct a complete balance sheet, rather than the one required under the Public Finance Act, which underpins the Scott–Smelt report. The full university balance sheet would include among its assets the buildings and other properties the university possesses, plus equipment and library resources, plus the market value of patent and similar intellectual property rights and so on, which already appear in the balance sheets required under the Public Finance Act. But the full list of assets would also include the human capital of the university, its work-in-progress, and its reputation, each of which is intangible.

There are a number of reasons why these items are not included in the conventional balance sheet. For one thing, they are not items of explicit interest to a commercialist strategy (not least because they challenge the premises it is based upon). For another, there is the conceptual difficulty of their definition and measurement. Here we sketch their central notions.

The human capital asset in the full balance sheet reflects the value of all the people that the university employs. The valuation of this asset is not easy, but it probably amounts to five to ten times the total market value of the physical capital. It should be noted that the value of the human capital may exceed the sum of the individual values, when there are synergies (or externalities) between the people involved. (Thus a department of economics can be more valuable than the total of the individual human capital of each economist if they worked by themselves.)

The work-in-progress asset covers research in progress, the teaching preparation, but by far the largest component is the value of the university to the students. The reason they may be thought as work-in-progress is because if for any reason the university were to terminate instantaneously, many students would be properly aggrieved because the effort they had put into obtaining a qualification would be sharply reduced in value. One can only guess at the value of the work-in-progress asset, but it probably exceeds that of the human capital asset by a factor of two or so.

The reputation of a university is a key element in its balance sheet, based upon its record, including the quality of its graduates, its degrees, and its research, as perceived by the relevant communities, including the overseas academy and potential staff and student recruits. It may be partly institutionalised in the entitlement to be called a university, but people are able to discriminate between the various universities, and between the various departments and specific activities of particular universities. This is obviously the most intangible item on the full balance sheet, but it affects the performance of the university (e.g. who it can recruit), and its costs (e.g. readiness to be recruited reduces the costs of appointment, and the staffer or student may come at a lower salary or maintenance costs).

It will be observed that while the precise magnitudes are unclear, there can be no doubt that the value of the physical assets in the balance sheet is only a small proportion—less than a twentieth—of the total value. Yet the commercialist solution is to focus almost exclusively on the physical assets.

This is nicely captured in the inadequate discussion in the Scott–Smelt report on the infrequency of profit-oriented successful universities.[5] A for-profit institution is not going to work if the majority of the institution's assets are not profit-generating, a point evident to all but those who insist on a narrow commercialist framework. Scott and Smelt have been captured by the commer-cialist paradigm, which defines a business in terms of its financial balance sheet, which is of considerable importance to the shareholders and one of a number of useful management tools, but which does not encompass the totality of the activity of a firm, and even less the totality of a tertiary education establishment.

WHO 'OWNS' THE UNIVERSITY?

It can be argued that most of the other assets in the full balance sheet (as distinct from the limited financial business sheet) are owned by someone else. For instance, the human capital and the work-in-progress are owned by the staff and students. That is only partly true in so far as the human capital of a university exceeds the value of the individual components, and there is also a sense that much work-in-progress is not entirely held by the individual doing it (course preparation may be much less valuable to the teacher if the university terminates).

But there is a more fundamental issue in the prior question of what does 'ownership' mean in the context of a university. Unfortunately the Scott–Smelt report does not explore this issue, assuming that the commercialist solution of ownership of the physical assets is equivalent to the 'ownership' of the university. The full balance sheet approach indicates that to jump to this conclusion is a fallacy.

A simple answer to the question of who owns the university is that all the stakeholders represented in the full balance sheet have some claims to 'ownership'. No single stakeholder nor group of stakeholders can claim to be *the* owner, except in the context of a particular political and economic environment.

The Scott–Smelt report makes the case that, in the context of a commercialist totalitarian public framework, the 'ownership' is determined solely by the university's relationship with the government (the Crown). Before describing the alternative of a liberal democracy, it is worth exploring the details of such an arrangement. The report is vague on these details, as was the corporatisation of state-owned enterprises at the same stage of development. But the commercialist logic in each case was plain, and its conclusion predictable.

The universities were to be turned into legal entities called trusts. The current physical and other assets of the universities, which appear in the Crown accounts as owned by the Crown, were to be transferred to the trusts, probably in exchange for debt and equity (as occurred for the corporatisation of trading enterprises and hospitals). The boards of the Trusts were to be appointed by the Crown (i.e. the government) and were to be responsible for the management of the universities to the Crown. Ominously, the Scott–Smelt report says that 'the Crown may meet its concerns that the incentives of the governing body may not align well with its own interests . . . by retaining the ability to nominate and dismiss some members of the body.'[6] In so far as the government has a commercialist totalitarian philosophy, it would be expected to mainly make business appointments to the university boards (as it did for CHEs).

Even ignoring the inappropriateness of having the government appoint the managers of a university (unacceptable in a liberal democracy, although not in a totalitarian state), one may ask about the efficiency of this management regime. The practice of corporatisation has been to appoint to boards people who have little competence in the activities in which the institution is involved, as has occurred with the RHAs and the CHEs in the health reforms. The justification for this has been the theory of the generic manager, which is an integral part of the philosophy of commercialism.

Recall that the assets not on the commercial balance sheet—the human capital, the work-in-progress, and the reputation—are far more important to a university than the assets which are there—the physical assets. To repeat the theme of the appendix to Chapter 10, the way in which the financial goals are defined and measured will have a substantial influence on the outcome. By focusing on the items that are in the commercial balance sheet, the boards will damage the management, and hence the quality and quantity of the other items. The result would be a deterioration in the efficiency and the efficacy of the university. (For instance, more would have to be paid to recruit staff following the deterioration in its reputation, there would be losses of synergies, and so on.) More generally there is no certainty that commercialist solutions will guarantee economic resource efficiency, even under the new goal (for commercialist strategies usually redefine the goal of the entity). It is only in select situations—typically where production conditions, goals, and markets conform to the standard economic assumptions—that some sort of efficiency will be attained (Chapter 2). Those conditions do not apply to universities.

A liberal democrat cannot ignore the political implications of the arrangements. Even if the appointments to these boards exclude, say, economic hotheads with their own political agendas, it will be practically impossible to prevent the boards from interfering in the academic activities of the university, since they will be responsible for the allocation of resources within the university and probably for the staffing. And since those appointments will be dominated by generic managers, they will bias the university teaching in that direction.

Unfortunately the Scott–Smelt report does not address this issue. Indeed at one point it slips up when it defines 'academic freedom (that is, individuals' freedom to express views on the subject they are assigned to teach and on their research topics). . . .'[7] Academics will bridle, since the passive construction nicely avoids saying who is to do the assigning. Faculty in a collegial university discuss and agree to the course program they teach. But the report's writers were so anxious to use a commercialist framework that they presented an uncomfortably narrow definition of academic freedom.

Contrast the ways that knowledge is held in the institutions of a traditional society. Traditionally knowledge was held hierarchically, the structure headed by high priests who controlled what was considered legitimate knowledge in the strata below. This may well be an appropriate means of organising knowledge in some of the institutions of a modern society—in a government department such as Treasury. Although universities have never been fully able to escape the hierarchy of knowledge, their shift over the years to a collegial structure reflects a more general shift in society towards knowledge being held collectively (horizontally), so that there are no persons or selected groups who by their status control access to it. The proposals in the Scott–Smelt report would further undermine the collegial university in favour of the hierarchical one, in an atavistic return to the power and structures of the traditional approach to knowledge.

In the end the financial balance sheet reflects a way of thinking about an economic activity, but it is not the only way of doing so. Often it is not the best way of doing so—certainly not for universities.

14

Science Policy

SCIENCE INTERFACES WITH BROAD ECONOMIC POLICY BECAUSE IT USES public resources and impacts on industrial policy. But even though the science community did not always help itself, Treasury's approach was fundamentally anti-science. There is an instructive article by a Treasury official who wrote:

> One leading United States researcher [Edward Mansfield][1] in this field has estimated that of the total cost of product innovation in United States industry, 40% on average is incurred for tooling and in design and construction of manufacturing facilities and 15% for manufacturing and marketing start up. In some industries only a small percentage of significant advances is estimated to be a direct outgrowth of corporate R&D [Research and Development] (17% in the railroad industry and 17% in housing). Because R&D is part of the investment package which achieves change, attention should therefore be primarily focused on conditions in the economy which will achieve efficient decisions on investment rather than R&D alone.[2]

The last sentence seriously misrepresents Mansfield's position, whose policy position is almost exactly the opposite. Scientist David Penny described the slip as 'an elementary form of deceit, using a quote from a recognised authority and then appending a different conclusion without indicating the end of the quote.'[3] It is more likely that the last sentence was meant to be unconnected to the rest of the paragraph, and express the official's own view. Even so, one is left with the uneasy feeling that Treasury colleagues did not identify the error because they did not notice that an authoritative overseas view conflicted with their own.

Penny went on to raise an issue which at first seems to contradict the argument that Treasury was dominated by the Chicago economists' analysis. Treasury analysis used a British economist, M. F. G. Scott, and neglected Americans Edward Dennison and Mansfield. Penny comments:

> The combined number of citations for 1983 and 1984 are Dennison 152, Mansfield 277, and Scott 16. . . . What (this) does show is that New Zealand is basing its R&D policy on a minority view, and neglecting the conclusions of the established workers in the field.[4]

Why did Treasury go to an unknown British source in favour of top-level American ones? The most likely explanation is they could not find a better one consistent with their tight prior. While Chicago economists have made some contributions in the area, there does not seem to be a major work that tackles the issues Scott and Mansfield were concerned about. The most obvious reason why the New Right economists seem not to have pursued R&D policy with any fervour is that it may suggest that their own research program is an anomaly in their own terms.

This inconsistency can be observed by considering the pile of articles supplied to the Beattie Working Party on Science and Technology by Treasury. It included a number of American ones whose author(s) acknowledged that their research had been made possible by funding from their National Science Foundation, or a similar funding body. This is not surprising, for US government funds are used extensively to promote public interest economic and other research. Without them, American economics would be the poorer and less interesting.

However, given that Treasury was arguing to the Beattie Committee, and elsewhere, that there should be no public funding of such economic and other research in New Zealand, one was left wondering what their attitude was to the funding of public interest research by the US government. There is, of course, no inconsistency in a government committed to the public interest nevertheless funding research the results of which may be interpreted as being opposed to such public funding. If the New Zealand Treasury had been the US Treasury, it would have refused to fund the research on which the New Zealand Treasury depended. Treasury's science policy was fraught with contradictions like this.

231

TOWARDS THE COMMERCIALISATION OF SCIENCE

Scientists also had their inconsistencies, when it came to the economics of science policy. Rather than using the scientific approach to assess the role of science, the tendency has been to grab convenient, but hardly secure, arguments and research findings which justify policy prejudices. By the usual scientific standards there is not a convincing case that increased expenditure on science will inevitably increase economic output of an economy. There is a lot of fragmentary evidence which makes this a plausible hypothesis, subject to numerous caveats, but the details of any causal mechanism are unclear, with insufficient evidence to trace each step.

Some scientists claimed Robert Solow's Nobel Prize work proved that research and development caused economic growth. But Solow's contribution to economics is much wider than the empirical estimation of the neoclassical production function. Moreover, while his research shows that economic growth cannot be wholly explained by increases in the stock of capital and labour hours worked, the remainder Solow attributed to 'technical change . . . a shorthand expression for *any kind of shift* in the production function. Thus slowdowns, speedups, improvements in the education of the labour force, and all sorts of things will appear as "technical change"' (italics in the original).[5] Subsequent work by Dennison has refined knowledge of this residual, but nevertheless it remains a 'coefficient of ignorance'.[6]

In contrast to this careful work overseas, the New Zealand tendency has been to make wild claims of the efficacy of (apparently all) scientific research in promoting economic growth. A backlash was inevitable. If it is argued that research and development (R&D) plays a similar role in economic performance as does capital, why then should not R&D be treated the same as capital investment for policy purposes? In particular, government does not subsidise most investment, even though it acknowledges that it generates economic progress. Should government treat R&D any differently? So Treasury's push towards the commercialisation of R&D in the 1980s led to a mutually uncomprehending dialogue between its own officials and the scientific community.

THE CHARACTERISTICS OF SCIENCE AND R&D

Science does not always have a commercial purpose. Some science is pursued for similar reasons to the reasons people pursue the arts. The intellectual and spiritual contributions of science lift us beyond that which the material world offers. With very few exceptions, we accept that the arts are valuable in their own right, if not commercially fundable. There are some areas in science like that too.

Second, sometimes the scientific research may not be a simple output, but a joint product, as when teachers feel compelled to research in order to keep up their teaching quality. The value of the research may be the improving of the scientific literacy and competence of the students rather than the research findings themselves.

Third, the client may not be able to pay for the work. Research on the environment may be most valued by yet-unborn generations. Poverty research can hardly be funded by the destitute.

Fourth, the client may have little competence in judging the need for research. Officials and politicians bemoan the shortage of hard evidence when they are under the pressure of policy making, but are unable to make the simple connection that the shortage is a consequence of their failure to fund the research in the past. Officials can be unbelievably short-sighted. Some years ago I regularly saw the head of a departmental research unit about its funding a research program in what is still a key policy area. The director only ever wanted to discuss the problems which had bothered his minister that morning. No research program ever developed.

But even the far-sighted may not predict all our future needs. Who a dozen years ago would have argued the possibility of a major epidemic as a justification for maintaining some of the research programs which are now fully committed to AIDS investigation? Some research competence has to be maintained for events which we are unable to foresee, just as a gene pool contains genes not in full use, but which may enable the species to adapt to an unexpected change in its environment.

Closely related to the above issues is that of political interference. Not all research is seen as politically sensitive, but particularly in the social, medical, and environmental sciences some can be acutely so. Ultimately science is about the possibility of creating revolutions in the way we think and what we do, something which politicians and officials are not enthusiastic about. Faced with the threat of the new, most will attempt to repress its source.

Yet a short time later they, or the next generation of politicians, will need and applaud the research findings.

In addition to the peculiarities of the demand for science, there are also some special features about the characteristics of the scientific process which mean that it is not simply analogous to the usual commercial processes.

Much of science is about uncertainty, not risk. These terms have quite distinct meanings in economics, but unfortunately they are often used interchangeably in the New Zealand science debate, even by some economists. Risk refers to an event which has a reasonably well-defined probability distribution. Uncertainty refers to an event which does not have such a well-defined probability distribution. The commercial world has evolved well-tried procedures for investing in risky events. Uncertainty requires quite different strategies—minimum regret rules are common—which are not handled at all well in commerce. It is no accident that so-called 'acts of God' are uninsurable.

There is also the problem of appropriability, the degree to which benefits of a piece of work can be captured—or sufficiently captured—by the producer or creator. One has the right to sell the commodities one produces, a feature which is so common in a market society that it is noticed only in the breach. In creative areas it is not always possible to ensure that the creator is the beneficiary. Intellectual property right laws are designed to meet some cases, but the scientific method with its emphasis on open publication is inconsistent with the commercial approach. Moreover, while ideas are not patentable, they can be immensely valuable to society. (I am paying no royalty for the use here of the concept of appropriability.) How then is society to ensure there is a sufficient supply of ideas? The commodity solution is simply not viable. Externalities may be a major feature of R&D.

We know little about how the benefits of R&D get transferred. Economists have so much trouble tracing the economic impact of R&D because it does not behave like ordinary investment. Studies which treat scientific knowledge like capital are very limited. The point is illustrated by Treasury's practice of importing overseas economic research into its economic policy making, without any intermediation from a local research process, which it discouraged by withdrawing public funding and tightly controlling consultancy work. Their view seemed to be that there were economic truths—independent of time, institution, culture, and location—which could be easily applied for our economic policy purposes. (They ended up with a theory which was peculiarly late-twentieth-century, raw capitalist, New Right, American.) Policy makers do not usually have research skills and experience, and if the research establishment had not been so gutted by the funding cutback, there would now be a lot of work showing the inadequacy of the resulting policy recommendations. Very often the imported technology has been already obsolete and rejected by the majority of the profession. The conclusion from the economics experience, which will be no surprise to scientists, is that an effective 'importation of technology for domestic applications' strategy, be it by firm or nation, still requires a high degree of local scientific competence. It is not obvious how to maintain this without an ongoing research program.

An excellent example of the misunderstanding of an imported idea is the application of 'contestability' to scientific research. The term has a well-defined meaning in economics. Basically, it refers to the situation where a market is under effective competitive threat from hit-and-run operators.[7] However, the term is frequently used loosely in public discussion without much reference to this rigorous notion. The idea that an ecology research group could be kept efficient by the threat of another research team appearing from nowhere, grabbing a few contracts, and then disappearing off to contest—say—the market for meteorological research is absurd. It may be argued that it does not matter that the economist's term is being abused. But that research is not contestable (in the rigorous sense) tells us a lot about why proposals for contestability (in the sloppy sense) are foolish.

A common feature of an industry which can make it noncontestable is capital specificity. That has both advantages (more specialised capital is likely to be more productive) and disadvantages (such capital can rarely be transferred profitably elsewhere). Thus, new entrants to an industry face higher costs than incumbent firms, while the latter find it expensive to leave the industry. In such cases the conditions for contestability do not apply. For instance, steel production is not particularly contestable; a steel mill cannot be easily converted into some other equally productive industrial plant. Although the illustrations apply to physical capital, they apply equally to human capital and, in the case of research, to the scientific skills and experi-

ences in the researchers. Human capital can be highly specific—
an economist cannot easily be converted into an ecologist, or
vice versa.

The rigorous notion of contestability is exactly the wrong notion to apply to this research process. There may well be a case
for regular assessments of each research unit's performance, with
the realistic possibility that if output and standards are too low or
the research area is no longer a priority then the unit may be cut
back or abandoned. There may be a case for some competition at
the margin for research funds. But the logic does not point to
contestability in research in any meaningful sense of the term.

Given all these complexities it is not surprising that
commercialisation of R&D is not a comprehensive solution to the
policy problem of sustaining the right level of progress of scientific and industrial knowledge. It is not even clear that R&D can
be treated as a single entity. Although some scientific endeavour
can operate under commercial conditions—the development of
pharmaceuticals is an obvious case—much cannot, including that
which is described as 'fundamental science'. But even dividing
scientific endeavour into two categories does not answer the crucial question—how much should the government spend on non-
commercial science activity?

THE SCIENCE REFORMS

The new structure had three characteristic features. There was a
policy-advising Ministry of Research, Science and Technology
(MRST, pronounced 'morst'), a funding Foundation of Research,
Science and Technology (FRST, pronounced 'forst'), and a number of state-owned providers called Crown research institutes
(CRIs, sometimes pronounced 'crises'), which are expected to be
run on business lines. The research funds are 'contestable', which
in this context means that private sector researchers can also seek
the funds, although the vast majority have gone to publicly
owned agencies (as would be expected if contestability did not
really apply).

In principle the funding is for 'public good research', but in
spite of a lot of effort it has proved difficult to define what that
means.[8] Obviously the intention is that which can be commercially funded is not to be publicly funded, but thereafter the no-

tion becomes vague. Instructively, the original scheme has had its rules changed, in order to fund 'fundamental research' and 'excellence' through the Marsden fund.

How to assess the success of the reforms? Unfortunately, research has such a long lead time that no definitive answer can be given after less than a decade since the reforms were initiated. It can be reported that there has been considerable rationalisation in establishments, presumably under the pressure to use capital efficiently (because CRIs have debt and equity servicing commitments). There have also been redundancies, sometimes involving scientists of considerable excellence, some of whom have been gratefully hired by foreign research institutions. The pattern of funding has changed. There is less funding of pastoral-related research, for the old system was not responding quickly enough to the new diversified economic structure.

On the downside, few of the CRIs are making profits (perhaps inevitably given that for the majority their sole funder is FRST, which is likely to use its monopsonistic position to squeeze profits). One CRI, the Institute of Social Research, went out of business before it went bankrupt. There is widespread unrest among the science community. A self-responding sample of scientists surveyed by the New Zealand Association of Scientists in 1994 thought on the whole that there had been a deterioration in international regard for New Zealand science, a reduction in the ability to attract and retain good scientists, and inferior access to facilities, support staff, and other working conditions as a result of the reforms. In summary, they thought there had been a decline in good science and a rise in bad science.[9]

Perhaps in a couple of decades we will have a better idea of whether the reforms have been successful or disastrous. As like as not, there will be further policy changes in the interim, which will make judgement about the earlier ones difficult. (Assessing the significance of a change is partly a question of judgement too. Is the Marsden fund a backdown or a progressive development?) One is struck, however, that they are not as evidently a disaster as the health reforms, although there are parallels.

One reason for the difference is that despite the upheavals, scientists have remained largely in control of MRST, FRST, and the running of the CRIs, unlike the generic management takeover in the health reforms. One might argue that the science sector is somewhat more under scientist capture than health is under medical capture. But is scientist capture worse than, say, Treasury capture?

FUNDING ACCOUNTABILITY AND CONTROL

Therein lies a deeper worry. Today the government is much more able to control the disposition of research resources, and hence influence what is researched upon and even what conclusions are reached. In the old days funding disappeared into the maw of the Department of Scientific and Industrial Research, where mysterious decisions were made about what it was to be spent on. Now the allocation is more transparent. However, that same accountability gives the government greater control over the direction of research, an effect reinforced by the pooling of university research into the FRST fund.

It is highly unlikely that this would lead to an episode like Lysenkoism in the Soviet Union, where a nutty theory was pushed at the behest of Stalin, doing considerable damage to the scientific community and to Soviet agriculture. However, if a sufficiently strong minister were to have some odd scientific theory, he or she could promote it through the various direction, funding, and appointment mechanisms.

An indication of this possibility arises in a speech by the Minister of Science in 1996, which a newspaper summarised as 'Avoid policy, Upton warns scientists'.[10] He said: 'Scientists should think carefully before they enter [climate change] policy debate because the move from scientific analysis to policy advocacy can be fraught with risks. . . . I am not saying scientists should become political eunuchs. But they must understand that their policy views are of no greater importance than anyone else's.' Perhaps one should pay as much attention to taxi drivers, or even politicians and Treasury, on the response to greenhouse warming (if it exists). There is a—probably unintentional—hint of menace in the minister's speech.

Social scientists are even more exposed. They are in much the same predicament as, the literary community was when it was uncertain how much it should protest against changes to the state literary fund, since protesters were likely to be omitted from funding allocations. This is not the place to traverse the story of political interference in social science research in New Zealand, a tale which goes back at least six decades. Nevertheless, a government committed to, say, commercialist economic principles and antagonistic to alternative accounts of the economy now has a further means of controlling the economics profession and the direction of the development of economic analysis in New Zealand, through its research policy (in addition to the direct funding of consultancy, and its own substantial outlays on policy advice). The accountability of commercialism is not that of a liberal society.

Towards an Alternative

Towards an Alternative

INITIALLY THERE WAS SOME SUCCESSFUL APPLICATION OF COMMERCIAL principles, especially to standard business activities. More recently their application to activities which are not essentially business—such as those described in this study—has led to inefficiency, disaster, chaos, and retreat. A policy based on commercialism has probably run its course. There will be some attempts to further it—such as privatisation of the water supply and some other government assets. There will be ideologists who will continue to parrot its nostrums, as will committed advocates who are the beneficiaries of commercialisation (such as the Business Roundtable and its acolytes), and consultants and policy advisers who like old dogs cannot learn new tricks. One is less confident about what will replace the commercialist policy paradigm. Hopefully it will be a more pragmatic approach, with its economic analysis based more in the centre of economics than the New Right extremism. Yet New Zealand policy makers were readily seduced by current fashions, and may be again.

Blitzkriegs are likely to become exceptions. Because the strategy is better understood, resistance will be more effective. Moreover, proportional representation has changed the operating context. It is not so much that the composition of Parliament will better reflect the aspirations and diversity of the voters. The hegemony of a Cabinet-dominated single-party government has been ended. In future at least two caucuses, who will compete against one another in other arenas, will have to be consulted in order to introduce policy.

Yet this study is not merely a history of policies that are becoming obsolete. It has described features of the policy process that are endemic in New Zealand, and are likely to remain so unless they are addressed. It is to these, and the development of alternative policy process, that this chapter is devoted. Here is a set of alternatives to Roger Douglas's blitzkrieg principles.

DON'T PANIC

At the beginning the Labour government confused a currency crisis, which is a short-term shortage of foreign exchange, with an economic crisis, which is a long-term structural issue. It suited the philosopher-kings not to make this distinction, but to use the air of crisis to promote their policies. The crisis strategy was repeated after the 1990 election, but with allegations of a 'budget blowout'.

Lange revelled in crisis management, so much so that he sometimes precipitated one, as in the revoking of the flat tax proposal and in foreign policy.[1] Some of his colleagues and advisers were more prone to lose their heads under pressure.

They would all have done well to have read a pamphlet by Michael Jensen and William Meckling, whose work was used to develop and justify some of the economic reforms, especially about corporate affairs, privatisation, and securities law. Published by an Australian New Right think-tank, the essay argues that people with policy agendas often claim crises to justify the adoption of their proposed courses of action.

> As entrepreneurs, politicians employ marketing strategies just as entrepreneurs do in the private economy. One such strategy in the political sector is the practice of creating crises or, more accurately, the impression of crises, which demand government action to save us all from the impending disaster. The creation of crises is an old political stratagem for turning contingencies into a resource for accumulating force in the government. In recent times, politicians in the United States have used the crisis ploy as a pretence for expanding their powers in one area after another.[2]

Understanding that 'politicians' is a more encompassing term than just parliamentarians, readers will recognise that this stratagem is exactly what the philosopher-kings pursued. Jensen and Meckling are pessimistic about the arresting 'the trend toward "Leviathan" government',[3] although they would be heartened by what occurred in New Zealand, where it was their side that used the crisis stratagem to increase its power. In some ways the writers foreshadow the strategy of the New Zealand reformers, for their pamphlet is titled *Democracy in Crisis*.

244

POLICY IS ABOUT PROBLEM SOLVING

A computer in *The Hitchhiker's Guide to the Galaxy* worked out that the answer to 'life, the universe, and everything' was '42'. Then it was that no one knew what the question was. Too often a policy is like that answer—none of its advocates are sure what policy problem it is they are dealing with. Very often they do not care, as is nicely captured by Jenny Stewart's story:

> A director of a childcare centre once told me that she found it very difficult to get the authorities in her field to concentrate on the actual problems they were encountering. 'All they want to do is talk about policy,' she complained. 'Policy' is all too often a form of words with little practical content. The current emphasis on 'strategic' statements for public sector bodies diverts attention from the fundamental question—what is the problem, and what, if anything can we do about it?[4]

Nor is it sufficient to resolve only part of a problem and ignore everything else. Recall the story of the seven blind men asked to report on an elephant. Each felt a different part of its body—trunk, tusk, mouth, ear, leg, belly, tail—and each reported that partial experience, which was totally misleading. It would have been even worse had one of the blind men eliminated the other six.

It is easy to shift perspective unintentionally, reversing the order so the policy defines the problem, just as innkeeper Procrustes observed the problem of visitor and bed not matching one another, and interpreted the failure as the guest's. As one of the readers of the draft text of this book commented, 'If commercialisation was the answer, it was the wrong question.'

Never forget the accountancy dictum 'how you score the game, affects the way it is played'. The score card may not have been the original problem, but it can become it—in both senses of the objective of the exercise, and the creator of new policy problems.

USE THEORIES CONSCIOUSLY

In an oft-repeated quotation, John Maynard Keynes said that 'Practical men, who believe themselves to be quite exempt from any intellectual influences, are usually the slaves of some defunct economist.'[5]

But one theory is insufficient. In the social sciences it is rare for one theory, or one discipline, to dominate all others, in the way that, say, physics dominates all our accounts of the physical world. Frequently there are competing theories. What is the policy adviser to do? One strategy is to choose one theory and apply it everywhere, tootling the only policy tune one knows on one's policy whistle. A second is to assess to what extent the different theories give different policy outcomes. In the 1970s there was a constant debate in Treasury between advisers with different perspectives. Policy recommendations were compromises between the different factions, but the compromises meant that the policies were thoroughly tested. When the commercialisers drove out their rivals, the policy advice became much less well worked through, and the policy outcomes poorer.

The central flaw of the commercialisation strategy was that comprehensive policy plans are doomed never to deliver what they promise. Karl Popper called such plans 'historicism'. Historicism is the notion there was some over-arching law that could be used to organise thinking about human society. While he applied it to the analysis of Hegel and Marx about historical processes, his criticism applies equally to the grandiose ideology on which commercialisation was based.

The decade of commercialisation was riddled with ironies, but perhaps the greatest was the New Zealand New Right celebrating Popper's achievements at a Mont Pelerin conference in Christchurch in 1989. Their policies—allowing no possibility of error, no possibility for correction, no self doubt—would have been an anathema to Popper. And while it is true that Popper vigorously attacked the Marxian left, he equally vigorously attacked Plato, from whom the New Right drew so much of their vision, including the belief that it was possible to construct a reality that is fundamentally mental in nature—a world ruled by the tight prior. Plato rejected government by the populace, advocating rule by a philosopher-king elite. The New Right tried to put it into practice in New Zealand.

In the end there is not a lot of difference between the practical politician who claims to have no theories, and the policy adviser who has only one. The Keynes quotation goes on: 'Madmen in authority, who hear voices in the air, are distilling their frenzy from some academic scribbler of a few years back.' Advisers who know only one theory may be likened to mad axemen whose frenzy is to hack at everything with the one tool they wield.

OPINION IS FREE, FACTS ARE SACRED[7]

Goethe wrote that 'facts and theories are natural enemies'. Faced with the conflict, a philosopher-king will abandon or ignore any uncomfortable fact. The Popperian will struggle to reconcile the theory with the facts. Thus C. P. Scott's dictum about journalism applies also to the policy process. One worrying characteristic of the commercialisation advocates was how casual they were with facts, using them like a drunk with a lamppost—for their support rather than their light. Anecdotes abound, as is well illustrated by Richard Prebble's book which relates numerous stories abut his time as Minister for State-Owned Enterprises.[8] He assures the reader they are all true. They must be, for the same stories are told elsewhere—Moscow, Warsaw, London, and Canberra—about their public enterprises.

The carelessness over facts is recalled by Stephen Jay Gould's 'Details are all that matters. God dwells there, and you never get to see Him if you don't struggle to get them right.'[9] And if you don't, you get consumed by the devil. New facts and changing facts need to be incorporated into the analysis, not ignored. As Keynes is alleged to have said, 'I change my mind in the light of new facts. What do you do?'

As a social statistician I have been especially outraged by the carelessness in the use of quantitative methods and data. Goethe also wrote that 'it has been said that figures rule the world. Maybe. I am quite sure that it is figures which show us whether it is being ruled well or badly.' Distorting figures corrupts the process of democratic government.

TOLERATE DIVERSITY, TOLERATE DISSENT

One of the earliest signals of the totalitarianism of the commercialisers was when they began using their political power to eliminate those who disagreed with them. The first people to be shot after the revolution are the public intellectuals, yet—or is it because?—the public intellectuals are the ones most likely to identify the failings in a policy. Popper went a step further when he advised us to be our own sternest critic. If you can see only one answer, 'take this as a sign that you have neither understood the theory, nor the problem it is intended to solve.'[10]

A key change occurred in 1984 when Treasury withdrew from the processes involving cooperation with officials from other departments. In the past, the main function of Treasury, and of officials in other departments, was to stop politicians and others from doing foolish things. They were not always successful, but numerous ill-conceived policies were blocked by well-trained, common-sense, pragmatic officials. A humble task, but one which saved the nation much heartbreak, when they were successful.

When Treasury became as arrogant as other policy advocates, there was nobody to caution against their defective policies. As Frank Hahn wrote, the principal achievement of economic theory has been 'disposing of claims and silly theories'.[11] (In my more melancholy moments, I think that perhaps the job of a policy adviser should simply be to discourage politicians from doing stupid things.)

The pretence of consultation is not sufficient. A legal case in 1993 concerned with Wellington Airport established three requirements for effective consultation, which were the exact opposite of the blitzkrieg strategy:

- sufficient time;
- sufficient information; and
- an open mind on the part of the decider.[12]

Totalitarians face the uncomfortable reality that New Zealand, like most other societies, is increasingly diverse. Attempting to obtain hegemony by an unpopular ideology that suppresses dissent (or uses populist chauvinism to ignore differences) will create unnecessary tensions in the short run, and is doomed in the long run.

IMPLEMENT POLICY INCREMENTALLY

Grand plans do not work, because no one is so clever as to know all the answers. Blitzkriegs do not work for the same reason. Ultimately revolutions consume the revolutionaries.

Consider the career of Geoffrey Palmer, Deputy Prime Minister and Prime Minister during the Fourth Labour government and also, before he was premier, Attorney-General and Leader of the House. In these various roles he played a central role in the reforms, driving through the administrative and legislative side of the blitzkriegs, usually by ignoring the implicit processes that underpinned the democracy and parliament. Before he entered Parliament he had written *Unbridled Power?*, in which he severely censured the political system for its neglect of democratic processes. The second edition, published while he was in office, dropped the question mark from the title. It was joked that the third edition would end with an exclamation mark. Instead, out of office he published a book entitled *New Zealand's Constitution in Crisis*, presumably a criticism of his six years of stewardship.[13]

Such inconsistencies are not confined to Palmer. In his 1986 prize-winning essay Simon Upton, who became a minister in the National government, wrote

the vast majority of citizens in the free world have come to believe that freedom is simply secured by majority rule. Provided a measure has been supported by a majority, it must be acceptable. The absurdity of this belief is taken one step further: if the governing party commands a majority of the electorate its actions are acceptable. Such an approach effectively confers on the government of the day the freedom to do *whatever it likes*.[14] (italics in the original)

It is a pity that Upton did not recall this and other cautious passages in his essay, as he sat in a Cabinet using its majority in Parliament, though it had none in the electorate, to take decisions which were not only unpopular but proved to be wrong.

Upton might also reflect on his: 'A market economy cannot survive if the prevailing system is hostile to it. If large numbers of citizens firmly believe in the collective organisation of labour, a socially "just" income as an entitlement and basic insulation from the pain of any hardship or adjustment, then the existence of an entrepreneurial caste will remain a peripheral and contingent one.'[15] The implication is that the success of the policies which Upton's government pursued required these citizens to change their beliefs. Not far from this is the overtone that 'we have our ways of making you love our individualistic freedom-loving ideology'.

AVOID THE CULTURAL CRINGE

The New Zealand commercialisers imitated what they thought foreigners were arguing, rolling over like puppy dogs whenever they were praised by them. Often they did not understand the foreign analysis, took a narrow version of it, or applied it in circumstances for which it was not designed. Even where it was relevant, it needed to be adapted for New Zealand conditions.

This is not to deny the relevance of overseas experience: that would be a further cutting off of New Zealand from the real world. The experience of Denmark is almost certainly as relevant as that of the US to the New Zealand economy. Yet the philosopher-kings tried to shoehorn New Zealand into their uninformed vision of an idealised United States of America. As Phillida Bunkle said,

> I met a large number of them [future commercialisers] in the United States. They're baby boomers, and they returned to this country with a vision that was very much gained from graduate school in the United States. They came home with a cosmopolitan view of New Zealand. They were going to transform this society. Now they thought they had 1960s student values, but they actually were very impressed by North America and its consumerism and its choice and civil rights and all that. They came back with that liberalised kind of vision. But it was also I think that they had a kind of sense of embarrassment about what a hick little place they had come from. They were in Chicago, they were in New York, they were in Harvard, and they were very aware that they came from 'Hicksville'. And part of it was their awareness that they were products of the welfare state because what the welfare state does in New Zealand is bring in social uniformity. It is deeply egalitarian. People end up having the same social services. They were not very sophisticated. And what they were going to do—they were going to bring us into the global village. They were going to bring McDonalds and all these wonderful slick things and transform 'Hicksville' into a sort of social paradise of the sort you would dream of in Cambridge, Massachusetts in 1968.[16]

In the end the New Zealand policy elite did not have enough confidence in themselves to create and apply their own analysis. Slavish copying leads to bad policy, and ultimately the subjugation by the imperium of the copiers, and of those on whom they imposed their crude imitations.

IN WHOSE INTEREST IS THE ADVICE?

It was easy for the blitzkriegers to discount any pressure groups opposed to them, no matter how competent, on the basis that they were acting out of self-interest. But so were the blitzkriegers. So are business lobbyists, confusing 'what is good for New Zealand is good for the Roundtable' with 'what is good for the Roundtable is good for New Zealand.' (The financial market commentators are especially prone to this mistake, for their advice is almost always in the interests of the business which pays them.) Treasury has constantly acted in its own interests while pretending it was the nation's. (Perhaps the only exceptions have been the university economists, who have hardly supported the universities' interests. However, it could be argued they confused their short-term interest with their long-term one.)

In the end the policy adviser can only ask, how does this advice align with my personal or institution's interest? Intellectual honesty and competition of ideas may be the only means of avoiding the corruption of the advice process, which goes with advisers who pretend independence to seek their own self-interest. A robust contribution from public intellectuals (even though they have their own agendas) may be the ultimate safeguard.

IF IT AIN'T BROKE DON'T FIX IT

Behind the folk wisdom is a set of questions which should be asked whenever policy is developed.

What exactly is the problem?

Who are involved? The problem will vary with the perception and interests of those involved. Identify all their exact problems.

What theory is being used?

What are the facts?

Who benefits, who loses?

What are the risks, and who bears them? A less likely outcome may have very different implications from the central, or the most likely, outcome. It was the asymmetry of the risk bearing in the Think Big projects that resulted in the government's fiscal position suffering when the oil price proved lower than expected.

What will be the benefits and the costs? Transition costs can outweigh long-term benefits. (A variation of this is 'if it ain't very broke, still don't fix it'.)

Why are things different from the last time? (Why did we cock up last time?) A knowledge of history is a key characteristic of the successful policy adviser.

Has the solution been tested out on someone independent of the policy maker? This is not simply a matter of consultation with those involved. No policy maker or group has all the wisdom, not even philosopher-kings.

Has there been adequate consultation?

Can the policy be explained (honestly) to the minister and the public? Alfred Marshall advised: '(1) Use mathematics as a shorthand language, rather than as an engine of inquiry. (2) Keep to them till you have done. (3) Translate into English. (4) Then illustrate by examples that are important in real life. (5) Burn the mathematics. (6) If you can't succeed in (4), burn (3). This last I did often.'[17]

How will outcomes be monitored? An easy way to distinguish between a good policy package and a poor one is whether there is a monitoring element in it. The policy will not be perfect—adjustments will have to be made. Not building in an evaluation component suggests the original conception is at least arrogant, and probably flawed.

Why are we panicking? See above.

Having answered all the above questions, is it still the same problem?

DON'T DISMISS ECONOMIC ANALYSIS

The commercialisers have given economics a bad name, by presenting an extremely narrow account of the subject's scope. Tibor Barna, one of my mentors, use to say that 'economics is good at asking questions'. The implication was that it is somewhat weaker at answering them. As a broad discipline economics rarely gives unique answers to questions. What economics—like other disciplines—does, is help us to understand the issues.

One might argue that no discipline, or subdiscipline, has a monopoly on answers to its questions, but perhaps mathematics is an exception. Bertrand Russell concluded that 'mathematics may be defined as the subject in which we never know what we are talking about, nor whether what we are saying is true.'[18] It is perhaps no accident that economics has increasingly set itself up to be a branch of applied mathematics.

And yet there is another sort of economics, which aims to understand the question without offering a single answer, which is cognisant—nay curious—about the actual world but does not ignore theory, which is affectionate towards people's aspirations but not naive about their behaviour, which is modest in what it can achieve and in that humility can be helpful. That is the economics that must not be dismissed. A humble economist may be thought an oxymoron, but such a person is worth her or his weight in gold in the policy process.

Frequently economics is dismissed, either because all of it is wrongly identified with the New Right, or else because it is a discipline that cannot be mastered without effort. Ironically, those who dismiss economics usually do so using even more incompetent economic theories than those they are criticising. And like the commercialisers they too are reduced to a sort of historicism, where the policy answer (albeit a different answer) is prescribed, even though the policy question is not understood.

. . . BUT DO NOT DISMISS THE OTHER SOCIAL SCIENCES EITHER . . .

George Akerlof wrote that

> economic theorists, like French chefs in regard to food, have developed stylised models whose ingredients are limited by some unwritten rules. Just as traditional French cooking does not use seaweed or raw fish, so neoclassical models do not make assumptions derived from psychology, anthropology, or sociology.[19]

Daniel Hausman added:

> If French chefs resembled neoclassical economists, French cuisine would be more monotonous, for chefs would use very few ingredients. They would also strenuously insist that food containing any other ingredients was not French.[20]

The unwillingness of economists to consider the possibility that there is anything to be learned about their world, other from their very narrow vision of economics, is as damaging to public policy as the denial by those from other disciplines that economics is relevant.

. . . NOR HISTORY . . .

Recalling history is not just a matter that if we do not learn the lessons of history we repeat the mistakes. As George Orwell sardonically observed, victors do not only write history, but they rewrite it, according to their current needs.[21]

New Zealand's philosopher-kings have gone a step further, not so much ignoring history, as using it selectively to hide their mistakes. They are always promising a glorious future, never recalling their shabby past. Historians, more than anyone else, can remind us that the emperor is wearing no clothes.

. . . USE ENGLISH . . .

As the writing of this book was nearly complete, a simmering row between the state agency for arts funding and the writers' community exploded. The reader can guess its broad outlines. The turn for the state funding of literature to be reformed had arrived. The rationalisation had involved concentration of power into the hands of some state-appointed generic managers, who seemed to know nothing about literature, but were earnestly imposing the commercialists' model.

The writers were outraged by the bureaucratic language. Gordon McLauchlan called it 'off-English'—'language which never quite says what it means, if it means anything at all'[22] Andrew Mason commented that off-English

> was not just professional jargon, but an attempt to obfuscate and confuse. It is the language of power: if you set the terms, others have to grapple with them in order to achieve their own aims.[23]

Even the new title of the funding agency, 'Creative New Zealand', has an Orwellian overtone. As John Ralston Saul wrote,

> The wordsmiths who serve our imagination are always devoted to communication. Clarity is always their method. Universality is their aim. The wordsmiths who serve established power, on the other hand, are always devoted to obscurity. They castrate the

public imagination by subjecting language to a complexity which renders it private. Elitism is always their aim. The undoubted sign of a society well under control or in decline is that language has ceased to be a means of communication and has become a shield for those who master it.[24]

. . . AND DON'T FORGET PEOPLE

A reader becomes aware of the images that are going through a writer's mind as he or she crafts the text. One can read New Zealand economists' reports and research papers without any impression that they were written with any tangible image: pages and pages bereft of people, of institutions, of reality. All the texts conjure up is over-idealised abstractions, whose content—if any—is only recognisable to the initiated.

Some of the worst crimes against humanity in the twentieth century, and in earlier times, arose because those making policy were able to distance themselves from those on whom the policy impacted. This is not to say that the commercialisation of New Zealand should be equated with the worst horrors of the twentieth century. But the parallel is the reducing of those who would suffer into abstractions whose humanness can be ignored in the interests of the grand, but inhuman, theory.

The motto on the New Zealand coat of arms is 'onward'—the promise of the blitzkrieg. Perhaps it should replaced with the Maori answer to the question of what is important: 'he tangata, he tangata, he tangata'.[25]

Appendix: Studying Policy

A major activity of government is problem solving. From this perspective policy is the set of rules and procedures used to resolve problems with common features. These rules may be very general or very specific, depending on how the policy is defined.

For example, consider the policy issue: what are we to do with people who have insufficient income from market earnings to sustain an adequate standard of living? Notice that this problem is imbedded in a wider problem: how to provide an adequate standard of living for everyone. The implicit solution to this question is that individuals should normally obtain income through market earnings. Because not everyone can do this, the particular problem identified here arises.

Moreover, the phenomenon of inadequate market income has been identified as a public policy problem, for as long as market earnings have been significant. Very often a policy problem is articulated as though it is brand new, whereas typically it has been around for some time in a not dissimilar form. Look at the history of a public policy problem in order to understand it better.

Note how a specific solution involves a hierarchy of policy institutions. In the case of income maintenance there is legislation such as the Social Security Act. Then there are the regulations which provide the detailed implementation of the legislative direction. Below these are the Department of Social Welfare's manuals and codes of practice by which individual decisions may be taken.

One of the purposes of policy is to enable problems with broadly the same features to be resolved in similar ways. Practically, solo-parent families in similar circumstances will obtain the same degree of income support. What is meant by circumstances depends on the policy. In New Zealand the over-arching principle was once 'need and degree of need',[1] although that has been undermined to some extent in recent years.

Furthermore, the consistency and comprehensiveness of policy varies. Consider the problem of the provision of an adequate standard of living to children. Today the entitlement is dependent upon family situation. Unlike income support for adults, the minimum support from the state (family support) is clearly not intended to be adequate by itself but to only be a part contribution to the total support of the child. Two children with the same needs, but in different family situations (such as in a two-parent family on low earnings, and a solo-parent family with no earners) may be treated differently in ways it is difficult to explain except by an involved historical account of how decisions were made.

One policy option is to declare there is no problem, or not a sufficient one to do anything about it. That is in effect what the homosexual law reform did. Previously, homosexual activities were seen to be a public problem. Subsequently, they were deemed to be a private issue.

Finally, the institutions of public policy can be imbedded into principles which may be more or less adequately codified. Although the Social Security Act was first passed in 1938, amended most years, and consolidated in 1962, it was not until the 1972 report of the Royal Commission on Social Security that a broad set of underlying principles was set down, so that it was some 34 years after the Act before the principles were systematically articulated. But that there was no articulation does not mean there were no principles.

DESCRIBING THE PROBLEM

Suppose a politician, or whoever, has a policy problem. Often it will be very vague but it should be possible to identify or construct the following features to it.

First there are constraints, of which there are two kinds. Some of these constraints are physical constraints—politicians cannot repeal the laws of thermodynamics, they cannot stop the incoming tide. The other set of constraints are political constraints arising from the various features of the community. For instance, a politician from a rural area could repeal a farm subsidy (for there is no physical constraint to prevent it being withdrawn), but be politically constrained because of depending upon campaign funds or votes from farmers who benefit from the subsidies. It is, of course, in the interests of those who support a political constraint to have everyone believe that it is a physical constraint, and therefore unavoidable. Some political constraints are practically unavoidable, in so far as they are outside the political (and economic and social) system. The New Zealand economy is strongly influenced by the existence of protection of domestic production of agricultural commodities in a number of Northern Hemisphere countries, which are the consequence of their political constraints, but there may be little that a New Zealand politician can do about it.

Subject to a given set of physical and political constraints, there are a number of possible options, called the 'feasible set'. If there is only one option—a very rare occurrence—then there is no alternative (TINA).

Once the options in the feasible set are identified, then it is a matter of choosing the best option. Usually economists and operations researchers have some notion of an objective function which is maximised to give the best option. Practically, in political situations it may be sufficient to 'satisfice'; that is, to achieve satisfactory aspiration levels of the objectives of decision making, without necessarily attempting to maximise anything.

If this seems a little abstract, consider the following problem. You are in a large, multi-storey rambling house, and you seek somewhere to sleep. First, there is the physical configuration of the house—the physical constraints. Second, there may be some political (social) constraints, such as 'don't sleep in other people's bedrooms', 'polite people don't sleep in the dining room', and so on. What is left is the feasible set of locations where one may sleep. Out of all the possibilities one is the best place, but you may choose a comfortable one rather than the best, in which case the decision is a 'satisficing' one. There are other features of this exercise which parallel policy. You may decide to break one of the political constraints—the sofa in the dining room looks attractive. You may not explore the whole house—you might decide the north wing is very damp, without looking at every room there. You may not understand the house well enough and overlook a critical feature which should have affected your choice—you chose a west-facing room, when you like being woken by the morning sun. Because you don't thoroughly explore the house, you miss some key elements of the feasible set—that small door opens into your ideal bedroom.

Wandering around the house may not be the best way to identify the feasible set. You need a plan of the house, or a model—a theory. With a good theory you are less likely to miss good options, or fail to observe crucial features. If it is a really complex house (feasible set), you are almost sure to fail to make a good choice unless you have a pretty good model/theory.

Note that this approach places little emphasis on the implementation stage, of getting into bed and falling asleep. Note that sometimes one will change one's mind. The chosen bed proves damp and bumpy, so the policy may have a back-up alternative. The relationship between policy and implementation is complex.

Now consider a change of policy. Any or some of the following may have happened:

- A new physical constraint has arisen, or an old one fallen;
- A new political constraint has originated, or an old one been abandoned;
- A better model/theory has enabled better identification of the feasible set;
- There are new criteria for choosing the best option within the feasible set.

Often new policy is not the result of policy advisers being cleverer than their predecessors, although that is the way they may want to present it. More often the circumstances have changed. Understanding the changed circumstances, why a policy worked in the past but does not work now, can be vital for developing a better policy.

In summary, the policy operation becomes a matter of identifying the feasible set of options, and choosing one within it, and then implementing it—going to bed.

POSITIVE AND NORMATIVE

At this point one of the key distinctions which Lionel Robbins introduced to economics raises its uncomfortable head. What he tried to do was distinguish between 'positive' and 'normative' analysis. Positive analysis is that which is concerned with 'the facts' of a situation, whereas normative analysis involves some moral judgement on them. The distinction seemed clear enough to Robbins, but is more difficult to maintain in practice.

Consider the following. In May 1996 the basic unemployment benefit for a single adult was about $138 a week. That we may take as a fact. A person living in another country or in another age may have difficulty relating to this figure, so here is another fact: at that time the average wage was about $456 a week after tax. From these two facts we may observe that the unemployment benefit was about 30 percent of the average wage. That is a third fact.

It is very unlikely that the reader will respond in a solely scientific way to this last fact. Perhaps the unemotional scientist might wonder what this ('replacement') ratio was like in other times of New Zealand history, or in other countries, or want to know more detail to check that the ratio is in some sense meaningful. However most readers are likely to think things like 'the unemployment benefit is not high compared to wages, so the unemployed must have a pretty miserable standard of living', or 'fancy getting almost a third of the average wage while doing nothing'. Here the observer is creeping from a statement about facts, about the world as it 'is', to moral judgements of the world as it 'ought' to be—from the positive to the normative.

Robbins was not saying that one should not make normative judgements. Rather his interest was in seeing to what extent economics could develop without making them. The student of public policy needs to be aware of the distinction between positive and normative, constantly looking for it, especially in any judgements he or she makes. It is not wrong to make normative judgements, but it is wrong to confuse them with positive ones. It is almost impossible to exclude normative judgements in some sense from public policy analysis. A human being has moral passions which cannot be suppressed. If one is studying the mechanics of a concentration camp, at the very least one expects to be in simmering moral outrage. Even so it may be of value to examine the mechanics from a scientific perspective—how did the thing work—though one can barely keep indignation in check. Usually policy analysis does not deal with such clear-cut offences to humanity, but the moral judgement is there. Analysis is clearer if it is explicit.

What is being rejected is an account of policy which purports to be value-free, with the policy analyst like a pathologist working on a cadaver unaffected by the knowledge that once it involved a living human being. Such an approach disguises value judgements, in the pretence that there are none. There is a well-run argument of some social scientists that the distinction between positive and normative analysis is virtually impossible in the study of society. Even the selection of facts involves value judgements. This, it could be argued, is a peculiarity of the social sciences. If distinguishing between the world as it is and the world as it ought to be is not any easy task, it is yet worth the attempt, even if we often fail. To do otherwise is to leave that which purports to be analysis in a miasma of confusion and dishonesty about the analyst's role and perspective.

POLICY AS PROCESS

If we stand far enough back, we become aware of policy as a process of ongoing evolution. Policy occurs in real time, and needs to be examined from this perspective. Once we move from the lowest level of policy implementation, policy as a process becomes very important. The policy adviser is continually advising in a context of change. The policy critic is continually trying to shoot a moving target. One of the standard gambits in the constant struggle between these two is for the critic to represent policy as it was, and the adviser to argue it has changed.

Consider Karl Popper's classic account of the scientific process:[2]

$$P_1 \rightarrow TT \rightarrow EE \rightarrow P_2$$

The meaning of the symbols is as follows:

P_1 problem 1;
TT tentative theory;
EE (attempted) error elimination;
P_2 problem 2.

The attraction of the Popperian schema is that it sees an ongoing process, to be represented by

$$P_1 \rightarrow TT_1 \rightarrow EE_1 \rightarrow P_2 \rightarrow TT_2 \rightarrow EE_2 \rightarrow P_3 \rightarrow TT_3 \rightarrow EE_3 \rightarrow P_4 \ldots$$

A crucial idea here is that each time the scientist goes through the cycle he or she modifies the theory that was being used. Typically the theory change is incremental, although sometimes it is revolutionary.

The policy process can also be characterised by this scheme, if we map some of the science concepts on to their policy equivalent. P remains a problem, but now we have PP, policy program, to replace TT, and PI, policy implementation, instead of EE. The schema becomes

P_1 problem 1;
PP policy program;
PI policy implementation;
P_2 problem 2.
$$P_1 \rightarrow PP_1 \rightarrow PI_1 \rightarrow P_2 \rightarrow PP_2 \rightarrow PI_2 \rightarrow P_3 \rightarrow PP_3 \rightarrow PI_3 \rightarrow P_4 \rightarrow PP_4 \ldots$$

Thus the Popperian approach focuses on the problem element of the policy process, rather than policy creation and implementation. The glory may be the latter, but the reality is captured in the story told by Jenny Stewart, quoted earlier: the pre-school teacher had problems, but all she got was policies, which apparently had little connection with her problems.

Even worse can be the situation where the policy defines the problem, as when a perfectly well-functioning institution is required to be reformed because it does not conform to the policy. Nevertheless, in the Popperian schema the theory, be it a scientific one or the one which is driving the policy program, has a central role. His advice to the scientific researcher applies also to those whose concerns are policy development:

> In any stage of your researches . . . be as clear as you can about the various theories you hold, and be aware that we all hold theories unconsciously, . . . although most of them are almost certain to be false. . . . Try to construct alternative theories. . . . Whenever a theory appears to you as the only possible one, take this as a sign that you have neither understood the theory nor the problem which it was intended to solve. . . . If an . . . observation seems to support a theory, remember that what it really does is to weaken some alternative theory—perhaps one you have not thought of before. And let it be your ambition to refute and replace your own theories. . . . But remember also that a good defence of a theory against criticism is a necessary part of any fruitful discussion since only by defending it can we find its strength. . . . There is no point in discussing or criticising a theory unless we try all the time to put it in its strongest form, and to argue against it only in that form.[3]

However, policy debates are usually settled in a different way from scientific ones. In one sense scientific debates are never settled. Rather the conventional wisdom is always open to challenge from new theories which give better accounts of the evidence, or which resolve new problems. Nevertheless, at some stage the conventional wisdom has to be written down in a text book—that is, a decision has to be made about what is the best theory available. Now as it happens there is no single best textbook—not in an open society anyway—so there is a potential for competition from others who will write textbooks with alternative theories. The intellectual market-place then chooses which books it judges best. In the short run it may make terrible mistakes, but Popper argues that the system is essentially progressive, and that ultimately better ideas will win.

However, policy implementation does not involve writing text-books (perhaps it would be more effective if it did), but introducing institutional change. Thus the selection process is quite different. It is not science's men of principle against gentlemen of honour, but a process of raw politics, in which there is only one winner, and few take prisoners. For those in the policy process, personal success and failure are intimately tied in to the policy success and failure and there is only one winner in a policy dispute. Thus the policy battles are far more ferocious than the science theory battles, more parallel to military ones. Rarely is there a place for the introversion and self-criticism that Popper advocates. On the contrary, having doubts about the efficacy of one's policies, or putting the opponent's policy in its strongest possible form, weakens the chance of successfully imposing the preferred policy.

POLICY CHANGE AS REVOLUTION

For the 1980s represented a policy revolution in New Zealand. This is still within the Popperian model. Students of Popper, such as Thomas Kuhn and Imre Lakatos,[4] have elaborated his model. For our purposes we observe that there is a process by which scientific theories evolve incrementally—what Kuhn calls 'normal science'. But on occasions the theories evolve very rapidly, in which some old theories are displaced by new ones in a sort of punctuated evolution. Yet from a distance the situation after the revolution has considerable continuity with the past. The reason is the problem-solving nature of the activity. The problems do not disappear. For one scientific theory to triumph completely over another, all the problems resolved by the old theory have to be at least equally well resolved by the new one. Perhaps some minor problems are forgotten or thought irrelevant, but the basic test of a new theory is whether it deals with all the issues of the old one, preferably better, and also resolves some problem which the old one could not, or could only by a sleight of hand or 'verbal shift', as Lakatos would call it.

Now there can be a crucial difference between a scientific revolution and a policy one. Policy changes do not always involve a change that incorporates the old one in its explanation. There may be every incentive in a debate involving a policy revolution, to play down any commonalities and continuities.

For example, in the shift towards more-market from the policies of Robert Muldoon to those of Roger Douglas in the 1980s the advocates of the change split into two camps. One argued that the old interventionist regime of Muldoon was wrong, and had been bad for New Zealand economic growth; the other argued that the circumstances under which the intervention evolved in the 1940s and 1950s had changed radically by the 1970s and 1980s, so that a different (i.e. more-market) approach was more appropriate. Which view is correct is not relevant here. What is relevant is to observe that both views are expressed in the policy debate and accounts of policy. In the natural sciences, accounts which destroy the validity of all past science are rarely argued, except at the journalist level. Scientists know their theories are going to be replaced by better ones. That generates a touch of humility. On the other hand policy debate encourages conceit. This is not a question of personality. Natural scientists are not meeker than policy advisers. But the latter's working situation leads to a greater display of arrogance.

CONCLUSION

Policy as a problem-solving process is one of the most effective ways of thinking about policy, once we move past accounts of what policy is, or what it ought to be. It is necessary for the academic interested in how policy is formed, and probably useful for those who are involved practically in the formation of policy, perhaps even for the committed advocate.

Yet it is not an approach which ignores the opportunism, the self-interestedness, of the people involved. In science development one might be able to overlook personality and personal circumstance. In the policy development one cannot do so, not just because the policy is usually about people, but more fundamentally because public policy is resolved in a different way from science. Arguments about public policy are a battle of wills. The monopolist nature of government, and the time pressures, tend to turn the theoretical dispassionate ideal into a reality more like a military campaign.

In the heat of policy battle, scepticism and critical insight may be an indulgence. But it is a luxury that those studying the process of policy creation cannot afford to be without.

Notes

Prologue: A Coiled Spring

1. This prologue is elaborated in Easton, *In Stormy Seas* (1997).
2. Gould (1985).
3. The examples come from Bollard & Easton (1985).
4. Johnstone & von Tunzelman (1982).
5. Olson (1982).

1 The Genesis of the Commercialisation Strategy

1. Deane, Nicholl, & Walsh (1981, Chapters 20–23).
2. e.g. Rosenberg (1993), reviewed in Easton, 'Prescription or Poison' (1993).
3. O'Dea (1981), Coleman (1992).
4. Easton and Marks (1983) illustrate the connections by showing how the removal of protection from CER generated demands for internal transport liberalisation.
5. For a survey see Easton, *Tariffs in the 1980s and 1990s* (1991).
6. Wells (1985).
7. Cameron & Duignan (1984).
8. Oliver (1989).
9. Ross (1986).
10. Douglas (1986).
11. Treasury (1986).
12. Douglas (1987: 226).

2 The Economic Theory of Commercialisation

1. Pusey (1993:15).

2. Harris (1989).
3. Galbraith (1972).
4. Jennings & Cameron (1988:144). The quotation begins 'With the exception of heavily regulated private sector firms . . .'.
5. Treasury (1987:113).
6. Domberger & Piggot (1986). See also Easton, 'What is so Good about the Private Sector Anyway?' (1989).
7. Duncan & Bollard (1992).

Appendix: Applying More-Market to the Environment

1. See Cooter & Ulen (1986).
2. I was involved in the 1983 deep-sea ITQs, and cannot recall a single mention of Maori interests. The justified Maori anger over the inshore ITQs was quite unexpected by the policy makers.
3. A major exception is extraction by the mining industry, for which the RMA does not require sustainability.

3 The Abandoning of Equity

1. Davey & Koopman-Boyden (1983:3).
2. RCSS (1972:65), original's italics.
3. Easton, *Pragmatism and Progress* (1980)
4. RCSP (1988, II:453–454). Omitted from the quotation are the Maori terms for the

concepts.
5. RCSP (1988, I:214–5).
6. Easton, 'Distribution' (1996).
7. Easton, 'Poverty in New Zealand: 1981–1993', (1995).
8. Measured by equivalent disposable income.
9. Easton (1995).

4 Commercialism versus Culture

1. Treasury (1985a:26–27).
2. Mill (1962:260).
3. RCB Evidence (29/11/85:149–150).
4. ibid. (4/12/85:58–59).
5. This illustration has been left even though it has become outdated. Perhaps the successor to the Goodnight Kiwi is 'Spot', appropriately a corporate image in a more commercialised system.
6. RCB Evidence (29/11/85:118–121).
7. ibid. (4/12/85:64–65).
8. ibid. (4/12/85:71).
9. Simpson was referring to the objectives set out in the Broadcasting Act 1976.
10. RCB Evidence (4/12/85:91).
11. ibid. (4/12/85:42).
12. See, for example, Barrone (1973).
13. RCB Evidence (4/12/85:103).

Appendix: The Broadcasting Reforms

1. Treasury (1985a, 1985b).
2. Carter (1993).
3. Perry (1994).
4. Day (1994).
5. See Smith (1996) for a broadcasting based account of the television reforms.
6. Harcourt (1994), Yeabsley, Duncan & James (1995).

5 The Troika and the Blitzkreig

1. A curious echo of the tight five appears in Lange's belief in 1996 that '[w]e have still 20 or 24 cabinet ministers, and you could run the show on four or five'. *Dominion*, 16 Oct. 1996.
2. Oliver (1989).
3. Prebble (1996).
4. Douglas (1993:215–238).
5. Flew (1989:17).

6 The Treasury: Philosopher-Kings for Commercialisation

1. McKinnon (1995).
2. Bertram (1993).
3. More examples are in Easton, 'From Reaganomics to Rogernomics' (1989).
4. Reder (1982:11).
5. Reder (1982:31).
6. Paque (1985:413).
7. Reilly (1988).
8. Reder (1982:13).
9. Weightman (1993).
10. Cameron & Duignan (1984).
11. Cameron & Begg (1984).
12. Fowler & Brenner (1982). For critiques see Easton, *Evidence to the Royal Commission on Broadcasting and Related Communications* (1986) and Barrone (1973).
13. Treasury, *Regulation of Company Takeovers*, 1984.
14. Richardson (1995).
15. Creech (1995).
16. Treasury (1987:47).
17. Treasury (1987:47).
18. Treasury (1987:42).
19. Treasury (1987:19).
20. Particularly Treasury (1987:12–19).
21. Treasury (1987:17).
22. Treasury (1987:26–34).
23. Treasury (1987:109–120).
24. Treasury (1987:10).
25. Treasury (1987:67).
26. Titmuss (1970)
27. Treasury (1987:49). The omitted words are 'to have a public

sector producing high quality advice'.

28. Treasury (1987), Section A, Chapter 2.
29. Treasury (1987:28).
30. A nice critique of this aspect of Plato's theories will be found in Scruton (1993).

Appendix: The Treasury View of the Labour Market

1. Easton, 'A Commentary on the Treasury View of the Labour Market', (1991).
2. Easton, 'What Were Economic Effects of the Employment Contracts Act?' (1997).
3. Before the 1987 Act, there would be industry-wide awards, which would be used as a base award in a firm, which was topped up with a second-tier agreement adding additional features such as higher remuneration or better working conditions.
4. Easton (1997) *op. cit.*
5. Easton (1997) *op. cit.*

7 The Private Sector

1. Roper (1993).
2. Stallybrass (1988:248).
3. Spicer *et al.* (1992:71).
4. Hawkins (1989:126)
5. Mansfield (1990).
6. Vowles & Aimer (1993).
7. Dahrendorf (1988:5).
8. Popper (1945).
9. Vowles *et al.* (1995), especially Chapters 5 and 6.

Appendix: The Growing Up of the Unions

1. The data on union size comes from the *New Zealand Official Yearbook* (various years), and Harbridge *et al.* (1995).
2. New Zealand Council of Trade Unions (1989).
3. Interpretations in this section are my own, and are not necessarily those of Dannin (1995), Franks (1991, 1994), Hill (1994), or Hill & Du Plessis (1993), on which much of the account is based.
4. Franks (1994:209).
5. Heal (1995:277).
6. Dannin (1995:85).
7. Roper (1995:269).
8. This section uses Harbridge *et al.* (1995) and Harbridge & Hince (1993).

8 Was There an Alternative?

1. Hawke (1989:99).
2. Jesson (1989:104–108).
3. Gordon (1986:92).
4. Jesson (1989:104–108).
5. Marshall (1965).
6. Sutch (1968, 1966, 1971).
7. Church Leaders' Social Justice Initiative (1993).
8. Walsh (1989).
9. Walsh (1993).
10. Easton, 'The Commercialisation of the New Zealand Economy' (1989).
11. Coleman (1992).
12. Klamer & Collander (1990).
13. Hyman (1994:47–48).
14. O'Dea (1981).
15. Jesson (1989:71), Kelsey (1993, 1995).
16. Keynes (1971–83, 3:3; originally published in *A Revision of the Treaty*, 1922).
17. Said (1994).
18. *Sunday Star-Times*, 14 July 1996, p.C1.
19. Easton, 'Piggy in the Middle' (1996).
20. Pearson (1974).
21. This section is based on Easton & Gerritsen (1995). I am grateful to Rolf Gerritsen for

allowing me to use some of his work.

22. Gerritsen (1986).
23. Gerritsen (1992).

9 The Health Reforms

1. Upton (1987:24, 26).
2. Hospital and Related Services Taskforce (1988).
3. Arthur Anderson (1987).
4. Easton, 'Faulty Figures' (1987), Scott (1991), Bowie (1992), Easton & Bowie (1992).
5. Upton (1990, 1991:8).
6. Upton (1991:132).
7. Danzon & Begg (1991:85, 57).
8. Oliver (1989:19).
9. WHAC (1993).
10. Coopers & Lybrand (1993).
11. OECD (1996:117).
12. P. D. Wilson, letter to the Ministers of Health, Crown Health Enterprises, and Finance, 17 December 1993, para 6.9.
13. Evening Post (9 October 1993:3).
14. Upton (1987:38).

Appendix: The Fallacy of the Generic Manager

1. Pollitt (1993).
2. A preferred medicine list usually involves the hospital doctor being able to prescribe from a limited list. Where it is necessary to go outside the list (to more expensive drugs), agreement is required from a senior clinician or a panel.
3. Frame (1996).

10 Central Government

1. See also Scott & Gorringe (1989), Scott et al. (1990).
2. Using a real discount rate of 10 percent p.a.
3. It is not relevant for this study's purposes but the government has a set of nine Strategic Results Areas (SRAs), alluded to in this outcome. In one sense the SRAs are platitudinous too, but they are not without their interest. It is instructive that the 1993 ones excluded any reference to culture, heritage, leisure, or nationhood, or to the requirements of a liberal democracy. The omissions are probably a start-up oversight, and will be included in some way in the next set of SRAs.
4. Boston et al. (1996).
5. Commission of Inquiry (1995).
6. Creech (1995).

Appendix: The Heritage Assets

1. Easton (1996) 'Archives and Public Policy'.
2. Financial Statements of the Government of New Zealand (1995:39).
3. op. cit. (1995:92).
4. Hubbard (1995).
5. The Trustees of the National Library have advisory powers only and are not responsible for the collections. Thus the National Library's collections are in the physical assets part of the FSGNZ, rather than the Crown entities part.

11 Local Government

1. For a detailed history see Bush (1996), which also describes the details of local government practice, and has informed this entire chapter.
2. Bush (1996:84).
3. Easton, 'What is so Great about the Private Sector?' (1989).
4. Easton, 'A Tale of Two Cities' (1996).
5. Putnam et al. (1993).
6. January/February 1996:26–30.

7. Johnson (1968).
8. Bowie & Easton (1994).

12 Core Education

1. Reprinted from *AJHR*, 1939, E.1, pp. 2–3, with amendments as suggested in Beeby (1992:189).
2. NZCER (1987), Part I.
3. NZCER (1987), Part II.
4. Renwick (1986).
5. Butterworth & Tarling (1994).
6. Easton, 'The Unmaking of Roger Douglas' (1989).
7. Taskforce (1988).
8. Lange (1988).
9. Treasury (1987).
10. Middleton *et al.* (1990).
11. Treasury (1987, II:293–4), 11.227
12. McQueen (1991).
13. Fougere (1974).

13 The Tertiary Education Reforms

1. Universities Review Committee (1986).
2. Universities Review Committee (1986:140).
3. Bairam (1991).
4. Hawke (1988:8).
5. Butterworth & Tarling (1994:119).
6. Reported in Butterworth & Tarling (1994:19).
7. Hawke (1988:9).
8. Ministerial Consultative Group (1994).

Appendix: A Question of Ownership

1. Scott & Smelt (1995).
2. Office of Treaty Settlements (1995:18).
3. Scott & Smelt (1995:3).
4. Easton, 'An Alternative Health System' (1992).
5. Scott & Smelt (1995:17–18).
6. Scott & Smelt (1995:22).
7. Scott & Smelt (1995:9).

14 Science Policy

1. Mansfield (1981).
2. Kerr (1985).
3. Penny (1986).
4. Penny (1986).
5. Solow (1957).
6. Dennison (1985), Balogh & Streeten (1963), Solow (1988).
7. Bollard & Easton (1985).
8. e.g. Strategic Consultative Group on Research (1994).
9. Berridge *et al.* (1995).
10. *Dominion*, 12 March 1996.

Epilogue: Towards an Alternative

1. Lange (1990).
2. Jensen & Meckling (1983:9–10).
3. Jensen & Meckling (1983:10).
4. Stewart (1994:237).
5. Keynes (1971–83, 7:383; originally published in *The General Theory of Employment, Interest and Money*, 1936).
6. Popper (1945, 1956).
7. Scott actually wrote 'Comment is free, but facts are sacred.' *Manchester Guardian*, 5 May 1921.
8. Prebble (1996).
9. Gould (1993:14).
10. Popper (1972).
11. Hahn (1971:viii).
12. *Wellington International Airport Ltd* v *Air New Zealand* (1993) NZLR 671 (CA).
13. Palmer (1979, 1987, 1992).
14. Upton (1987:19).
15. Upton (1987:34–5).
16. CBC *Ideas* program, 'The Remaking of New Zealand' (first broadcast on October 1994).
17. Reported in Coase (1994:174).
18. Russell (1953).
19. Akerlof (1984:2).
20. Hausman (1992:260).
21. Orwell (1950).
22. McLauchlan (1996:90).

23. Mason (1996:15).
24. Saul (1992:8-9).
25. Final lines often have another book behind them. In 1986 I discussed with the Prime Minister's Office the possibilities for the proposed Royal Commission on Social Policy, remarking that a good summary title for its report should be 'He Tangata, He Tangata, He Tangata', a phrase I first came across in Sutch (1969). I heard nothing following this conversation, but shortly after the phrase popped up in one of Lange's speeches, becoming popular among politicians of all colours for a while.

Appendix: Studying Policy

1. Royal Commission on Social Security (1972:65).
2. Popper (1972:287).
3. Popper (1972:265).
4. Kuhn (1962), Lakatos (1970).

Bibliography

Akerlof, G. (1984) *An Economic Theorist's Book of Tales*, Cambridge University Press.

Arthur Anderson & Co (1987) *Public Hospital Performance*, New Zealand Department of Health, Wellington.

Atkinson, J. (1994) 'The State, the Media, and Thin Democracy', in A. Sharp (1994), pp. 146–77.

Bairam, E. (1991) *Publication Rates and Research Productivity in New Zealand University Economics Departments, 1984–88*, Department of Economics, University of Otago.

Balogh, T., & P.P. Streeten (1963) 'The Coefficient of Ignorance', *Bulletin of the Oxford University Institute of Economic and Statistics*, May 1963, pp. 99–107.

Barrone, J.A. (1973) *Freedom of the Press for Whom? The Right of Access to the Mass Media*, Indiana University Press, Bloomington.

Barry, A. (1996) *Someone Else's Country*, Community Media Trust, Wellington, (video).

Beeby, C.E. (1992) *The Biography of an Idea: Beeby on Education*, NZCER, Wellington.

Berridge, M.V., C.H. Sissons, H. Offenberger, & R.P. Davies (1995) '1994 NZAS Survey of Scientists' Perception of New Zealand Science: Results', *New Zealand Science*, 52, pp. 7–28.

Bertram, G. (1993) 'Keynesianism, Neoclassicism, and the State', in B. Roper & C. Rudd (1993).

Bolger, J.B., R. Richardson, and W.F. Birch (1990) *Economic and Social Initiative—December 1990*, Statement to the House of Representatives, Wellington.

Bollard, A.E. (ed.) (1989) *The Influence of American Economics on New Zealand Thinking and Policy*, NZ–US Educational Foundation & NZ Institute of Economic Research Monograph 42, Wellington.

Bollard, A.E., & R.A. Buckle (1988) *Economic Liberalisation in New Zealand*, Allen and Unwin, Wellington.

Bollard, A.E., & B.H. Easton (1985) *Markets, Regulation, and Pricing*, NZIER Research Paper 31.

Borren, P., & Alan Maynard (1993) *Searching for the Holy Grail in the Antipodes: The Market Reform of the New Zealand Health Care System*, Centre for Health Economics Discussion Paper 103, York.

Boston, J. (ed.) (1995) *The State Under Contract*, Bridget Williams Books, Wellington.

Boston, J., & P. Dalziel (eds) (1992) *The Decent Society*, Oxford University Press, Auckland.

Boston, J., & M. Holland (eds) (1987) *The Fourth Labour Government,* Oxford University Press, Auckland.

Boston, J., & M. Holland (eds) (1990) *The Fourth Labour Government: Second Edition,* Oxford University Press, Auckland.

Boston, J., J. Martin, J. Pallot, & P. Walsh (eds) (1991) *Reshaping the State: New Zealand's Bureaucratic Revolution,* Oxford University Press, Auckland.

Boston, J., J. Martin, J. Pallot, & P. Walsh (1996) *Public Sector Management: The New Zealand Model,* Oxford University Press, Auckland.

Bowie, R.D. (1992) 'Health Expenditure and Health Reforms: A Comment', *NZMJ,* 11 November, p. 458.

Bowie, R.D., & B.H. Easton (1994) 'Vexation in the Voluntary Sector', *NZMJ,* 9 March, pp. 76–7.

Bowie, R.D., & I. Shirley (1994) 'Political and Economic Perspectives on Recent Health Policy', in J. Spicer, A. Trlin, & J. Walton (eds) *Social Dimensions of Health and Disease: New Zealand Perspectives,* Dunmore Press, Palmerston North, pp. 298–322.

Brook, P. (1990) *Freedom at Work,* Oxford University Press, Auckland.

Bush, G.W.A. (1995) *Local Government and Politics in New Zealand,* 2nd edn, Auckland University Press.

Butterworth, R., & N. Tarling (1994) *A Shakeup Anyway: Government and the Universities in New Zealand in a Decade of Reform,* Auckland University Press.

Cameron, R.L. (1988) 'An Often Misunderstood but Beautiful Concept', *NBR,* 20 June, p. 12.

Cameron, R.L. (1988) 'The Sharemarket', in G. Karacaolugu (ed.) *An Introduction to Financial Markets in New Zealand,* Victoria University Press, Wellington, pp. 22–43.

Cameron, R.L., & S.J. Begg (1984) *Venture Capital: Some Recent Theoretical Perspectives and Policy Implications,* Treasury, Wellington.

Cameron, R.L., & P.J. Duignan (1984) *Government Owned Enterprises: Theory, Performance and Efficiency,* Treasury, Wellington.

Cameron, R.L., & P. Duignan (1986) 'Principal/Agent Theory Key Factor in Economic Performance', *NBR,* 20 June.

Carter, I. (1993) *Gadfly: The Life and Times of James Shelley,* Auckland University Press.

Castles, F.G., R. Gerritsen, & J. Vowles (eds) *The Great Experiment: Labour Parties and Public Policy Transformation,* Allen & Unwin, Sydney and Auckland University Press.

Church Leaders' Social Justice Initiative (1993) *Social Justice for Our Times,* NZCCSS, Wellington.

Coase, R.H. (1994) *Essays on Economics and Economists,* University of Chicago Press.

Coleman, W. (1992) 'Concord and Discord Amongst New Zealand Economists: The Results of an Opinion Survey', *NZEP,* 26(1), June, pp. 47–82.

Commission of Inquiry (1995) *Report of the Commission of Inquiry into the Collapse of a Viewing Platform at Cave Creek,* Department of Internal Affairs, Wellington (Noble Report).

Coopers & Lybrand (1993) *Future Establishment of CHEs: Organisation and Management Turnaround,* Wellington.

Cooter, R., & T. Ulen (1986) *Law and Economics,* Scott, Foreman, & Co, Glenview, Illinois.

Creech, W. (1995) 'A Number of Differences', *New Zealand Listener*, 11 November, p. 28.

Dannin, E. (1995) 'We Can't Overcome? A Case Study of Freedom of Contract and Labour Law Reform', *Berkeley Journal of Employment and Labour Law*, 16, 1, pp. 1–168.

Danzon, P., & S. Begg (1991) *Options for Health Care in New Zealand*, Report for the New Zealand Business Roundtable, CS First Boston NZ Ltd, Wellington.

Dahrendorf, R. (1988) *The Modern Social Conflict: An Essay on the Politics of Liberty*, Weidenfeld & Nicholson, London.

Davey, J., & P.G. Koopman-Boyden (1983) *Issues in Social Equity*, NZPC, Wellington.

Day, P. (1994) *The Radio Years: A History of Broadcasting Vol. I*, Auckland University Press & the Broadcasting History Trust, Auckland.

Deane, R.S., P.W.E. Nicholl, & M.J. Walsh (eds) (1981) *External Economic Structure and Policy*, Reserve Bank of New Zealand, Wellington.

Deeks, J., & N. Perry (eds) (1992) *Controlling Interests*, Auckland University Press.

Dennison, E.F. (1985) *Trends in American Economic Growth 1929–1982*, The Brookings Institution, Washington.

Devlin, N., P. Hansen, & S. Knowles (1994) *Universities: Who Benefits from Them and Who Should Pay? A Response to the 1994 Todd Report*, Economics Discussion Papers 9418, University of Otago, Dunedin.

Domberger, S., & J. Piggot (1986) 'Privatization and Public Enterprise: A Survey', *Economic Record*, June, pp. 145–62.

Douglas, R.O. (1980) *There's Got To Be a Better Way!*, Wellington, Fourth Estate Books.

Douglas, R.O. (1986) *Principles Guiding the 1986 Expenditure Review* (March 1986), Wellington.

Douglas, R.O., with L. Callen (1987) *Towards Prosperity*, David Bateman, Auckland.

Douglas, R.O. (1993) *Unfinished Business*, Random House, Auckland.

Duncan, I., & A.E. Bollard (1992) *Corporatization and Privatization: Lessons from New Zealand*, Oxford University Press, Auckland.

Economic Development Commission (1989) *Privatising State Owned Enterprises*, Wellington.

Easton, B.H.: see separate list below, pp. 280–282.

Easton, B.H., & R.D.Bowie (1992) *Some Aggregate Health Statistics: Through Time and Between Countries*, Department of Public Health, Wellington School of Medicine.

Easton, B.H., & R. Gerritsen (1995) 'Economic Reform: Parallels and Divergences' in Castles *et al.* (1995), pp. 22–47.

Easton, B.H., & P.A. Marks (1983) *By Rail or Road: A Case Study*, NZIER Research Paper 27, 1983.

Financial Statements of the Government of New Zealand for the Year Ended 30 June 1995, Wellington

Flew, A. (1989) *An Introduction to Western Philosophy: Ideas and Argument from Plato to Popper*, revised edn, Thames & Hudson, London.

Fougere, G. (1974) 'Medical Care the Market's Quiet Revolution', in D.W.

Beavan and B.H. Easton (eds) *The Future of New Zealand Medicine: A Progressive View*, Peryer, Christchurch.

Fougere, G. (1988) *Health Policy and the Gibbs Report: An Analysis*, Department of Sociology, University of Canterbury, Christchurch.

Fougere, G. (1991) *Analysing the Issues: Health Care Funding and Organisation in 'Your Health and the Public Health'*, Department of Sociology, University of Canterbury, Christchurch.

Fowler, M.S., & D.L. Brenner (1982) 'A Marketplace Approach to Broadcast Regulation', *Texas Law Review*, 60, pp. 207–57.

Frame, I. (1996) 'The Changes Occurring at Christchurch Hospital and Why They Must Work,' *The Press*, 2 March, p. 19.

Franks, P. (1991) 'Organising the "Unorganisable": The Formation of Clerical Unions and the Labour Press' in J.E. Martin & K. Taylor (eds) *Culture and the Labour Movement*, Dunmore Press, Palmerston North.

Franks, P. (1994) 'The Employments Contracts Act and the Demise of the New Zealand Clerical Workers Union', *NZ Journal of History*, 28, 2, October, pp. 194–210.

Galbraith, J.K. (1972) *The New Industrial State*, 2nd edn, Andre Deutsch, New York.

Gee, M. (1994) *Crime Story*, Penguin, Auckland.

Gerritsen, R. (1986) 'The Necessity of "Corporatism": The Case of the Hawke Labor Government', *Politics* 21, pp. 45–54.

Gerritsen, R. (1992) 'The Politics of Microeconomic Reform: Structuring a General Model', *Australian Journal of Public Administration* 51, 1, March.

Gordon, I. (1986) 'En(in)quire Within', *New Zealand Listener*, 18 October.

Gould, J. (1985) *The Muldoon Years: An Essay on New Zealand's Recent Economic Growth Record*, Hodder & Stoughton, Auckland.

Gould, S.J. (1993) *Eight Little Piggies*, Jonathan Cape, London.

Hahn, F. (1971) *Readings in the Theory of Growth*, Macmillan Student Editions, Macmillan, London.

Harbridge, R. (ed.) (1993) *Employment Contracts: New Zealand Experiences*, Victoria University Press, Wellington.

Harbridge, R., & K. Hince (1993) 'Organising Workers: The Effects of the Act on Union Membership and Organization', in Harbridge (1993), pp. 224–36.

Harbridge, R., K. Hince, & A. Honeybone (1995) 'Unions and Union Membership in New Zealand: Annual Review for 1994', Working Paper 2/95, Industrial Relations Centre, Wellington.

Harcourt, D. (1994) *How Should Broadcasting be Funded?*, Ministry of Commerce, Wellington.

Harris, P. (1989) 'Asset Sales and the Management of the Public Debt and Fiscal Deficit', in Public Service Association (1989).

Hausman, D.M. (1992) *The Exact and Separate Science of Economics*, Cambridge University Press.

Hawke, G. R. (1988) *Report on Post Compulsory Education and Training in New Zealand*, Government Printer, Wellington (Hawke Report).

Hawke, G.R. (ed.) (1991) *Access to the Airwaves: Issues in Public Sector Broadcasting*, Institute of Policy Studies, Wellington.

Hawkins, A. (1989) *The Hawk: Alan Hawkins Tells His Story to Gordon*

McLauchlan, Four Star Books, Auckland.

Heal, S. (1995) 'The Struggle over the Employment Contracts Act 1987–1991', in P.S. Morrison (1995).

Hill, L. (1994) 'Feminism and Unionism in New Zealand: Organising the Markets for Women's Work', PhD thesis, University of Canterbury, Christchurch.

Hill, L., & R. Du Plessis (1993) 'Tracing the Similarities, Identifying the Differences: Women and the Employment Contracts Act', *New Zealand Journal of Industrial Relations*, 18, 1.

Hospital and Related Services Taskforce, *Unshackling the Hospitals*, Wellington, 1988 (Gibbs report).

Hubbard, A. (1994) 'The Treasury and the Books', *New Zealand Listener*, 4 June, pp. 40–1.

Hyman, P. (1994) *Women and Economics*, Bridget Williams Books, Wellington.

James, C. (1986) *The Quiet Revolution*, Allen & Unwin, Wellington.

James, C. (1992) *New Territory: The Transformation of New Zealand 1984–1992*, Bridget Williams Books, Wellington.

Jarey, D., & J. Jarey (1991) *Dictionary of Sociology*, HarperCollins, London.

Jennings, S., & R.L. Cameron (1988) 'State-Owned Enterprise Reform in New Zealand', in Bollard & Buckle (1988), pp. 121–52.

Jensen, M.C., & W.H. Meckling (1983) *Democracy in Crisis*, Centre for Independent Studies, Sydney.

Jesson, B. (1987) *Behind the Mirror Glass*, Penguin, Auckland.

Jesson, B. (1989) *Fragments of Labour*, Penguin, Auckland.

Jesson, B., A. Ryan, & P. Spoonley (1988) *Revival of the Right*, Heinemann Reed, Auckland.

Johnson, H.G. (ed.) (1968) *Economic Nationalism in Old and New States*, Allen & Unwin, London.

Johnston, J., & A. von Tunzelmann (1982) *The State in Business: Public Enterprise in New Zealand*, NZPC, Planning Paper No 15, Wellington.

Kalmer, A., & D. Colander (1990) *The Making of an Economist*, Westview Press, Boulder, Colorado.

Kelsey, J. (1990) *A Question of Honour? Labour and the Treaty: 1984–1989*, Allen and Unwin, Wellington.

Kelsey, J. (1993) *Rolling Back the State*, Bridget William Books, Wellington.

Kelsey, J. (1995) *The New Zealand Experiment*, Auckland University Press/Bridget Williams Books.

Kerr, R.L. (1985) 'Government Involvement in Research and Development', *New Zealand Science Review*, 42, pp. 4–9.

Keynes, J.M. (1971–83) *The Collected Writings of John Maynard Keynes*, 30 volumes, Macmillan, for the Royal Economic Society, London.

Kidman, F. (1990) *True Stars*, Random Century, Auckland.

Kuhn, T.S. (1962) *The Structure of Scientific Revolutions*, University of Chicago.

Lakatos, I. (1970) 'Falsification and the Methodology of Scientific Research Programmes', in I. Lakatos & A. Musgrave (eds) *Criticism and the Growth of Knowledge*, Cambridge University Press.

Lange D. (1988) *Tomorrow's Schools: The Reform of Education Administration in New Zealand*, Wellington.

Lange D. (1990) *Nuclear Free—The New Zealand Way*, Penguin, Auckland.

McKinnon, M. (1993) *Independence and Foreign Policy*, Auckland University Press.

McLauchlan, G. (1996) 'Writer's Block', *Metro*, October, pp. 90–7.

McQueen, H. (1991) *The Ninth Floor: Inside the Prime Minister's Office—A Political Experience*, Penguin, Auckland.

Mansfield, A. (1990) 'The Power Elite', M.A. thesis in Political Science, University of Canterbury, Christchurch.

Mansfield, E. (1981) 'How Economists See R&D', *Harvard Business Review*, November–December, pp. 98–106.

Marshall, T.H. (1965) *Social Policy in the Twentieth Century*, Hutchinson, London.

Mason, A. (1996) 'Biting the Hand that Feeds', *Quote Unquote*, October, pp. 11–13.

Middleton, S., J. Codd, & A. Jones (eds) (1990) *New Zealand Education Policy Today: Critical Perspectives*, Allen & Unwin, Wellington.

Mill, J.S. (1962) *Utilitarianism*, ed. M. Warnock, Collins, London.

Ministerial Consultative Group (1994) *Funding Growth in Tertiary Education and Training*, Ministry of Education, Wellington (Todd Report).

Morrison, P.S. (ed.) (1995) *Labour, Employment and Work in New Zealand 1994: Proceedings of the Sixth Conference*, Department of Geography, VUW, Wellington.

New Zealand Centre for Educational Research (1987) *How Fair is New Zealand? Part I & II*, Report for the Royal Commission on Social Policy, Wellington.

New Zealand Council of Trade Unions (1989) *Strategies for Change: Challenges for the Trade Union Movement of Today*, Wellington.

OECD (1996) *New Zealand*, OECD Economic Surveys 1995/96, Paris.

O'Dea, D.J. (1981) 'A Survey of What Economists Think', *Recent Research Results*, NZIER, Wellington, 1981, pp. 41–6.

Office of Treaty Settlements (1995) *Crown Proposals for the Settlement of Treaty of Waitangi Claims: Detailed Proposals*, Wellington.

Oliver, W. Hugh. (1989) 'The Labour Caucus and Economic Policy formation, 1981 to 1984', in Easton, *The Making of Rogernomics* (1989), pp. 11–52.

Olson, M. (1982) *The Rise and Decline of Nations: Economic Growth, Stagflation and Social Rigidities*, Yale University Press, New Haven.

Orwell, G. (1950) *Nineteen Eighty Four*, Secker & Warburg, London.

Palmer, G. (1979) *Unbridled Power?* Oxford University Press, Auckland.

Palmer, G. (1987) *Unbridled Power*, Oxford University Press, Auckland.

Palmer, G. (1992) *New Zealand's Constitution in Crisis: Reforming our Political System*, John McIndoe, Dunedin.

Paque, K-H. (1985) 'How Far is Vienna from Chicago? An Essay on the Methodology of Two Schools of Dogmatic Liberalism', *Kyklos*, 38, pp. 412–34.

Pearson, W.H. (1952, 1974) 'Fretful Sleepers: A Sketch of New Zealand Behaviour and its Implications for the Artist', *Landfall*, September 1952, reprinted in *Fretful Sleepers and Other Essays*, Heinemann Educational Books, Auckland.

Penny, D. (1986) 'Expected Economic Benefits of R&D', *New Zealand Science Review*, 42.

Perry, N. (1994) *The Dominion of Signs*, Auckland University Press.

Pollitt, C. (1993) *Managerialism and the Public Services: Cuts or Cultural Change in the 1990s?* 2nd edn, Blackwell Business, Oxford.

Popper, K.R. (1945) *The Open Society and its Enemies*, Routledge & Kegan Paul, London.

Popper, K.R. (1957) *The Poverty of Historicism*, Routledge & Kegan Paul, London.

Popper, K.R. (1972) *Objective Knowledge*, Clarendon Press, Oxford.

Prebble, R. (1996) *I've Been Thinking*, Seaview Publishing, Auckland.

Public Service Association (1989) *Private Power or Public Interest? Proceedings from a Conference on Privatisation*, Dunmore Press, Palmerston North.

Pusey, M. (1993) 'Reclaiming the Middle Ground . . . From New Right Economic Rationalism', in S. King and P. Lloyd (eds), *Economic Rationalism: Dead End or Way Forward?*, Allen & Unwin, Sydney.

Putnam, R.D., with R. Leonard & R.Y. Nannetti (1993) *Making Democracy Work: Civic Traditions in Modern Italy*, Princeton University Press.

Reder, M.W. (1982) 'Chicago Economics: Permanence and Change', *Journal of Economic Literature*, 20, pp. 1–38.

Rees, S., & G. Rodley (eds) (1995) *The Human Costs of Managerialism*, Pluto Press, Leichardt, NSW.

Rees, S., G. Rodley, & F. Stillwell (eds) (1993) *Beyond the Market: Alternatives to Economic Rationalism*, Pluto Press, Leichardt, NSW.

Reilly, S. (1988) 'The Right', in A. Bullock, O. Stallybrass, & S. Trombley (eds) *The Fontana Dictionary of Modern Thought*, Fontana, London.

Renwick, W. (1986) 'Forty Years On in New Zealand Education: A New Net Goes Fishing', *Bulletin of the Regional Office for Education in Asia and the Pacific*, No. 27, November 1986, pp. 103–20.

Richardson, R. (1995) *Making a Difference*, Shoal Bay Press, Christchurch.

Roper, B. (1993) 'A Level Playing Field? Business Political Activism and State Policy Formation', in B. Roper & C. Rudd (1993).

Roper, B. (1995) 'Leading from the Rear? A Theoretical Analysis of the Contingent Conservatism of the NZCTU Leadership', in P.S. Morrison (1995).

Roper, B. & C. Rudd (eds) (1993) *State and Economy in New Zealand*, Oxford University Press, Auckland.

Rosenberg, W. (1993) *New Zealand Can Be Different and Better*, New Zealand Monthly Review Society, Christchurch.

Ross, B.J. (1986) *Report of the Steering Committee Established to Advise on the Proposed Industrial Development Board*, Wellington.

Royal Commission on Broadcasting (1986) *Broadcasting and Related Telecommunications in New Zealand*, Government Printer, Wellington.

Royal Commission on Electoral Reform (1986) *Towards a Better Democracy*, Government Printer, Wellington.

Royal Commission on Social Policy (1988) *The April Report*, 4 volumes, Government Printer, Wellington.

Royal Commission on Social Security (1972) *Social Security in New Zealand*, Government Printer, Wellington.

Russell, B. (1953) *Mysticism and Logic*, Penguin, London. (First published 1917.)

Russell, M. (1996) *Revolution*, Hodder Moa Beckett, Auckland.

Said, E. (1994) *Representations of the Intellectual*, Vintage, London.

Saul, J.R. (1992) *Voltaire's Bastards: The Dictatorship of Reason in the West*, Vintage, New York.

Schick, A. (1996) *The Spirit of Reform: Managing the New Zealand State Sector in a Time of Change*, State Services Commission, Wellington.

Schwarz, H.M. (1994) 'Public Choice Theory and Public Choices: Bureaucratic and State Reorganization in Australia, Denmark, New Zealand, and Sweden in the 1980s', *Administration & Society*, 26, 1, May 1994 pp. 48–77.

Schwarz, H.M. (1994) 'Small States in Big Trouble: State Reorganization in Australia, Denmark, New Zealand, and Sweden in the 1980s', *World Politics* 46, July, pp. 527–55.

Scott, G.C., P. Bushnell, & N. Sallee (1990) 'Reform of the Core Public Sector: The New Zealand Experience', *Governance*, 3: pp. 81–92.

Scott, G.C., & P. Gorringe (1989) 'Reform of the Core Public Sector: The New Zealand Experience', *Australian Journal of Public Administration*, 48:81–92.

Scott, G.C., & S. Smelt (1995) *Ownership of Universities*, New Zealand Vice-chancellors' Committee, Wellington.

Scott, W.G. (1991) 'A Note on Trends in Area Health and Hospital Board Real Expenditure', *NZEP*, 25(1), pp. 127–30.

Scruton, R. (1993) *Xanthippic Dialogues*, Sinclair-Stevenson, London.

Sharp, A. (ed.) (1994) *Leap into the Dark: The Changing Role of the State Since 1984*, Auckland University Press.

Shirley, I., B. Easton, C. Briar, & S. Chatterjee (1990) *Unemployment in New Zealand*, Dunmore Press.

Smith, P. (1996) *Revolution in the Air*, Longman, Auckland.

Solow, R.M. (1957) 'Technical Change and the Aggregate Production Function', *Review of Economics and Statistics*, 39, August, pp. 312–20.

Solow, R.M. (1988) 'Growth Theory and After', *American Economic Review*, 78, 3, June, pp. 307–12.

Spicer, B., R. Bowan, D. Emanuel, & A. Hunt (1992) *The Power to Manage*, Oxford University Press, Auckland.

Stallybrass, O. (1988) 'The Establishment', in A. Bullock, O. Stallybrass, & S. Trombley (eds) *The Fontana Dictionary of Modern Thought*, Fontana, London.

Stewart, J. (1994) *The Lie of the Level Playing Field: Industry Policy and Australia's Future*, The Text Publishing Company, Melbourne.

Strategic Consultative Group on Research (1994) *For the Public Good: Directions for Investment through the Public Science Fund: A Strategic Statement*, prepared for MRST, Wellington.

Sutch, W.B. (1966) *The Quest for Security in New Zealand: 1840 to 1966*, Oxford University Press, Wellington.

Sutch, W.B. (1969) *Poverty and Progress in New Zealand: A Re-assessment*, A.H. & A.W. Reed, Wellington.

Sutch, W.B. (1971) *The Responsible Society in New Zealand*, Whitcombe &

Tombs, Christchurch.

Taskforce to Review Education Administration (1988) *Administering for Excellence*, Wellington. (Picot Report)

Titmuss, R.M. (1970) *The Gift Relationship: From Human Blood to Social Policy*, Allen and Unwin, London.

Treasury (1984) *Economic Management, Post Election Briefing to the Incoming Government*, Wellington.

Treasury (1984) *Regulation of Company Takeovers*, Submission to the Securities Commission, Wellington.

Treasury (1985a) *Submission to the Royal Commission on Broadcasting and Related Telecommunications*, September.

Treasury (1985b) *Synopsis of the Treasury Submission to the Royal Commission on Broadcasting and Related Telecommunications*, November.

Treasury (1986) *Statement on Government Expenditure Reform* (May), Wellington.

Treasury (1987) *Post Election Briefing to the Incoming Government: Vol I, Government Management; Vol II, Educational Issues*, Wellington.

Universities Review Committee (1987) *New Zealand's Universities: Partners in National Development*, New Zealand Vice Chancellors' Committee, Wellington (Watts Report).

Upton, S. (1987) *The Withering of the State*, Allen and Unwin/Port Nicholson Press, Wellington.

Upton, S. (1990) 'The Politics of Rogernomics' in Walker (1990).

Upton, S. (1991) *Your Health and the Public Health*, Wellington.

Vowles, J., & P. Aimer (1993) *Voters' Vengeance: The 1990 Election in New Zealand and the Fate of the Fourth Labour Government*, Auckland University Press.

Vowles, J., P. Aimer, H. Catt, J. Lamare, & R. Miller (1995) *Towards Consensus: The 1993 Election in New Zealand and the Transition to Proportional Representation*, Auckland University Press.

Walker, S. (ed.) (1989) *Rogernomics: Reshaping New Zealand's Economy*, GP Books, Wellington.

Walsh, P. (1989) 'A Family Fight? Industrial Relations Reform Under the Fourth Labour Government', in Easton, *The Making of Rogernomics* (1989), pp. 149–70.

Walsh, P. (1993) 'The State Sector Act', in Boston *et al.* (1993), pp. 52–80.

Weightman, J. (1993) 'Fatal Attraction', *New York Review of Books*, 11 February, 1993.

Wellington Health Action Group (1993) *A Second Opinion*, Wellington.

Wells, G.M. (1985) 'Evaluating the Policymakers' Theories', *NBR*, 8 April.

Working Party on Science and Technology (1987) *Key To Prosperity*, Government Printer, Wellington (Beattie Report)

Yeabsley, J., I. Duncan, & D. James (1994) *Broadcasting in New Zealand: Waves of Change*, NZIER Contract Report No 634, Ministry of Commerce, New Zealand.

Publications by B. H. Easton

'An Alternative Health System', NBR, May 22, 1992.

'Archives and Public Policy' in New Zealand Archives Futures: Essays in Honour of Michael Hoare, Archifacts, October 1996.

'The Broadcasting Funding Debate: A New Zealand Perspective', Proceedings of the Communications Research Forum 1994, 2, Bureau of Transport and Communication, Canberra, 1995, pp. 521–39.

'Broadcasting Policy: Two Views', Proceedings of the 1991 Conference of the Sociological Association of Aotearoa, Dec 1991, University of Waikato.

'A Commentary on the Treasury View of the Labour Market' Submissions to the Labour Select Committee on Employment Contracts Bill, 1990, New Zealand Engineering Union, February 1991.

'The Commercialisation of the New Zealand Economy: From Think Big to Privatisation', in Easton, The Making of Rogernomics (1989) pp. 114–31.

'The Commercialisation of Tertiary Education', in J.D. Marshall (ed.) The Economics of Education, University of Auckland Faculty of Education Annual Lectures, 1995, pp. 18–49.

'Distribution', in A. Bollard, R. Lattimore, & B. Silverstone (eds) A Study of Economic Reform: The Case of New Zealand, North Holland, 1996.

'Development Strategies for the Eighties', New Zealand Monthly Review, November 1980.

'Economic and Other Ideas Behind the New Zealand Reforms', The Oxford Review of Economic Policy, 10, 3, 1994.

'Economic Rationalism in New Zealand', Australia, New Zealand and Economic Rationalism: Parallel of Diverging Tracks? Occasional Paper Number 7, Institute of Ethics and Public Policy, Monash University, 1994, pp. 15–30.

Evidence to the Royal Commission on Broadcasting and Related Communications, NZIER Working Paper 86/12, 1986, Wellington.

'Faulty Figures', New Zealand Listener, 31 October 1987, p. 94.

'From Reaganomics to Rogernomics', in Bollard (1989), pp. 69–95.

'From Rogernomics to Ruthanasia', in Rees et al. (1993), pp. 149–62.

Getting the Supply-side to Work, New Zealand Engineering Union, Wellington. 1994.

'"Government Management": A Review of its Political Content', Political Science, 42, 2, December 1990, pp. 35–42.

'How Commercial Should Science Research Be?' New Zealand Science Review, 46, 1, 1989.

'How Did the Health Reforms Blitzkrieg Fail?' Political Science, 46, 2, December 1994, pp. 214–33.

'How the Market was Introduced into Resource Management and the Environment', Agriculture and the Environment: Proceedings of the 1995 Conference of the New Zealand Agricultural Economics Society, AERU Discussion Paper No 142, Lincoln University, Canterbury, pp. 54–61.

Is Health an Economic Commodity?, 1992 Nordmeyer Memorial Lecture, Wellington Medical School.

In Stormy Seas: The Post-War New Zealand Economy, University of Otago Press, Dunedin, forthcoming.

The Making of Rogernomics, Auckland University Press, 1989.

'Narrow Focus: Review of "Corporatization and Privatization: Lessons From New Zealand" by Ian Duncan and Alan Bollard', *New Zealand Books*, 3, 1, 1993, pp. 20–1.

Open Growth: A Response to the Ministerial Task Force on International Competitiveness, New Zealand Engineering Union, 1990.

'Philosopher Kings and Public Intellectuals', Auckland University Winter Lecture, 20 August 1996.

'Piggy in the Middle', *Metro*, August 1996, pp. 82–7.

'Planning or the Market?' *Planning Quarterly*, September 1991, pp. 10–13.

'Poverty in New Zealand: 1981–1993', *New Zealand Sociology*, 10, 2, November 1995, pp. 182–213.

Pragmatism and Progress: Social Security in the Seventies, University of Canterbury Press, Christchurch, 1981.

'Prescription or Poison: Review of "New Zealand Can be Different and Better" by Wolfgang Rosenberg', *New Zealand Books*, 3, 3, 1993, pp. 5–6.

'The Rise of the Generic Manager', in Rees & Rodley (1995), pp. 39–48.

'Royal Commissions as Policy Creators: The New Zealand Experience', in P. Weller (ed.) *Royal Commissions and the Making of Public Policy*, CAPSM, Brisbane, 1994, pp. 230–43.

'The Sellers of Instruments' *Terra Nova*, July 1991, pp. 50–1.

'A Tale of Two Cities', *New Zealand Listener*, 7 September 1996, pp. 50.

Tariffs in the 1980s and 1990s: Evidence, Analysis, and Policy, New Zealand Engineering Union, 1991.

Towards a Political Economy of New Zealand, Hocken Library, Dunedin, 1996.

'The Unmaking of Roger Douglas?', in Easton, *The Making of Rogernomics* (1989), pp. 171–87.

'What Is So Great About the Private Sector?', in Public Service Association (1989), pp. 36–54.

'What Were the Economic Effects of the Employment Contracts Act?', in P.S. Morrison (ed.) *Labour, Employment, and Work in New Zealand: Proceedings of the Seventh Conference*, Dept of Geography, Victoria University of Wellington, Wellington, 1997.

Index

academic freedom, 215, 229
Access to the Airwaves (ed. Hawke), 132–34
ACT, 117, 121
Administering for Excellence (Picot report), 202, 204, 206
Akerlof, George, 253
Anderton, Jim, 117
area health boards (AHBs), 154, 156, 162, 190
Arthur Anderson, 152
arts funding, 254

Barna, Tibor, 252
Beeby, Clarence, 200, 220
    See also Fraser–Beeby statement
Begg, Susan, 157
Bentham, Jeremy, 55
Birch, Bill, 83, 161
blitzkrieg approach
    of 1984 Labour government, 50, 79–81, 82–83, 193, 214
    of 1990 National government, 81–83
    alternatives to, 243–55
Bolger, Jim, 83, 121
border protection. *See* protection
Briefing to the Incoming Government: 1990 (Treasury 1990 PEB), 99–111
broadcasting
    commercialisation of, 58–61
    cultural role of, 55–58, 66–67
    economic characteristics of, 64–66
    editorial independence of, 67–68
    evaluation of reforms, 68–70
    Maori, 67, 69–70
    Royal Commission on, 54–61, 62–64, 138
Broadcasting Commission, 70
Broadcasting Corporation of New Zealand, 137
Bunkle, Phillida, 250
Business Roundtable (NZBR), 93,

114–17, 118, 141, 157–58
Butterworth, Ruth. *See A Shakeup Anyway* (Butterworth and Tarling)

Capital Power, 194, 195–96
Cave Creek tragedy, 178, 180
Caygill, David, 74, 77
    See also 'Troika'
central government, reform of. *See* Public Finance Act; State Sector' Act
Chicago school, Treasury influenced by, 20, 88–89, 90, 91–93, 202
Christchurch City Council, 195–97
civic virtue, 197–99 *passim*
Clark, Helen, 78
Close, David, 196
Closer Economic Relations (CER), 9
Coalition for Public Health, 159–60
Coase Theorem, 37–39, 41
Commerce Commission, 194, 196
commercialisation
    defined, 25–26
    economic theory, 25–35
commercialisation strategy
    compared with Australian corporatist strategy, 142–47
    genesis of, 13–24
    opposition to, 136–42 *passim*
    revolt of populace against, 119–21
    totalitarian tendencies of, 214–17, 238–39, 247–48
    Treasury's adoption of, 20–21
Conservation, Department of, 40, 42, 178, 180, 186, 187
conservation estate, 184–88 *passim*
contestability, 105, 235–36
Corkery, Pam, 199
corporatisation
    defined, 13–14
    of SOEs, 22–23
cost–benefit analysis (CBA), 15–17, 20, 21, 30, 40
Council of Trade Unions (CTU), 123–

282